Advanced Social Research Series
The Center for the Study of Social Research for the Enhancement of Human Well-being
Kwansei Gakuin University, Nishinomiya, Japan
Volume 1

A Sociology of Happiness

Advanced Social Research Series

The Center for the Study of Social Research for the Enhancement of Human Well-being
Kwansei Gakuin University, Nishinomiya, Japan

Series editor: Eishō Ōmura

A Sociology of Happiness: Japanese Perspectives
Kenji Kosaka

Advanced Social Research Series
The Center for the Study of Social Research for the Enhancement of Human Well-being
Kwansei Gakuin University, Nishinomiya, Japan
Volume 1

A Sociology of Happiness

Japanese Perspectives

Edited by

Kenji Kosaka

MASTERY FOR SERVICE

TRANS PACIFIC PRESS

This English edition first published in 2006 by
Trans Pacific Press, PO Box 120, Rosanna, Melbourne, Victoria 3084, Australia
Telephone: +61 3 9459 3021 Fax: +61 3 9457 5923
Email: info@transpacificpress.com
Web: http://www.transpacificpress.com

Designed and set by digital environs, Melbourne. www.digitalenvirons.com

Printed by BPA Print Group, Burwood, Victoria, Australia

Distributors

Asia and the Pacific
Kinokuniya Company Ltd.

Head office:
38-1 Sakuragaoka 5-chome, Setagaya-ku, Tokyo
156-8691, Japan
Telephone: +81 (0)3 3439 0161
Fax: +81 (0)3 3439 0839
Email: bkimp@kinokuniya.co.jp
Web: www.kinokuniya.co.jp

Asia-Pacific office:
Kinokuniya Book Stores of Singapore Pte., Ltd.
391B Orchard Road #13-06/07/08
Ngee Ann City Tower B
Singapore 238874
Telephone: +65 6276 5558
Fax: +65 6276 5570
Email: SSO@kinokuniya.co.jp

Australia and New Zealand
UNIREPS
University of New South Wales
Sydney, NSW 2052
Australia
Telephone: +61(0)2-9664-0999
Fax: +61(0)2-9664-5420
Email: info.press@unsw.edu.au
Web: http://www.unireps.com.au

UK and Europe
Asian Studies Book Services
Franseweg 55B, 3921 DE Elst, Utrecht,
The Netherlands
Telephone: +31 318 470 030
Fax: +31 318 470 073
Email: info@asianstudiesbooks.com
Web: http://www.asianstudiesbooks.com

USA and Canada
International Specialized Book
Services (ISBS)
920 NE 58th Avenue, Suite 300
Portland, Oregon 97213-3786
USA
Telephone: (800) 944-6190
Fax: (503) 280-8832
Email: orders@isbs.com
Web: http://www.isbs.com

ISBN 1-876843-27-6, 978-1-876843-27-4 (Hardback)
ISBN 1-876843-28-4, 978-1-876843-28-1 (Paperback)

Contents

Figures

Tables

List of Contributors

Kiyoshi Abe is Professor, Graduate School of Sociology and Social Work; Kwansei Gakuin University. His main research interests lie in the field of cultural studies, critical theory, and media and communication studies.

He received B.A. in Sociology from Kwansei Gakuin University and M.A. and Ph.D. in Sociology from the University of Tokyo.

His main publications are: (2000), *Samayoeru nashonarizumu* (Wondering nationalism), Kyoto: Sekaishisosha; (2000), *Nichijō no nakano komyunikēshon* (Communication in everyday life), Tokyo: Hokuju Shuppan; and (1998), *Kōkyō-ken to komyunikēshon* (Public sphere and communication), Kyoto: Minerva Publishing.

Hiroshi Hamada is Associate Professor, School of Sociology and Social Work, Kwansei Gakuin University. His main interests lie in the field of mathematical sociology, indices of economic inequality, relative deprivation, income distribution modeling, and theories of distributive justice.

He received B.A. in Politics, M.A. in Sociology and Ph.D. in Sociology from Kwansei Gakuin University.

His latest works are: (with Atsushi Ishida, 2003), 'Fubyōdō shakai to kikai no kintō (Social inequality and equal opportunity)', *Japanese Sociological Review*, Vol. 54, No. 3: 232–249; (2004), 'A Generative Model of Income Distribution 2: Inequality of the Iterated Investment Game', *Journal of Mathematical Sociology*, 28 (1): 1–24; (2005), 'Parametric Decomposition of the Gini Coefficient: How Change of

Subgroup Affects an Overall Inequality', *Sociological Theory and Methods*, vol. 20 No. 2: 241–56.

Nobutaka Kamei is COE Associate Professor, Graduate School of Sociology and Social Work, Kwansei Gakuin University. His main interests lie in field research on linguistic and cultural minorities in West and Central Africa including the Deaf and traditional hunter-gatherers.

He received B.A., M.A. and Doctoral Degree in Science from Kyoto University.

His recent publications are: (2005), 'Play among Baka children in Cameroon', in Barry S. Hewlett and Michael E. Lamb (eds), *Hunter-Gatherer Childhoods: Evolutionary, Developmental & Cultural Perspectives*, New Brunswick, NJ: Transaction Publishers, pp. 343–59; (with Nami Akiyama, 2004), *Shuwa de ikou* (Shall We Sign?), Kyoto: Minerva Publishing; (2001), 'Play of the children of the Baka hunter-gatherers', in Mitsuo Ichikawa and Hiroaki Satō (eds), *Mori to hito no kyōzon-sekai* (Hunter-gatherers in the Central African forests), Kyoto: Kyoto University Press, pp. 93–139.

Kenji Kosaka is Professor, Graduate School of Sociology and Social Work, Kwansei Gakuin University, and Director of the COE (Center of Excellence) Program on Human Well-being. His main interests lie in the field of mathematical sociology, social stratification, and applied sociology.

He received B.A. and M.A. in Sociology from Kwansei Gakuin University and Ph.D. in Sociology from the University of Pittsburgh, USA. He has been President of the Asia Pacific Sociological Association (1999–2002), and President of the Japanese Association for Mathematical Sociology (1989–1993).

His main publications are: (2006), *Shakaigaku ni okeru fōmaru seorī: Kaisō imēji ni kansuru FK moderu, kaiteiban*, (Formal theory in sociology: FK model of images of stratification, revised edition), Tokyo: Harvest-sha; editor (with Kazuo Misumi, 2005), *Symbolic debaisu: Imisekai eno fōmaru apurōchi* (Symbolic device: Formal approaches to meaning), Tokyo: Keisoshobo; (with Thomas J. Fararo, 2003), *Generating Images of Stratification: A Formal Theory*, Netherland: Kluwer Academic Publishers; and editor (1994), *Social Stratification in Contemporary Japan*, London: Kegan Paul International.

Kojiro Miyahara is Professor, Graduate School of Sociology and Social Work, Kwansei Gakuin University. His main interests lie in the field of social theory (Nietzsche, Weber, Simmel and Foucault), sociology of knowledge, and cultural sociology. He is currently exploring a theory and practice of "social aesthetics".

He received B.A. in Law from the University of Tokyo, and M.A. and Ph.D. from the University of Wisconsin-Madison, USA.

His main publications are: (2005), *Ronryoku no jidai* (The hegemony of rational discourse), Tokyo: Keisoshobo; (1999), *Henshin ganbō* (The metamorphoses of the body), Tokyo: Chikuma Shobo Publishing; (1998), *Kotoba no rinshō shakaigaku* (Clinical sociology of speech acts), Kyoto: Nakanishiya Shuppan; (1998), *Nīche* (Nietzsche), Tokyo: PHP Institute; (1992), *Kijinron* (On the noble persons), Tokyo: Sin-yo-sha; and (1983), 'Charisma: From Weber to Contemporary Sociology', in *Sociological Inquiry*, 53 (4): 368–88.

Masahiro Ogino is Professor, Graduate School of Sociology and Social Work; Kwansei Gakuin University. His main interests lie in the field of the sociology of culture, capitalism, and history of social theory.

He received B.A. in Sociology from the University of Monpellier III, M.A in Sociology from the University of Paris X and Ph.D in Sociology from the University of Paris VII, France. He has been President of la Société japono-française de Sociologie since 2004.

His main publications are: (2005), *Rei-do no shakai: Sagi to zōyo no shakaigaku* (Society at zero: The sociology of swindles and gifts), Kyoto: Sekaishisosha; editor (2002), *Bunka isan no shakaigaku: Rūburu Bijutsukan kara Genbaku Dōmu made* (The sociology of a cultural heritage: From the Louvre Museum to the Atomic Bomb Dome), Tokyo: Sin-yo-sha; (1998), *Shihonshugi to tasha* (Capitalism and others), Nishinomiya: Kwansei Gakuin University Press; and (1998), *Fissures*, Paris, Editions de la Villette.

Eishō Ōmura is Professor, Graduate School of Sociology and Social Work; Kwansei Gakuin University. His main interests lie in the field of social pathology, religious consciousness and clinical sociology.

He received B.A. and M.A. in Literature from Kyoto University and Ph.D in Sociology from Kwansei Gakuin University. He has been Director of the Japanese Association for Religious Studies (1996–), and President of the Kansai Sociological Association (2003–).

His main publications are: (2002), *Hikō no riaritī: Futsū no danshi no ikizurasa* (Reality of delinquency: Hardships of life for ordinary boys), Kyoto: Sekaishisosha; and (1996), *Gendai shakai to shūkyō: Shūkyō ishiki no hen'yō*, (Modern society and religion: Transformation of religious consciousness), Tokyo: Iwanami Shoten.

Yoshiyuki Yama is Associate Professor, School of Sociology and Social Work; Kwansei Gakuin University. His main interests lie in the field of cultural anthropology and folklore in East Asia.

He received B.A. in Archeology from Kyushu University, M.A. in Anthropology from Osaka University and Ph.D in Sociology from Kwansei Gakuin University.

His recent work is (co-author with Masahiro Ogino, Nobuhiko Ogawa, Henri-Pierre Jeudy and Ken'ichi Wakita, 2002), *Bunka isan no shakaigaku: Rūburu Bijutsukan kara Genbaku Dōmu made* (The sociology of a cultural heritage: From the Louvre Museum to A-Bomb Dome), Tokyo: Sin-yo-sha.

Introduction

Kenji Kosaka

Sociology as a science originated from a criticism of utilitarianism. For example, Durkheim criticized Spencer's utilitarianism by arguing that it lacked insights into the 'non-contractual elements of contract'. Issues and subjects that are unique to sociology were conceived to make up for such deficiencies. To that end, Parsons put forward the question of social order—the Hobbesian problem—and defined an inquiry into the basis for its formation as the issue to be resolved by sociology. Underlying this view was a criticism of utilitarianism for ignoring social norms and values. Parsons and Durkheim have one thing in common, their criticism of Spencer (Durkheim 2000; Parsons 1937). We of later generations, however, need to look at the positional relationships of their theories carefully because Spencer himself also began from a criticism of utilitarianism. Spencer was consistently critical of the view of human beings that underpinned Bentham's idea of 'the greatest happiness of the greatest number'. Spencer felt that the utilitarian view of human beings was but a step from egoism. He described his own solution to the problem (i.e., happiness exists where the function of the state is limited to prevention of injustice) in his *Social Statics* (1851), which was subtitled *The Conditions Essential To Human Happiness.*

As a science, sociology set out to confront utilitarianism on two issues—'social order' and 'happiness'—and propose alternatives. Yet in the process of sociology's theoretical development, methodological refinement and scope expansion, the social order issue was explored in depth whereas the issue of happiness was either forgotten or left behind. Hardly any sociological studies have addressed the happiness issue squarely. While studies of happiness have been accumulating in psychology and economics, they have been absent in the field of sociology.[1] This is obvious when, for example, one reviews both old and new dictionaries and encyclopedias of sociology. Terms like 'social order', 'alienation' and 'welfare' appear, but not 'happiness'. You may argue that 'happiness' is not a sociological term, but not all of the terms in these references are sociological in the strict sense, for example 'crime' and 'war'. There must be a good reason in terms of the sociology of knowledge for the exclusion of 'happiness'. The issue of 'justice' has been an interdisciplinary topic of discussions in sociology as well as philosophy, economics and ethics in recent years. There has been growing interest in 'goodness' too, which may have something to do with the recent resurgence of communitarianism. In contrast, 'happiness' has never been a discussion subject by itself. Happiness and unhappiness have failed to become a main subject of sociology even though they occupy an extremely substantial part of people's simple, everyday interest. This situation can only be described as unnatural.

Given this situation, we would like to propose the 'sociology of happiness'. This proposition means revisiting the starting point of sociology, the criticism of utilitarianism, but it also goes beyond that. Sociology has a 170 year history since the time of Comte and it has been one hundred years since the so-called second generation of sociologists including Durkheim. The American Sociological Association has just convened its 2005 annual meeting celebrating the Centennial year of the association. Academic studies accumulated over this history cannot be ignored even though almost none of them are directly useful from the standpoint of studying happiness. The contemporary concept of the sociology of happiness entails a complete overhaul of all academic advances in sociology.

Now, what kind of viewpoint are we developing in this journal? What kind of 'view of happiness' is our sociological viewpoint?

It appears that there are two basic views of happiness: let us call them the 'active view of happiness' and the 'passive view of happiness'.[2] The active view of happiness is the view that happiness can be obtained by actively searching for it and brought on by the satisfaction of obtaining it. In contrast, the passive view of happiness is based on the sense that happiness is transient and life is full of misfortunes. Priority has been given to the active view until now, whether consciously or subconsciously, and the passive view has not received due attention despite its real existence. This has been the case in terms of the view of happiness of ordinary people as well as sociological studies. I will elaborate on this below.

Human culture has created myriad forms of desire. A desire to be wealthier. A desire to live in security and comfort. A desire to lead a meaningful and joyful life. A desire to live a worthwhile life, etc. These desires, however, come with the involvement of 'others' (Girard 1961) and are never satisfied. This inability to satisfy usually intensifies the desires further. The trouble is that satisfaction of some people's desires may result in the sacrifices—abandonment or delay—of other people's desires.

On the other hand, there is a fundamentally different view. It is a desire to pray for *buji* (trouble-free), the word discovered by Japanese folklore studies. For example, one would wish others (family members) a safe journey when seeing them off. A family would wish that its breadwinner would come home safely when seeing him or her off every morning to work. The modern world is so unpredictable and full of danger that anyone can get caught up in some sort of incident or accident. This desire is therefore not limited to old, traditional communities. *Buji* means the absence of misfortunes. Nothing happens: that's the true sense of the word. This may sound rather passive from the active view of happiness but this is regarded as the greatest happiness. And the concept of *buji* involves concern not only for oneself or the people around. Trouble-free nature means a trouble-free community. A trouble-free community means a trouble-free home and family. It is a spirally encompassing concept (Furukawa 2004). The view of happiness that wishes for the absence of misfortunes therefore cannot be understood by an element-based approach that directly asks about the conditions of happiness (Glatzer et al. 2004). For example, empirical studies that attempt to identify determinant factors for happiness from the 'life satisfaction' point of view often provide pre-selected answers for respondents to pick from. It is also clear that even those studies that place more emphasis on free answers by respondents are not designed to pick up degrees of spiral 'life satisfaction' that are rooted in the concept of happiness based on the *buji* criteria (Easterlin 2004).

The dichotomy of 'materialistic values' and 'post-materialistic values' set forth by Ronald Inglehart seems at first glance to correspond to the active view of happiness and the passive view of happiness respectively. However, post-materialistic values consist of many items, including having more say in government decisions, protecting freedom of speech, having more say about how things are done at work, making cities and countryside more beautiful, progressing towards a more humane society and progressing to a society that respects ideas (Inglehart 1990). In order to realize these post-materialistic values, we must actively do something. This is where it differs from what we call the passive view of happiness based on the absence of misfortunes. Some people may be tempted to relate these types of the view of happiness to empirical and historical society types. For example, the active view of happiness is European whereas the passive view is Asian, or the former is elitist whereas the latter is populist. Or some may hypothesize that the passive view of happiness becomes dominant in more cohesive societies. However, we realize that things cannot be generalized so easily as we learn more about localized characteristics of various societies. Two views of happiness must co-exist in any society in any age. And that is all the more reason to point out the imbalance in sociological studies and research that have focused on only one of these views.

All of the papers included in the present volume focus on the passive view of happiness and at the same time emphasize the need for sociological studies and research premised on localized knowledge of the passive view of happiness. Influences of localized knowledge on sociological knowledge claims of universality are unavoidable. Or rather, I should say that universal sociological knowledge can only be established by fully reflecting localized knowledge. Therefore I argue that it is imperative to devise a theoretical framework for a sociological study design that can reflect local knowledge. With this point in mind, I would like to briefly explain the sociological approach of each of the studies in this volume.

Kosaka argues, in 'Killing Many Innocent People', that reducing unhappiness is more important than adding happiness based on observations of the history of theoretical concepts and points to the importance of the sociology-of-knowledge approach to 'missed opportunities' in order to reduce unhappiness. It would be best if nothing happens from the passive view of happiness but what do we do with misfortunes that have already happened? The article touches on the Vietnamese experiences regarding this question.

In response to Kosaka's proposition, Hamada's 'An Axiomatic Approach to the Disadvantage Index' takes up a challenge to mathematically formularize the degree of ill-being in society in general. Although using the poverty measure proposed by Sen et al. as a hint, this study is an original contribution that incorporates multiple resources such as education, health and social capital as well as poverty as various factors that cause ill-being to introduce the theoretical 'disadvantage boundary'. A person whose resources fall below this standard is considered to be in a disadvantaged environment.

In 'Violence in Modern Society', Ogino explores what lays behind the unhappy life of a person who couldn't get free from trouble through the personal history of a woman he calls K. In the end Ogino found that the state of capitalism, violence in modern society and unpredictable social structures fraught with uncertainties were the central themes in her story. This study plays a dual role of searching for structural and historical factors through a personal history while proposing a bidirectional sociological method of re-interpreting the latter by the former.

Re-reading Nietzsche, Miyahara points out three types of happiness in 'Nietzsche and the Height of Happiness'. In the low form of happiness the slave finds 'comfort and rest', in contrast to the high form of happiness sought by the master in 'fighting and conquest' and the highest form of happiness the young child finds in 'play and creativity'. While the happiness of the master and slave are both based on the active view of happiness, the young child's happiness—which Miyahara regards as the ultimate goal—is supported by the passive view of happiness.

Kamei's 'Language and Well-being' puts forward a clear, realistic and practical point of view on what constitutes human happiness in relation to the use of a language, particularly a sign language. According to Kamei, there are three basic requirements of language rights: biological, developmental and cultural. In contrast with the pursuit of an utopian multilingual democracy by intellectuals, the attempt to resolve the pains and deprivation of actual language users (including making Sign Language an official language) originates from what we call the passive view of happiness.

Yama's 'On Facts' looks at the relationship between 'faith' and 'knowledge' from the perspective of folklore by analyzing the similarities between Kunio Yanagita and Norinaga Motoori. He concludes that their relationship is mediated by what he calls 'own culture', a kind of localized knowledge, and argues that the folklore of happiness and unhappiness may be developed by deconstructing modern knowledge which lacks the perspective of the dead.

'Conditions for Well-being in Surveillance Society', by Abe, is a theoretical examination of contradictions inherent to surveillance society, one of the most striking contemporary phenomena, using Habermas' discourse on Benjamin for clues. While the attempt to prevent obvious violence by thorough mutual surveillance ('politics of security') is rooted in the active view of happiness, Abe persistently calls for 'politicization of peace' by analyzing the mechanism of violence hidden in the 'happiness of being watched over'.

In his 'Happiness and Unhappiness: A Clinical Sociological Approach', Ōmura argues that traditional Western social science in general could only speak in terms of an active view of happiness because it was founded on functionalistic behavioral theories. He introduces Goffman's dramaturgical approach and emphasizes that a real feeling of happiness can only be realized between 'I as a performer' and 'I as a spectator'. What he calls 'agitating culture' corresponds to the active view of happiness and 'calming culture' to the passive view of happiness. Ōmura states that a sense of resignation that happiness in this world is 'transient' by nature was born out of the Japanese Buddhist view of life as something transient and empty.

I believe that in the near future the sociology of happiness will have to begin discussions on happiness in various subordinate fields of study, including criteria, theories, mathematical modeling, history, social philosophy, practice, methodology, data, social criticism, etc. This journal has not yet attained that level of specialization. Still, even though all of the studies in this issue are loosely tied together with a common understanding of the view of happiness, each of them exhibits a certain level of specialization and orientation. Hamada's paper is on mathematical modeling, Ogino's on methodology, Miyahara's on social philosophy, Kamei's on practice, Yama's and Ōmura's about the relationship between theories and the (passive) views of happiness, and Kosaka's is an overview.

The present volume is one of the outcomes of Kwansei Gakuin University's 21st Century COE Program (program director: Kenji Kosaka) selected by the Ministry of Education, Culture, Sports, Technology and Science of Japan in 2003. The program is titled The

Study of Social Research for the Enhancement of Human Well-being. This issue is largely a collection of reflective essays presenting the main points of human well-being. Thanks are due to Karl Smith who conducted editorial work and to Rui Nakai who undertook administrative tasks for this volume. The next volume in the series will address theory and practice of social research that contributes to human well-being, including the 'sociology of social research'.

Kenji Kosaka
April 2006

1
Killing Many Innocent People: An Introduction to the Sociology of Well-being and Ill-being

Kenji Kosaka

Introduction

In front of me is a newspaper cutting from *The Kōbe Shinbun* dated 8 April 2003, a photograph of an injured Iraqi boy in a Baghdad hospital. He was injured in an American air-raid. Both of his arms have been amputated just below the shoulders. The photo does not show his legs, but his upper body below the chest appears to be charred, and the skin color darkens in the lower body. What pains me most is the boy's expression—he is holding back his tears (of pain or grief I cannot tell) while looking straight ahead. It is clear that, even with the latest science and medical technologies, this boy will never regain his arms. What will be in his mind in the coming days and for the rest of his life? I cannot fathom the thoughts of someone who has lost his arms under such circumstances. What I can say with some certainty, though, is that there was no apparent justification for his suffering and no one had any right to make him suffer so. As I contemplate this image, other images come to mind and begin to overlap—the A-bomb victims and the children who became victims in the recent terrorism in Chechen, Russia in late October 2002 and other places (Chūgoku Shinbunsha 1980; Naono 2004).

The title of this essay—'Killing many innocent people (*Shikiri ni, muko o, sasshō shi*)'—is taken from a special issue of the *Asahi Graph*,

6 August 1952. This was the first publication in Japan to detail the extent of the atrocities caused by the A-bombs dropped on Hiroshima and Nagasaki. Its editorial concludes:

> Setting aside arguments for and against rearmament, we hope that anyone who dares to discuss future wars will keep in mind that the devastation shown in these pages—and perhaps even worse—could fall upon us once again.

This was seven years after the bombs were dropped. Under the Occupation, reports and photographs of the devastation were banned from publication. As a result, apart from the locals and a handful of other concerned people, the Japanese public lived through the ruins and confusion in the wake of the war ignorant of both the true nature of the bombs and their effects. It is no coincidence, perhaps, that this special issue apparently sold out on the day of publication.

The title 'killing many innocent people' delineates the object of the sociology of well-being and ill-being: numbers of innocent people are suddenly inflicted with fear or pain. If they escape death, they continue to suffer from after-effects. They suffer not only physically but psychologically and socially, often encountering prejudice and discrimination in later life. In cases such as the widespread use of defoliant (Agent Orange), the suffering continues for generations. Of course, death and injuries are not the only causes of unhappiness. As Munesuke Mita outlined in his 'types of ill-being', there are various types of ill-being with various histories. He delineated, through the analysis of advice columns in a popular newspaper, apathy/ennui, anxiety/impatience, solitude/hostility and paucity/dissatisfaction as four main pair types of ill-being and alienation in capitalist Japanese society (Mita 1963). Furthermore, while sometimes ill-being affects only a few individuals by accident, at other times it is not accidental and it affects many. A large number of victims does not necessarily make it a misfortune for 'humanity' *per se*, but our concern is with the 'well-being and ill-being of humanity' rather than the suffering of individuals.

Before we proceed, though, the title requires further explanation, for it is also a quote from the Shōwa Emperor's Rescript to announce the end of the war, which was broadcast on 15 August 1945. The complete sentence in which the phrase appeared was: 'The enemy has begun to employ a new and most cruel bomb, resulting in killing many innocent people, which is indeed incalculable'. To define the sociology of well-being and ill-being by quoting from the Imperial Rescript may, understandably, incite some criticism, for the Rescript was premised on ideas such as the protection of the national polity, maintenance of the Imperial system, that the war was (justifiably) waged for the purpose of 'liberating Asia', continuing sympathy for Japan's allies, faith in the 'divinity of the nation', etc.[1] It conveys a sense of being the victim, rather than the aggressor. At the time, apparently one teacher explained the significance of the announcement to his students at a primary school: '...the atomic bomb is so powerful that it would kill all Japanese people within a few days... If the Japanese people perished, there would be no national polity. If that happened, we would fail all our ancestral gods. So we surrender now so that we can fight again and win next time.' Upon hearing this, one boy responded: 'This war is the war of science, so we study science and mathematics to invent new technology. It is our task now. I study science and mathematics and invent powerful bombs that would blow up the whole enemy land...' (Nishio 1999: 623)

In short, the original expression of the phrase 'killing many innocent people' did not equate the catastrophe with the 'ill-being of humanity': its concern has to be interpreted in the above historical context. In this essay, however, the phrase is used independently of this historical context. As we interpret the phrase, it provides clues for examining the characteristics, contents and borders of the sociology of well-being and ill-being. Although we specifically employ the expression in these independent terms, we must of course bear in mind that it might still be used by others in its original sense.

Welfare, happiness and comfortable living

Before discussing the objects of the sociology of well-being and ill-being, it will be useful to briefly examine the terms 'well-being' [*kōfuku*] and 'ill-being' [*fukō*] in both Japanese and English. While the term *fukushi* '(social) welfare' is (academic) sociological terminology, the Japanese words *kōfuku* and *fukō* are in general, rather than academic, use. As everyday words, however, they have a semi-formal status: in a casual conversation, *shiawase* rather than *kōfuku* is more commonly used. Furthermore, *kōfuku* has different connotations according to individuals, societies and cultures. Surveying the various ways that people perceive or have perceived what counts as *kōfuku* and related expressions is a fascinating subject of study in itself. This has already been addressed, though, in Akira

Furukawa's *Kōfuku no fīrudowāku* ('The fieldwork of *kōfuku*'), so I will not expand on it here, merely noting its importance.

Another issue that requires clarification is the appropriate English equivalent for *kōfuku*, which corresponds to both 'well-being' and 'happiness'. Although the meanings of the two overlap, their origins are different: 'happiness' came from 'hap', which denotes 'chance', 'fortune' and 'luck', while 'well-being' of course originates in 'well'. Popular dictionaries (such as Webster) give, as synonyms of 'happiness', words such as 'glad', 'cheerful', 'joyful', 'joyous' and so on, but not 'well-being'.

'Happy' typically describes a state of an individual. It can be used to describe the state of a society, but when used this way, it implies either the average of individual self-evaluation or the perception of the sum of individuals belonging to a society. In contrast, 'well-being', which can be used to refer to a personal condition, principally refers to the condition of society as a whole as well as individuals. While the general well-being of humanity cannot exist without the well-being of individuals (i.e. 'happiness'), for the purpose of this essay I consider 'well-being' more appropriate. 'Well-being' has been translated differently into Japanese, as *fukushi* [welfare] (Sen [1992] 1999: 59 and in 'Translator's notes') and *kurashi-yosa* [level of comfort in living] (OECD 1974).

The most active area of the current study of 'well-being' is subjective well-being or SWB (OECD 1974; Strack et al., 1991; Ormel et al., 1999). Psychology and those branches of politics that research public opinion about values are the mainstream of SWB studies. It seems that the researchers in those areas form a loose 'theoretical working group' creating SWB barometers, using them to compare and rank countries. SWB is similar to 'happiness' in that its departure point is the individual. However, SWB studies are not concerned with individuals, but rather defects and issues of social systems (such as market democracy) and the roles of government (for example, Lane 2000), in order to identify the reasons why people cannot enjoy happiness but are, according to my research, increasingly feeling unhappy. The starting point for SWB research, however, is subjective well-being, which means that many forms of objective ill-being are excluded from these studies, with the exception of the effects of some universal, economic factors of ill-being such as poverty, or of social ill-being such as lack of companionship. This essay is concerned with objective ill-being, and thus SWB is beyond its scope. The research program 'Comparative study of happiness', conducted for six years from 1992 and led by Yoshida

Tamito at the International Advanced Research Centre (Kokusai Kōtō Kenkyūjo) can be described as a pioneering project in the sociology of well-being (Yoshida 1999). Yet, Yoshida's work revolves around perceptions of happiness, and as such belongs to a wider type of SWB study (i.e., of greater scope than those of psychology and politics). Similarly, Veenhoven's (1994) series of qualitative studies, which aims to verify the notion that 'a better society does not always make more people happy' and closely examines the relationship between SWB and objective social conditions, can also be considered to belong to a wider SWB approach.

The three elements of the 'ill-being of humanity'

The expression 'killing many innocent people' consists of three elements: 'many', 'casualties' (caused by killing) and 'the innocent people'. The object of the sociology of well-being and ill-being requires that ill-being entails all three elements.

Many

Our concern is whether an incident or a condition affects many people or limited individual/s. Individual ill-being undoubtedly exists. For the individual concerned it affects his/her whole life, and no one can say that it does not deserve attention. Furthermore, a problem concerning the whole of humanity may manifest itself in one individual. 'Many' in the title is translated from the Japanese *shikiri ni* (see note 1). *Shikiri ni* cannot be understood only in terms of quantity: its attributes include 'intentional', 'intensive', 'planned', 'repetitive', 'frequent', 'continuous', 'constant', 'continual', 'excessive' and 'purposeful'. The quantitative aspect, however, cannot be ignored as the modern translation of *shikiri ni* properly suggests.

It is not easy to measure ill-being or devastation precisely. Even the final number of victims of a specific disaster or disease (e.g. the Minamata Disease, a disease of the central nervous system caused by industrial discharges of organic mercury compound from Chisso Company in a city named Minamata in Kumamoto Prefecture, Japan) cannot easily be determined. Admitting the necessarily arbitrary nature of such figures, let us look at the numbers of deaths in a few examples.

The deaths of Japanese nationals during WWII consisted of 1,740,000 combatants and 1,000,000 non-combatants. The total of

2,700,000 constituted 3.6 percent of the total Japanese population (approx. 74,433,000) in 1944 (Kyodai Nihonshijiten Hensankai, 1990: 1301). Deaths from the atomic bombs are estimated at 150,000 in Hiroshima and 80,000 in Nagasaki.

The Vietnam War resulted in the deaths of 3,000,000 Vietnamese and 58,000 Americans. The term 'Vietnamese' here is rather vague, as it includes the soldiers of the then Republic of South Vietnam, Viet Cong, North Vietnamese army and farming villagers. For a more precise figure, the deaths of military personnel from Korea and Australia must also be taken into account.

Minamata Disease took the lives of about 1200 people. The Great Hanshin-Awaji Earthquake ('the Kobe earthquake') of 1995 killed about 6434 people. Although numbers vary according to different sources, Iraq Body Count—which has been cited by President Bush—reports that as of 23 December 2005, between 27,569 and 31,088 Iraqi civilians had been killed by the military intervention in Iraq since March 2003. President Bush announced on 12 December that 2,140 US service-members had died in the war in Iraq over the same period. The terrorist attack in New York City on 11 September 2001 killed about 3,000 people.

In the following equation, the number of deaths caused by the incident i is D_i with parameters a and n:

$$D_i = a\,10^n \; (0.1 < a \leqq 1, n = 0, 1, 2 \ldots),$$

$$M = n + a.$$

The parameter n denotes power, and a the scale of power. Thus, the equation is a measure for the size of devastation (death toll) caused by an incident, just as one can measure the size of an earthquake by the Richter scale. Using the Vietnam War (for the Vietnamese) as an example:

n (power of the death toll) = 7 and a (the scale of power) = 0.3

Thus the magnitude of deaths M is 7.3, implying 3 million and 7 thousand death toll. To express the deaths figure as an index means that, as the power increases, the absolute value of each unit also increases. From the egalitarian point of view, this equation may appear irrational. However, perhaps by coincidence, the highest scale of seismic intensity is 7 (severe): the 1995 Hanshin-Awaji Earthquake recorded the maximum 7, and the recent Niigata earthquake (23 October 2004) recorded 6. As in the earthquake, the fact that the death scale of the Vietnam War is rated at 7 would help one grasp the proportion of the disaster at an experiential level, making it an effective guide to understanding the relative size of a natural disaster or war.

The nature of disaster will be discussed in the next section. Here I just point out that the death toll is not the only indication of a disaster: a disaster can be damages to body or mind, or pain and suffering of family and loved ones. These can be incorporated in the equation by changing the definition and interpretation of *Di*. Casualties to future generations can also be conceived by introducing a time-based variable. A low *n* value does not necessarily mean that the incident was less serious; an accident that killed a handful of people could have involved millions of people under different circumstances. Had the Hanshin-Awaji Earthquake occurred during peak-hour rather than at 5:46 am, the casualties would have been much greater. Still, a high parameter *n* carries gravity: 'the dialectic leitmotif conversion of quantity to quality' (Adorno 1966) also applies here.

Shikiri ni can also contain a notion that appears contrary to quantitative significance. Sacrificing the few for the well-being of the majority is a case in point. In this instance, only few suffer from ill-being. Therefore, such a case may seem outside the scope of this study. However, let us remember that in defining *shikiri ni* we eliminated 'accidental ill-being of an individual'. 'Accidental' here means that statistically no intentional factor is at work. This rule also applies when the 'individual' is expanded to 'a few'. In other words, 'a few' become a means to replace 'many'. Put in Marxist terms, to sacrifice well-being of a few as a means to achieve well-being of many is to deny the well-being of humanity as a whole. Our definition of *shikiri ni* should entail this as well. Therefore, 'many' here implies that an incident or a condition involves 'a large number of people' or is not an 'accidental occurrence'.

Casualties

Here 'casualties' refer to ill-being as a whole. Opinions of what constitutes ill-being can vary. In reality, the objective state of well-being and ill-being, and subjective perception of this state are closely related, but in a somewhat convoluted way, which complicates the matter. For our purpose, we define ill-being as the 'deprivation of life opportunities'. Deprivation can mean a change from 'not deprived' to 'deprived' states, as well as the 'deprived' condition irrespective of the process of deprivation.

Human life is finite, so natural death cannot be described as ill-being. Death of one's family or friends causes grief, but natural death is not what we define as ill-being. On the other hand, premature deaths, deaths due to medical mistakes, murders (war, terrorism or other forms), suicide etc., are not natural deaths and are thus ill-being. There are other types of death—capital punishment, death away from home, meaningless death, immolation, death in prison, death from indignation, death from starvation, etc. Arguably, 'The controlled death of a mass' (Adorno 1966) is the most harrowing death witnessed by human history.

Ill-being can deprive life opportunities without depriving life: child abuse, bullying, domestic violence, abuse of elderly people etc., all deprive life opportunities. Unemployment, homelessness, poverty and inequality, discrimination and prejudice also deprive one of social opportunities and life opportunities, and thus constitute forms of (contributors to) ill-being. Abortion deprives the fetus the opportunity of life prior to becoming fully human. Of course, not all instances of ill-being are as obvious as these. For example, the philosopher Comte-Sponville says: 'our ill-being is not limited to those worst conditions'—i.e., massacres in Rwanda or the former Yugoslavia, East Timor, poverty and unemployment, expulsion, serious illnesses, and having family members in a deathbed, for example. 'In many cases, people are not happy even when things in general seem to be satisfactory' (Comte-Sponville 2000). We entirely agree. But what we want to emphasize here is that such 'worst conditions' have become part of our everyday life, constantly threatening us. As clear from the frequent terrorist attacks and their causes, we can no longer see those 'worst conditions' as unusual.

Ill-being cannot always be discussed in terms of the control or distribution of resources. We need to emphasize this point. As I will mention below, utilitarian economists have long dominated the discourse of human well-being, as a result of which the discussion is typically conducted only in terms of resource distribution. While it is possible to sustain this argument by expanding the notion of resources beyond economics to include social resources and those of human relations, 'worst conditions' cannot be reduced to the question of resource distribution.

Innocent

The third condition of ill-being that concerns us is that the victims are not responsible for their predicament. If a person is aware of a typhoon warning and knows its implications and still goes rock fishing, that is a reckless act. If, as a result, the fisherman is swept by the waves off the rock and drowned, while it would be a tragedy for himself and his family, the fisherman was responsible for his own death and thus his fate is outside of our concern. In another instance, if residents of a disaster-prone area were not 'prepared' for possible natural disasters and as a result became victims of a landslide, the answer is less straightforward. Their share of responsibility for their own fate depends upon whether the local authorities had warned of possible calamity and whether all residents properly understood such warnings. In recent years, manufacturers have been held responsible for problems caused by their products, which has led to excessive warnings on products—reflecting the manufacturers' intention to ensure that consumers share responsibility. With growing numbers of foreign workers in Japan, the contested grounds for workplace injuries includes whether or not appropriate warnings have been issued with due consideration for the language and cultural backgrounds of the workers.

In practice, then, it is not always possible to establish the 'innocence' of the victim; border cases will continue to appear and need to be determined. If, for example, one child kills another in a personal conflict, one cannot assume that the victim was 'innocent' and the perpetrator wholly responsible. There are always particular circumstances that lead to such actions.

For our purpose, we need to consider two issues here. One is the so-called 'historical necessity'. To view an incident as 'a historical necessity' or 'historically determined' is to consider it as a natural disaster. Such a view excludes any scope for human responsibility, of either the victim or the perpetrator. If the victims are deemed innocent, but there is no perpetrator, the meaning of 'innocence' is lost, and the incident becomes a matter of destiny, or Divine Providence or similar. Thus, our discussion of 'innocence' as an element of ill-being necessarily excludes the idea of historical necessity or historical determinism.

The other issue is that it is not always possible to determine where responsibility lies. War responsibility has never been clear at any time in history. As Masao Maruyama pointed out, in Japan after the war the discussion on 'infinite responsibility' had simply evaporated into 'non-responsibility' (Maruyama 1961). The point is that where there was a calamity someone was responsible for it. Responsibility does not always rest on (an) individual(s): in some cases, it clearly lies with a system, which 'transmits and expands a small, localized original mistake' (Nakaoka 1979: 9). In practice, determining responsibility often becomes a political issue, and an extended investigation does not necessarily result in clear identification of who or what is responsible. Nevertheless, the difficulty in placing responsibility does not mean that no one is responsible.

To further complicate the issue, ill-being can be a result of both individual choices and outside factors. If the victim is 100 percent innocent or 100 percent responsible, the issue is simple. However, when both individual and outside factors are involved, we need to determine the extent to which an incident was caused by the victim's own actions as well as by other factors. If this is done successfully, the portion of the resultant ill-being that was caused by those other than the victim is subject to compensation. This idea was the basis for the 'distributional justice' developed and applied by Roemer (1996).

Roemer's argument is as follows (cf. Hamada and Ishida 2003): for example, a decision to smoke is determined partly by individual choice and partly by environmental factors (ethnicity, profession, parents' habits and customs, social class etc.) that are outside the control of the individual. Roemer divides a society into factions of equivalent classes according to environmental factors. For example, if the environmental factor was 'gender, ethnicity, profession and age', the faction of equivalent classes will be people with similar attributes such as 'female, white, university professor, sixty years old', or 'male, black, steel worker, sixty years old'. A society can be divided into a composite of those exclusive groups. Each group shows its own typical pattern of smoking, which is a characteristic of that group, not of an individual. Among the sixty-year-old black steel workers, each has been smoking for a different length of time. That difference is considered a personal choice.

Attempts such as Roemer's to quantify the size of personal responsibility in a resultant ill-being directly relates to compensation issues. Practical applications of studies like this will be discussed in a later section. The point to be made here is that incidents and conditions of ill-being in which the victim is innocent can be studied objectively.

We now have the object of the sociology of well-being and ill-being. We are dealing with ill-being that satisfies three elements: that the incident/condition is *shikri-ni*, adversely affecting 'the innocent' by inflicting 'casualties' on them. Some may object to the fact that we are not paying enough attention to well-being. However, if we examine past studies of well-being, we observe that discussions of well-being ultimately lead to discussion of ill-being. Of course, well-being and ill-being are not always polar opposites: not all of the issues concerning well-being apply to ill-being. On the other hand, human well-being cannot be achieved without addressing issues of ill-being.

Importantly, the following discussion assumes that ill-being must be reduced. There may be some positive affects of ill-being—e.g., some see it as a challenge necessary for character building. Here, however, ill-being is understood as a social ill that must be either avoided or minimized.

From the increase of well-being to reduction of ill-being

The search for human well-being has been the fundamental theme of philosophy since ancient Greece. For our purpose, it will suffice to begin our survey with nineteenth century utilitarianism.[2] The ultimate goal of utilitarianism was 'the greatest happiness of the greatest number'. It held that individual happiness could be measured in terms of utility, and one needs only to obtain the sum of the whole. Aside from the question whether or not 'happiness' can be measured, this naïve theory leaves some questions unanswered: is there a limit to the amount of utility individuals can increase?; should a large increase of utility for some people justify a smaller increase for others?; is the 'greatest number' a compromise for 'all'?; would leaving out some people be acceptable as 'inevitable'?

Pareto, an economist and sociologist, offered some answers to these questions, which have come to be called the 'Pareto optimum'. The 'Pareto optimum' is the state in which further increase of utility for some is not possible without reduction of utility for others. According to this line of thinking, if a society maintains the 'Pareto optimum', no one is disadvantaged. I want to point that there is no guarantee that inequality does not exist under the 'Pareto optimum'. Furthermore, if changes occur in resource constraints (i.e., if the 'pie gets bigger'), the 'Pareto optimum' will also shift. For example, if one person's wage is doubled while others' remain the same, unless there is some convincing reason for the others to accept his/her rise, they would perceive it to be 'unfair'. In sociology this phenomenon has been referred to as 'relative deprivation'.

From a sociological perspective, the 'Pareto optimum' remains a vague concept. Because utilitarianism aimed at maximizing total utility, it was unable to discuss the distribution of wealth and problems arising from changes in distribution. As a result, it failed to offer a framework for discussion of basic issues such as poverty.

Modern economics has developed a tradition of measuring well-being via Gross National Product. This approach, like utilitarianism, is inadequate because it fails to solve problems stemming from the distribution of wealth. It cannot see beyond total or average wealth. It cannot deal with other kinds of wealth that relate to assets and income, such as life expectancy, infant mortality, quality of relationships in terms of race or gender, etc. It is now commonly understood that GNP is a poor measure of well-being.

An alternative approach to the utilitarian's pursuit of maximum total utility is to equalize certain essentials (whatever they may be) while allowing disparity in non-essentials. Rawls's 'justice theory' and Nussbaum's 'capabilities approach' are based on this way of thinking.

Rawls identifies a category of 'primary goods' (1971) and later (1982) specifies their contents: basic freedoms including freedom of association, freedom of choice of domicile and job, power and privilege associated with responsible positions, income and assets, and human dignity. The reason for calling these goods 'basic' is that any rational human being would consider them to be essential. All citizens, therefore, must have them. The first two 'primary goods'—the freedoms—are of particular importance. When the two freedoms are enjoyed by all, improvements in the remaining three social 'goods' indices will be addressed, starting from the least wealthy.

Of the critical comments on Rawls's theory, I will mention just one (Kukathas and Pettit 1990). For Rawls, the responsibility to bring 'justice' lies with the nation. In an effort to satisfy the 'primary goods', therefore, the 'least wealthy' are identified by their relative position within the nation. Let us consider two nations, one (A), wealthier than the other (B). When Rawls's theory is applied to the combined population of A and B, any attempts at redistribution of resources to improve the 'least wealthy' within each nation will be inadequate, because the 'least wealthy' of A is not equal to the least wealthy of B.

Nussbaum adapted her 'capabilities approach' from Sen. Her approach shares Rawls' view that certain minimum requirements must be satisfied. But she criticizes Rawls for ignoring the fact that people vary in both their need for resources and their abilities to turn available resources to their advantage: for example, an ordinary person and a person confined to a wheelchair have different needs for resources in moving the same distance. Nussbaum has incorporated such factors into her approach.

Sen observes that the dominant evaluation criteria for social welfare has long been wealth and utility (Sen 1985). However, he says, wealth is not welfare itself, but merely its means; having goods is different from enjoying good health, and for sick people social welfare does not guarantee well-being. What people want and what makes them happy changes with environment and circumstance. Feeling the same standard of subjective well-being does not mean the same standard of social welfare. 'Function' means 'what a person can do and what he/she can be'. For example, a car has a function to move people. Its owner, as long as he/she satisfies physical and other requirements, is capable of driving a car, which makes the person feel well-being (joy). Sen calls the total of the functional vector of an individual 'capabilities', and an approach to welfare based on those functions the 'capabilities approach'. The core question of the 'capabilities approach' is not 'is this person satisfied?' (utilitarianism) nor 'how much resources does this person have under control?' (resource distribution approach). Rather, the 'capabilities approach' asks 'what is this person capable of?' and, 'who is this person?'[3]

Through a number of publications, Sen's 'capabilities approach' has become widely known, and has been partially incorporated in the United Nation's *Report on Human Development*. Nussbaum's approach is a more realistic and practical refinement of Sen's. She expands the 'functions vector' through observing the lives of women in India. Her list of the main human functional capabilities is as follows (Nussbaum 2000: 78–80; note that I have altered each sentence into question form and simplified some of the concepts):

1. Life: Do they die prematurely?
2. Bodily health: Do they have good health that allows them to reproduce and bring up offspring? Are they adequately nourished? Do they have adequate shelter?
3. Bodily integrity: Are they able to move freely from place to place? Are they safe against assault (including sexual assault, child sexual abuse and domestic violence)? Do they have opportunities for sexual satisfaction?
4. Senses, imagination and thought: Are they able to use the senses? Can they imagine, think and reason in a 'truly human' way?
5. Emotions: Are they able to have attachments to things and people other than themselves? Are they free from overwhelming fear, anxiety of abuse, neglect or traumatic events?
6. Practical reason: Can they form a conception of the good? Can they engage in critical reflection in planning their life?

7. Affiliation:
   a) Can they live with and towards others? Can they recognize and express their concern for other people? Can they engage in various forms of social interaction? Can they imagine and have compassion for the situation of another? Are they capable of justice and friendship?
   b) Do they have social bases of self-respect and non-humiliation? Are they treated as a dignified being of equal worth to others? This entails, at a minimum, protection against discrimination on the basis of race, sex, sexual orientation, religion, caste, ethnicity or national origin. Are they able to work as a human being, exercising practical reason and entering into meaningful relationships of mutual recognition with other workers?
8. Other species: Can they live with concern for and in relation to animals, plants and the world of nature?
9. Play: Can they laugh, play or enjoy recreational activities?
10. Control over their environment:
    a) Political: Can they participate effectively in political choices that govern their life? Do they have the right of political participation, protections of free speech and association?
    b) Material: Can they hold property (both land and movable goods), not just formally but in terms of real opportunity? Do they have property rights on an equal basis with others? Do they have freedom from unwarranted search and seizure?

Nussbaum claims that the items in this list are separate components: they are not interchangeable, thereby limiting trade-offs and the applicability of quantitative cost-benefit analysis. They are all critical: fully satisfying one item is not a substitute for another item in the list. What a government can do is to provide social bases for those capabilities. Where differences exist, the provision of a base for later improvement becomes its task. Finally, each item has its 'threshold', a level which must be available to citizens (Nussbaum 2000: 6).

She proposes to use these capabilities as 'measures for quality of life'. These capabilities can vary in countries, regions, race or sexes. Our task in hand is to examine the reasons for the differences: government policies can deal with some but not others, but the basic principle of government is to provide social bases upon which all of these capabilities can be achieved by all of its citizens.

Although Nussbaum maintains that all ten capabilities must be satisfied, she considers 'practical reason' and 'affiliation' to be particularly important because together they organize and suffuse all the others (Nussbaum 2000: 82).

Some of these items may appear to be a bit too abstract, ambiguous, or ad hoc, but they are nevertheless clearly well thought out in terms of global application. Nussbaum explains that her starting point for determining these characteristics developed while interviewing two Indian women. She says:

> Critical moral principles are especially urgent when we consider women's situation, as particularly vulnerable people in a time of rapid economic change. If we consider each person as worthy of regard, as an end and not just a means, we cannot in any simple way praise Gujarat's rapid economic growth, which has left many powerless people behind and caused many self-employed women to lose their livelihoods. (Nussbaum 2000: 32)

> Vasanti and Jayamma, like many women in India and in the rest of the world, have lacked support for many of the most central human functions, and that lack of support is at least to some extent caused by their being women. But women, unlike rocks and trees and horses, have the potential to become capable of these human functions, given sufficient nutrition, education, and other support. That is why their unequal failure in capability is a problem of justice. It is up to all human beings to solve this problem. I claim that a universal conception of human capability gives us excellent guidance as we pursue this difficult task. (Nussbaum 2000: 110)

Her description of ideals and tasks corresponds to our idea of humanity's well-being and ill-being: the state in which all human beings' capabilities are satisfied, at least above the minimum level, is well-being and the state in which they are not satisfied is ill-being. As she notes, these two women are not responsible for their ill-being: their ill-being stems 'mostly from the fact that they are women'. This concept of ill-being satisfies the three elements discussed earlier: it affects many, they are innocent, and casualties (i.e., deprivation of life opportunities) have been incurred.

Although Nussbaum does not explicitly say so, she appears to maintain that the important task is not to increase well-being but to reduce ill-being. Pursuit of increased well-being leads to utilitarianism, which is not a bad thing in itself. But if we are trapped in the pursuit of increased well-being we fail to address ill-being in practice. We are not dealing only with the ill-being of unequal distribution such as poverty, economic inequality or disparity, but also, importantly, with the ill-being of unfulfilled human capabilities.

Nussbaum's primary aim is the elimination of the ill-being of being prevented from realizing one's full human capabilities.

Although Nussbaum is a philosopher, basing her research on poor Indian women and her inclination towards real human actions and government policies brings her thought close to sociology. What, then, has sociology proper had to say about well-being and ill-being?

The sociological perspective on well-being and ill-being is directly related to the question of what sociology is. Let us briefly look at Comte and Spencer, the first generation of sociologists, before moving on to the twentieth century.

For Comte, order was the fundamental condition of progress, and progress was the inevitable purpose of order (Comte 1844). Comte saw history as progress, so it was obvious for him that progress meant 'human well-being'. As he saw it, however, in the confusion in the middle of the French Revolution, the social situation was made worse by the 'mistake of the king', who sought order without aspiring for progress, and the 'mistake of the people' who aspired for progress but disregarded order (Comte 1822). Comte hoped that sociology as empirical science would correct those mistakes and play a major part in conceiving a new social condition.

That Spencer's major publication *Social Statics* (1851) was subtitled '*or the Conditions Essential to Human Happiness*' is not widely known. Spencer was always critical of Bentham's view of humanity, expressed in his maxim, the 'greatest happiness of the greatest number', and held that the task of his 'social statics' was to decide what laws are required in order to achieve perfect happiness. He considered it wrong for an individual to achieve happiness by sacrificing the happiness of others and formulated a conception of a social condition, or 'justice', that would not disadvantage any of its members even though every member has faults.

Weber, a second generation sociologist, was concerned about modern rationalism, specifically the universal historical question of why modern capitalism emerged in the Western world (Weber 1920). He attributed the foundations of modern capitalism to the religious ethics or ethos of Protestantism. According to Weber, for the people who attempted to secure salvation through becoming 'means to the glory and majesty of God', it was necessary to engage in labor (a "calling") accompanied by worldly asceticism. Seeing an affinity between this ethos and the capitalist 'spirit', Weber argued that modern capitalism was based on the life philosophy derived from this religious ethic. In this realm, individual salvation (well-being) and social prosperity (well-being) happily coexist. Weber's religious/sociological analysis has established this. But how has world history evolved since then?

'In the field of its highest development, in the United States, the pursuit of wealth, stripped of its religious and ethical meaning, tends to become associated with purely mundane passions, which often actually give it the character of sport' (Weber 1920: S.204 [1930: 182]). Ubiquitous in this realm are 'specialists without spirit' and 'sensualists without hearts'. Weber called this social condition the 'iron cage'. If modern rationalism aimed for the 'elimination of magic', the end of the pursuit of rationalism is what Mannheim (1940) calls 'actual irrationality'. Here, rationalization and irrationality exist hand-in-hand. In the 'iron cage', both well-being and ill-being have become secularized. While religious asceticism was alive and well, even unequal distribution of wealth in the real world seemed justified by an assurance that it was a 'dispensation of Divine Providence'; now when worldly desires and life's vanities have increased, it is nothing more than a result of victory or defeat in competition.

Durkheim referred to 'progress in well-being' in his discussion of the origin of the social division of labor (Durkheim 1893). Durkheim's main argument was that the pursuit of well-being, contrary to what economists claim, does not necessarily accelerate the division of labor. One must look between the lines to detect what Durkheim considered well-being to be. In his view, well-being (*bonheur*) is a healthy state (*l'état de santé*), balanced actions in which all human faculties develop in harmony. Because well-being is culturally and socially relative, what was considered well-being in the past could well be considered painful in the present. 'According to Pascal, happiness for men is different from happiness for women. Likewise, happiness in a lower society is not happiness in a modern society, and vice versa. This does not mean that one happiness is greater than the other' (1893/1971: 242). In an affluent society in which the division of labor is highly developed, one can find the social ailments that Durkheim called anomie: 'The result of the endless conflicts and all kinds of disorderly state displayed by the terrible vista of the world of business' (1893/1971: 2). One of the more extreme affects of anomie is suicide. He thus concludes that 'progress does not dramatically increase happiness' (1893/1971: 242).

All is not beyond salvation, however. Anomie can be countered if society re-establishes cohesion and order by balancing various functions. For example, he says, in order to construct the missing rules structure, rebuilding cooperatives or occupational groups would be effective. Occupational groups are most appropriate because they 'have direct interest in economic life, thus they can detect all possible desires', and 'have the continuity of the family' (1893/1971: Preface to the second edition).

We must leave it to another occasion to conduct a comprehensive survey of well-being in the history of sociology. Here, we need to confirm a few points concerning Weber and Durkheim. First, they both view history and the state of human being in dichotomous terms: positive and negative history, well-being and ill-being. For Weber, the 'elimination of magic' was positive history but irrationalism was negative history; for Durkheim, the progressive division of labor which allows organic unity is positive history while abnormal forms of the division of labor are negative history. They both see positive and negative, well-being and ill-being, as inseparable and synchronous. Furthermore, unlike the simple utilitarian, they do not advocate the pursuit of increased well-being.

We must question, however, the extent of the synchronicity or concomitance between well-being and ill-being, for this concerns the very possibility of increasing well-being and reducing ill-being at the same time. There seem to be two different types of concomitance in their writing; substantial and conceptual. In substantial concomitance, well-being and ill-being go side by side as an entity of two sides of a coin. When well-being increases, then so does ill-being. In the latter, the increase of well-being automatically means the decrease of ill-being, and the decrease of well-being automatically means the increase of ill-being—i.e., the concepts are defined as forming a duality. If well-being and ill-being are absolutely inseparable and substantially concomitant, a kind of divine dispensation in which human intervention is impossible, we must resign ourselves to experiencing ill-being forever. This is the case with Weber's and Durkheim's views of historical progress. My belief is that we must reject the idea that well-being and ill-being are substantially inseparable. They are separable, and it is possible to increase well-being and reduce ill-being at the same time. We can intervene in both, and it is sociology's task to probe the precise extent to which we can.

This section has been inspired by Saburō Ichii's (1971) excellent discussion 'What is the progress of history?' He argues that, although pleasure and pain are complementary, 'perhaps the standard ethics of human society should aim at reducing the typical "pain" specific to the period rather than increasing the total "pleasure"' (Ichii 1971: 139).

The difficulty in calibrating well-being and ill-being is not his only reason. He also notes that 'pleasure' is subjective, and even for the same person, it is subject to the law of diminishing marginal utility: the amount of 'pleasure' (utility) a person takes from additional satisfaction does not remain the same but gradually decreases. Pursuing increased pleasure also raises the problem of 'relative deprivation': an increase in some people's 'pleasure' may be linked to a decrease in other people's 'pleasure', that is, the pleasure necessarily causes pain to others.

From this perspective, Ichii arrives at the ethical principle: 'we must strive as much as possible to decrease the pain each person (homo-sapiens) suffers due to reasons for which the person should not be held responsible' (Ichii 1971: 143). This principle is central to what we have expressed in the phrase 'killing many innocent people'.

Types and historical characteristics of ill-being

Mita (1963) presented an empirical and inductive structure that he called 'Patterns of unhappiness in contemporary society', derived from his analysis of the personal advice columns in newspapers. As indicated earlier, Mita identified four patterns of ill-being: 'apathy/ennui', 'anxiety/impatience', 'solitude/hostility' and 'paucity/dissatisfaction'. As discussed, Nussbaum outlined ten 'central capabilities' of human functioning that must be satisfied. For Mita, ill-being took the form of consciousness and reactions to the alienation which occurs in capitalist societies. Nussbaum's approach claims to be universal, while sensitive to pluralism and cultural differences. But she recognizes that these are relative values and that her research was deeply colored by the specific problems of women in India. Further research is required to determine whether her capabilities approach is truly universal. They will suffice at present for us to create general types of ill-being.

Types of ill-being can be determined by whether each of Nussbaum's ten items is satisfied above the minimum threshold. If we conceptualize them according to Ragin's (1987) Boolean algebra, the results are as follows. We mark each item with '1' if it is satisfied, and '0' if not. Thus we have two to the tenth power of cases (see Table 1.1). Case one, where all items show '1', means that all the capabilities are satisfied. This case is not considered ill-being. Case 1024, where all items show '0', means none of the capabilities are satisfied. Between the two extremes are cases where some items are satisfied and others

Table 1.1: Various types of unhappiness imagined on the basis of the Nussbaum criteria

	Requite									
Case	**1**	**2**	**3**	**4**	**5**	**6**	**7**	**8**	**9**	**10**
1	1	1	1	1	1	1	1	1	1	1
2	1	1	1	1	1	1	1	1	1	0
3	1	1	1	1	1	1	1	1	0	1
…	…	…	…	…	…	…	…	…	…	…
…	…	…	…	…	…	…	…	…	…	…
…	…	…	…	…	…	…	…	…	…	…
1023	1	0	0	0	0	0	0	0	0	0
1024	0	0	0	0	0	0	0	0	0	0

are not. The number of logically possible types of ill-being is, therefore, two to the tenth power minus one (2^{10-1}).

If we can apply appropriate dependent variables (such as actions of dissatisfaction) to this with relevant data, we can empirically draw out the patterns of ill-being that cause the dependent variables. In Nussbaum's image, the poor Indian women, for whom none of the capabilities are satisfied, are in dire straits. But which pattern of ill-being is most dominant among them? This is a reasonable question and is answerable if we could manipulate the variables and obtain matching empirical data. We must leave that for a future task.

As for the types of ill-being, in addition to the general/logical type and empirical type, it is possible to construct them from a historical perspective. For example, some have claimed that equality in basic commodities has been achieved in Japan (Hara and Seiyama 2005). What they mean is that Japanese society has overcome starvation and become an affluent society. Around the globe, however, starvation remains a serious problem. We can attribute phenomena such as starvation to the 'ill-being of poverty'.

We can similarly consider the disparity between rich and poor. Disparity may be a serious problem in one nation, but a regional problem in another. Disparity can also exist between countries. It can take the form of assets or income. It might also be non-economic, as in levels of education or power. In general, disparity refers to the availability of control of resources. Any such disparity between groups of people translates into disparity in life opportunities, and thus ill-being. Of course, the 'distress of the rich' is also a real social problem, but we shall limit our discussion to the problem of those who are deprived of life opportunities.

If we turn to economic disparities between countries, such as the 'north-south problem', responsibility for the mal-distribution is unclear. These may therefore be better classified as a fourth type of ill-being. However, as they are also problems of disparity, we include them here for discussion. Let us call this type 'the ill-being of social disparity'.

Changes in society produce various distortions to the distribution of resources. One of Nussbaum's informants reported that economic development was the beginning of ill-being. Although not often cited today, Ogburn observed that the disparities between technological and cultural developments bring various types of ill-being (Ogburn 1922). Changes in lifestyle, inter-generational conflicts, changes in medical technology and drug poisoning and so on cause depravation of life opportunities at various levels—individual, inter-personal relationships, family, company and community. In postwar Japan, the 'high economic growth' and the 'bubble economy', which eventually 'burst', created a type of ill-being distinct from 'the ill-being of poverty' and 'the ill-being of social disparity' (Suzuki and Nakamichi 1997). Let us call this 'the ill-being of affluence'. The term may sound too general, but it is a distinct type of its own.

Finally, there is a kind of ill-being that does not fit in any of the three types outlined so far. Globalization, depending on how it is defined, is not only a recent phenomenon. What Wallerstein (1974) calls the 'modern world system' dates back to the sixteenth century. Colonialism was part of this system, and a prominent manifestation of globalization. Wars have always mediated the flow of people, goods and money across national borders. However, the emergence of anti-globalization campaigns, the defense of identity by threatened peoples and cultures, threats from more powerful nations to those peoples and cultures, the daily advance of postcolonialism and rampant terrorism all indicate that a type of ill-being specific to the twenty-first century is produced alongside and within globalization (Žižek 2002; Cohen and Kennedy 2000). Most of these states of ill-being can be classified as specific to contemporary globalization, but there are others that do not quite fit into this classification (such as the victims of atomic bombs or Minamata Disease). We therefore tentatively call this type 'non-obvious ill-being'. 'Non-obvious' can be from either a common social or lay perspective, or from a sociological perspective. We will discuss this term in more detail later. For the moment, we will locate any type of ill-being that cannot be classified in the other three types into this category.

We have now identified four types of ill-being:

- the ill-being of poverty
- the ill-being of social disparity
- the ill-being of affluence
- non-obvious ill-being.

Ichii observed that there are 'typical pains specific to each period' (1971). This typology of ill-being might be suggestive of Maslow's 'hierarchy of needs': they somehow appear to be 'grades of ill-being'. But we cannot grade ill-being according to any such theoretical hierarchy. The hierarchy of needs assumes that satisfaction of lower-level needs will lead to higher-level needs. This does not apply to ill-being. Resolving specific ill-being in a particular historical period does not necessarily require resolving the ill-being of an earlier period: rather, in the long-term all types of ill-being simply accumulate. But this accumulation is not simply linear: plural non-contemporaneous types of ill-being coexist contemporaneously (Mannheim).

What should the sociology of well-being and ill-being do?

So far, I have roughly outlined the targets of the sociology of well-being and ill-being. Now I turn to a discussion of how sociology should engage these targets.

Each study has its own course of development. Beginning with identification of the problem, data must be collected, theories, models and hypotheses constructed, data analyzed (which may include developing or innovating analytical methods), conclusions verified, and policy recommendations proposed and followed-up. What, then, should the sociology of well-being and ill-being do at each stage of its development?

The object of study

The very first and most important problem of a study at the outset is to identify its object and determine how to approach it. I have already defined the three conditions of the object of the sociology of well-being and ill-being. Now we need to identify particular incidents or states of ill-being—which, at this stage, may be concrete and empirical or abstract and logical concepts such as poverty (as designated in the Gini coefficient)—and examine whether or not they fulfill the three conditions. Given that not all sociology is concerned with ill-being, it is worth considering what proportion of studies in sociology are of ill-being. For example, although war may be the ultimate state of ill-being, surprisingly few sociological studies deal with this subject. The International Sociology Association (ISA) has a division on 'Army and Conflict Resolution', but it presupposes the post-WWII Cold War and arms race. Similarly, while studies of the 9/11 terrorist attack have recently emerged within this division, as a whole it continues to focus on the Cold War, which leaves the division rather outdated. Studies of war in particular and ill-being more generally, seem to be given far too little attention in proportion to its gravity.

When ill-being is treated as an abstract and logical concept, the sociology of ill-being is conducted under a 'generalizing strategy'. The generalizing strategy attempts to describe and clarify the base mechanism of the matter independently of specific time and space (Fararo and Kosaka 2003). Under such circumstances, mechanisms that were previously deemed irrelevant may still be worth re-examining for the purpose of identifying ill-being. For example, from our perspective, the well-established category of a 'social dilemma' can be re-interpreted as a mechanism by which each player seeks well-being, while its aggregate produces ill-being for the group.

Another approach is to seek ill-being in empirical episodes. In this case, ill-being has occurred at a point in the past. Although the precise point is not always obvious, conceptually, ill-being occurs at one moment in time and evolves. Although this is often overlooked, ill-being evolves in some way. It may expand or converge: it follows its own course.

In Figure 1.1, the course of ill-being is shown above the horizontal line (time moves from left to right). The sociology of ill-being must follow the diverse evolution of ill-being: the death of people as direct victims of war in turn deprives their families of life opportunities, which becomes the next object of study. Ill-being diffuses through time and space, eventually converging at a point that seems to become

Figure 1.1: Studies on unhappiness and missed opportunities

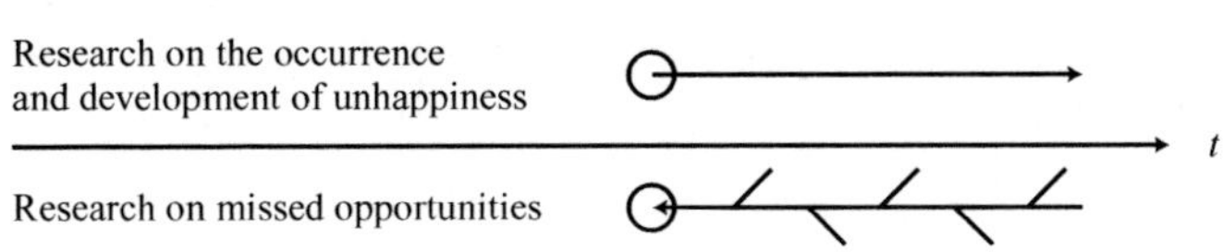

Figure 1.2: Two stages of activities to pursue happiness

	Realization of happiness	**Mitigation of unhappiness**
What should we do as citizens?	1	2
What should sociology do?	3	4

a normal part of life. However, that convergence point would not have existed had the ill-being not occurred, and it is necessary to reveal the actual diffusion of the ill-being by comparing the new convergence point with the imaginary convergence point; in this case, how it changes the life of the surviving family, the mental care of soldiers, re-habilitation of returned soldiers and so on.

At the time of writing, we are beginning a research project in conjunction with Vietnamese NGOs. The study covers fourteen topics including: how the families of the children affected by the defoliant Agent Orange are situated and how they are adapting to the situation; how, thirty years after the war ended, the Vietnamese people see the war; and what roles the former soldiers play in the community. The paucity of sociological studies on the Vietnam War is conspicuous in light of the richness of other material such as publications by photojournalists, news reports, novels and films. Such paucity is also common to studies of other types of ill-being.

An empirical approach to the study of ill-being should include an important area, namely the 'study of missed opportunity'.

The pursuit of how well-being can be achieved and how ill-being is reduced takes the following two questions:

The two questions are: 'what should citizens do?' and 'what should sociology do?' Here, from a sociological perspective, we shall focus on cell 4. To identify and recognize an instance of ill-being plays the same role as 'hope' in the pursuit of well-being: what occurred in the past could occur in the present or future. Conversely, to figure out what to do when it occurs, we need to look back to see what should have been done to prevent or reduce the instance of ill-being. Let us call this kind of inquiry 'the study of missed opportunity'.[4] Its aim is to visit past instances of ill-being in order to learn from them and find ways to reduce present and future ill-being.

Let us briefly look at four examples that have been objects of the study of missed opportunity.

Example 1: Missed opportunity in the Vietnam War

On 24 December 2003, some Japanese Department of Foreign Affairs Secret Documents became available to the public. The documents revealed that, at the time of the Tonkin Gulf Incident, which triggered the Vietnam War, the second attack by North Vietnam did not in fact occur, and that some members of the Japanese government were skeptical about the US claim that it had. This revelation made it clear that the justification for the war, which continued for the next ten years, was a fiction forged by the US government; and that the Japanese government supported the US government's decision, even though it was not totally convinced of its justification. To be blunt, the truth was hidden from both the American and Japanese publics.

The documents also revealed other, more serious matters. For example, an immense misunderstanding occurred in interpreting the 'Pleiku incident'. In February 1965, on President Johnson's order, Special Assistant to the President McGeorge Bundy arrived in Vietnam. His mission was to assess the situation and advise the president on three options for the US: to expand military intervention, to maintain the status quo or to gradually withdraw troops. In the early hours of the morning after his arrival, the air base at Pleiku in central Vietnam was attacked. Bundy interpreted this attack as provocation by the North Vietnamese, and immediately advised the president to expand military intervention. The carpet bombing of North Vietnam followed, producing a large proportion of the war's victims. Somewhat ironically, perhaps, it is now clear that the North Vietnamese government did not know at the time that Bundy was in Saigon on such a mission; which means that the bombing of the Pleiku air base could not have been a deliberate provocation.

Nguyen Co Thach, the then North Vietnam Foreign Minister, says:

> You must bear in mind that our economy is an agricultural economy, not an industrial economy, nor did it develop like the US economy... With an agricultural economy there is always decentralization, because communication is so difficult. But industrialization leads to urbanization and centralization. So you see: you were very centralized in your decisions and commands, and we were very decentralized in ours. (cited in Higashi 2000)

Example 2: Missed opportunity in an accident at a petrochemical complex
On 16 September 1973, the second day of holidays, black smoke rose over Senboku petrochemical complex. An electrical blackout inside the complex triggered a number of systems to shut out as a safety measure, but the raw material that was in the system was automatically sent to the flare stack and burnt, emitting the smoke. Later investigation revealed that it was a 'threefold accident' that occurred in the period of half a day (Nakaoka 1979): (1) The electrical blackout was due to a mistake by a subcontract electrical technician; (2) There was an accident in an ethylene plant caused by the combination of the blackout and emergency computer control system; (3) A boiler exploded initiated by the environment of both blackout and the ethylene plant accident. Each of these incidents was triggered by 'a minor mistake'. Although the accident did not lead to a major catastrophe, the incident exposed the vulnerability of large and complex systems.

The first accident occurred in the following sequence:

1. The electrical technician's hand slipped and let go of a cable.
2. The cable hit a copper conductor bar causing a short circuit, giving the worker an electrical shock.
3. By chance, an electrical conductor installed to disperse unusual pressure broke down.
4. The first transformer broke down.
5. The second transformer broke down.
6. The boiler stopped working.
7. The in-house generator stopped.

This sequence of events reveals how the entire system 'functioned to carry and expand what was originally a small, localized mistake' (Nakaoka 1979: 9).

The second accident occurred as follows:

1. Faced with the emergency blackout, the chief operator immediately shut-down the heating systems of the odd-numbered (of 15) furnaces, and put the even-numbered furnaces on stand-by.
2. The computer shut itself down in response to the blackout.
3. Reducing the heat of the furnaces required closing a fuel valve, which was usually done automatically by the computers; the computer's failure to complete this operation increased the heat/temperature.
4. As a result, the centrifugal casting pipe melted.

The third accident: out of the twenty-seven fuel-jet valves closed manually, two valves were not completely closed. Because it was Sunday night, the normal staff of around 100 had been reduced to ten, and it was the least experienced worker who remained at the panel to keep watch.

Example 3: The missed opportunity to end the Pacific War

In February 1945 the then Prime Minister Konoe Fumimaro suggested surrender to the Emperor. The Emperor, however, rejected this recommendation, saying that it would be difficult to surrender before achieving another substantial military result in battle (Oguma 2002: 58; Mori 1993: 289). During the following six months the battle of Okinawa was fought, many kamikaze pilots were dispatched, Japan suffered heavy air-raids, atomic bombs were dropped on Hiroshima and Nagasaki, the Soviet Union declared war, the Korean peninsula was divided and a huge number of people were either killed or starved to death on the southern fronts. A large proportion of Japan's total war deaths, in particular, most of the civilian deaths, occurred during these six months.

Example 4: The missed opportunity to minimise Minamata Disease

"Strange disease" was first found widely among cats as early as 1952, and among human beings in 1953 in Minamata City, Kumamoto Prefecture. It was a serious nerve disease that sometimes caused death. At the beginning, people suspected an epidemic or endemic disease, but it was eventually determined that the disease, later named 'Minamata Disease', was due to organic mercury poisoning in the waste water discharged from a plant of Chisso Company, a producer of nitrogenous fertilizer. It turned out that more than 10 thousand people were severely affected by the disease in Minamata. If the fishermen's petition to stop the waste draining from the factory (17 January 1957) had been heeded, Miyazawa (1997) argues, the damages could have been kept to a minimum and perhaps terminated within one year.

Nishida, a Chisso plant manager, and others at the Minamata plant had suspected that the discharge from the plant was the cause of the disease judging from his proposal to improve the drainage of the acetaldehyde acid disposal system to collect the mercury (17 April 1957). But the Kumamoto prefectural government decided that the disease was unrelated to the factory—perhaps to avoid potential problems of responsibility and indemnity. At a time when preventing serious damage to human life should have been the priority, the government prioritized an inquiry into the cause of the disease ahead of stopping the discharge of polluted water. In the meantime, the damage spread. 'As a scientist, I refrained from making statements unless I was sure of the fact' (statement by witness Hosokawa). This scientism coupled with political interests, led to a failure to grasp available opportunities to avoid the deterioration of the situation.

In the spring of 1957, Tokuomi Haruhiko of the research team at Kumamoto University learned that the symptoms of the Minamata Disease were also present in cases of alkyl mercury poisoning. Yet he 'did not pay attention' to the connection because he 'thought a profit-making company would not drain an expensive substance such as mercury into the sea' (Miyazawa 1997: 131).

The first measure that should have been taken at the time was, as the Minamata fishermen requested, to stop the discharge. There was no need to stop all outflows from the factory: only acetaldehyde acid needed to be stopped. Or, they could have at least tested the water discharged from the plant. Within at most three months, the cause could have been found, and the damage contained within one year or so.

The Chisso plant itself was in the best position to take corrective measures or to conduct an investigation. The parties that were in a position to apply pressure on it to do so were primarily the Ministry of International Trade and Industry and the Kumamoto prefectural government. However, both maintained that investigating the cause was the first priority and took no action. In other words, they took the position that unless the cause was determined they were not obliged to act. This 'determination of the cause first' approach was the explanation provided at the national level ministerial meeting on 10 April 1957 for their failure to act (Miyazawa 1997: 111, 115, 144–5).

In short, the Minamata Disease could have been controlled within one year, rather than the fifty years it actually took.

In each of these examples, either the participants or outside observers have traced the history of the incident. In Figure 1.2, the arrow indicating the 'study of missed opportunities' points in the opposite direction to the factual development of ill-being. Also, while the factual development of ill-being may appear as a straight line, when we investigate it further, we find numerous crossroads of choices. The 'fishbone-like' branching represents these crossroads. We are then led to consider the possible courses of events if different choices had been made at each point (what Weber calls 'objective possibility judgment'). We probe the points which might have led to evading or reducing the incidents of ill-being: e.g., if, at one point choice B was taken instead of A, further ill-being might have been avoided. Of course, this is all hypothetical because certain choices were made to bring us to the situation we are in today. We cannot directly reverse these choices, but by pursuing hypotheses of 'objective possibility' we may be able to identify choices (that were not taken) that would have avoided or reduced the incidents of ill-being, and to use this knowledge to evade or reduce current or future ill-being.

Hence, the sociological study of missed opportunities is not simply about tracing the events that produced ill-being, finding the relevant 'crossroads' and making objective judgments. It is not, in the examples above, about pointing out that Bundy made the wrong decision, that the chief engineer and factory manager of the Chisso plant made mistakes, that Emperor Shōwa made a bad choice, and so on. Rather, the point is to unveil why those 'bad' decisions, from the perspective of reducing ill-being, were made in the first place. I shall return to this.

Meta-methods

In the previous section we discussed what the courses of study that sociology of well-being and ill-being should take. They are, in summary:

- identify the ill-being
- for discussing the abstract conception of ill-being, employ a 'generalizing strategy'
- for discussing empirical episodes of ill-being, to trace the origins and development of the particular ill-being
- trace the process of development backwards and identify 'missed opportunities'.

I have discussed the 'generalized strategy' elsewhere (although not specifically pertaining to ill-being) (Fararo and Kosaka 2003). Here, I will introduce the application of the 'meta-methods' for the study of empirical episodes of ill-being. Calling the methods 'meta' allows us to leave aside technical questions about methods—quality, quantity, or imagery—and focus on basic methodology.

Non-obvious

The term 'non-obvious' is borrowed from Collins, who advocated 'non-obvious sociology'. The mission of this approach, he holds, is to reveal some of the important factors that drive the world, which are 'not obvious to everyone' (Collins 1982).[5] Collins seems to suggest that sociologists, particularly great sociologists, can see truths that drive the world, and should teach those truths to ignorant lay people. While recognizing the significance of 'non-obvious sociology', I feel that what we really need is a sociology of what is 'non-obvious to sociologists'. This is particularly true with the sociology of well-being and ill-being.

Let me give two examples—the Vietnam War and 'the Hmong tragedy' (Takeuchi 1999). We call the former the 'Vietnam War', but if we were to mention a 'Vietnam War' in Vietnam, we would be met with a blank look. In Vietnam, this war is variously referred to as: 'the War against America to save Vietnam', 'the war of Vietnamese independence', 'the anti-American war' or simply, in English, 'the American War'. Japan, bound by the Japan–US Security Treaty, sided with the US, and therefore has adopted the American term 'Vietnam War'. The differences in perspective here go beyond the name of the war, too. While the US periodizes the war from 1965 to 1975, the high school history textbooks widely used in Vietnam show this historical period to be from 1954 to 1975 (Dinh 2004). For the Vietnamese, this period begins with their victorious battle at Dien Bien Phu, which signaled the end of French colonial rule, and ends with the meeting at Geneva and the peace treaty at Paris, and should be understood as a historically continuous 'struggle for independence and unification'. The American view of the Vietnam War (1965–75), in other words, represents a different history from the one seen by the Vietnamese people.

The Hmong had been a minority ethnic group in China, where they were called the Miao Tribe. They were expelled by the Qing dynasty (1644–1911) and spread throughout South East Asia, especially Vietnam, Laos, and Cambodia. When US President Kennedy's New Frontier program was implemented, the Hmong were recruited, under a 'Hmong injection plan', to be trained as the main unit of a special strike force to fight against the North Vietnamese. In practice, they were used to reduce the numbers of American casualties. The Vietnam War Memorial in Washington DC does not include their names among the soldiers killed in the war (Takeuchi 1999).

Obviously the Vietnam War produced many forms of ill-being, yet ill-being varies depending on the perspective from which it is considered: the war produced ill-being for the American soldiers killed in the war and their families, but the Vietnamese people suffered greater ill-being. The Korean soldiers, who fought and were injured in Vietnam, would justifiably feel that the ill-being they suffered as a consequence of the war was unreasonable. The problem is that each perspective presents a different view of the incident, and that by adopting any one view, all of the others are automatically excluded. The Hmong perspective, for example, is not accounted for by any of the major representations of the Vietnam War. The war clearly amounts to a destruction of the Hmong people and their culture, yet this perspective remains 'non-obvious' even to sociologists. The 'Tragedy of the Hmong' and the Vietnam War thus represent examples of ill-being that cannot be ignored.

The three-tier pattern of 'structure–action–image'

The examples of 'missed opportunity' presented above vary significantly from one another. Yet we can conceptualize them in a three-tiered pattern in which 'actions' mediate 'structures' and 'images'. Simply put, the 'structure' is given first. 'Structure' is the objective system in which the world functions. Labor systems and technology are included. Various ministerial authorities and politics also fall into this category. So do international relationships between nation-states. 'Image', in contrast, is about how people perceive those structures. 'Image' can sometimes be substituted by 'knowledge'. Fact judgments, value judgments and action judgments fall into this category. Ethics and ambitions also contribute to the image. Certain images may be socially established as law, or may exist only within

Figure 1.3: Images, action and structure

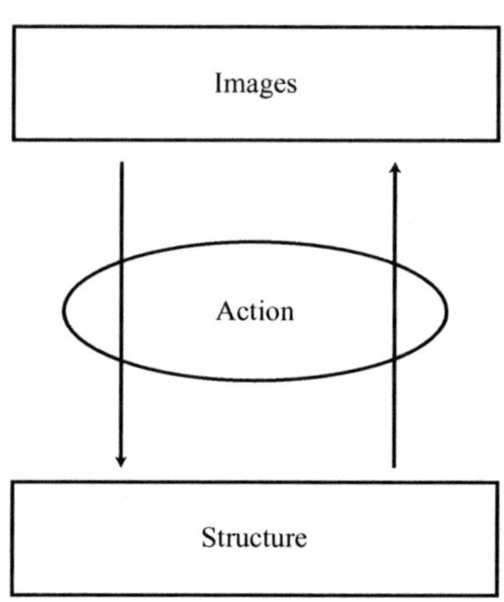

people's consciousness. People with power and authority have certain images of an issue or matter that are frequently different from those held by people with no such power or influence. Different images may not reflect objective facts. Usually, those images are biased in some way; we are therefore concerned with the nature of that particular bias. People do not take action under a given structure without mediation: they act in accordance with the image/knowledge they have of the structure. In his idea of 'dual structures', Giddens stresses that structure and actions regulate each other (Giddens 1984). However, it is more correct to say that actions are regulated by images, rather than being unmediated reactions to the structure. It follows that the study of images is very important. Among individual actions, some are more influential than others; but the aggregate of all of those actions produce certain consequences. These consequences, in turn, affect the maintenance or changes in a structure.

The study of 'missed opportunities' should be understood in this three-tier context: what were the objective circumstances? (structure); how were the circumstances perceived? (image); who acted in accordance with what image? (action/inaction). Our task is to analyze how the incidents or situation of ill-being occurred in terms of the interaction of the three tiers. Here I can only point out the necessity for such a study and its direction, leaving detailed analysis of such episodes for another occasion.

Non-homogeneity

'Missed opportunities' here of course refers to opportunities for avoiding or reducing ill-being. In reality, we often miss or catch opportunities. This means that, unless prevented by physical conditions, there were some alternative choices that existed in terms of either 'image' or 'action'.

Here, A and B are separate entities: they exist non-simultaneously in time and are extraneous to each other in space. Each one has its own environment, expressed by the circle around it. A 'missed opportunity' means that choice B was taken where choice A should have been taken or vice versa. In Example 1, the choice was 'the commanding system and viewpoint in an agricultural country' versus 'the commanding system and viewpoint in an industrial country'. In Example 2, the choice was 'tightening the fuel valve to reduce heat' versus 'following the computer program and not reducing heat'. In Example 3, it was 'after achieving another outstanding military activ-

Figure 1.4: Two options and a missed opportunity

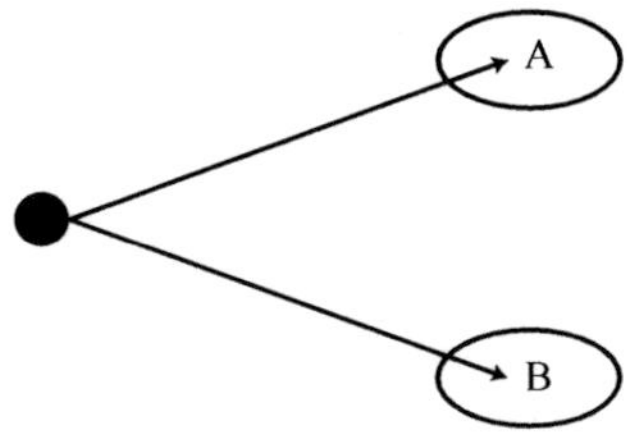

ity' versus 'surrender now'. In Example 4, it was 'determine the cause first' versus 'stop the outflow first'.

Decisions to take one choice over another (or others) are reached following certain processes. While recognizing that those processes are never simple, the choices are extraneous or non-simultaneous. The meta-method to study 'missed opportunities' can focus on the 'simultaneity of extraneous matters' or the 'simultaneity of non-simultaneous matters'. For convenience we will call the combination of the two 'non-homogeneity'. This does not point to actual methods such as quantitative versus qualitative methods, but is prior to that stage. That is, it does not matter whether qualitative or quantitative methods are used, as long as the simultaneity of extraneous or non-simultaneous matters can be identified.

When we live with a purpose, whether well- or ill-intended, we become sensitive to both 'extraneous matters' and 'non-simultaneous matters'. For example, a person intending to deceive someone would study the 'world' of the intending victim—relevant technologies, the victim's knowledge, the values held by the victim, and so on. The victim, on the other hand, is much less aware of living in his/her obvious world. In sociological studies, too, when we embark on a study with intention to take actions (with no ill-intention of course), we are more sensitive to non-homogeneity than when we are without such intent. Being 'contemporary' only means that the entities are sharing physical time (now) and space (the earth as maximum), not that they are homogeneous.

Schütz termed those who co-exist in the same world 'contemporaries' (Schütz 1967: 221). But it is difficult for us to imagine 'others' who do not share the earth with us. So I would like to use the term 'simultaneity' (contemporary) to mean sharing time and space. The extraneousness within this simultaneity is endless—affluence and poverty, life and death, major and minor countries, industrial and agricultural nations, center and periphery, normal and abnormal, different ethnicities, different cultures and so on.

Mannheim emphasized the 'contemporaneity of the non-contemporaneous' in his book *Man and Society in an Age of Reconstruction* (Mannheim 1940). The 'non-contemporaneous' here does not refer only to people but includes technologies or systems with origins at different times. In human society, he uses an example of a person harboring a barbarous motif in a highly developed technological environment. His point was that such non-contemporaneity would lead to catastrophe. The non-homogeneity in our meta-methods focuses our attention to the ill-being that was rooted in ignoring the existence of extraneous or non-simultaneous matters. To emphasize the point, it is not non-homogeneity *per se* that causes ill-being, but its neglect.

The barometer and data

I noted above that for our theme of objective ill-being, the barometers for subjective well-being are not directly useful and remain beyond our consideration. Could we, however, create a barometer for objective well- and ill-being?

The United Nations employs the Human Development Index (HDI) and related indices for measuring human developments. The 'capabilities approach' developed by Sen and Nussbaum has contributed significantly to the development of this index. The HDI is a composite barometer consisting of three indices: average life expectancy, education level (measured by literacy rates and attendance at primary/ secondary/ tertiary education) and standard of living (measured by GDP). Weightings and other technicalities can be found in the UNDP Report (available at http://hdr.undp.org/reports). The influence of the capabilities approach is not obvious in those indices, but it is apparent in some thirty other barometers including: gender-related development criteria, gender empowerment criteria, poverty criteria, access to water, sanitation, nutrition and so on. The 'reasonable living standard' criterion has sub-criteria of: supply of safe water, access to health services and the percentage of children under five with below average weight.

The Human Poverty Index (HPI) was developed as a means to examine the deprivation of the three factors reflected in HDI. It may be called the barometer of ill-being, but despite some influence of Sen and Nussbaum, it does not contain all of the many facets of ill-being, such as the gross numbers and rates of suicide (the World Health Organization compiles this data), illnesses caused by chemicals (particularly cancer) and murders. To consolidate those items and contribute to the formation of a more comprehensive barometer of ill-being should become a central aim of sociology.

Aside from the difficulties and problems concerning the collection of data for creating such a barometer, which I will discuss shortly, it is important to outline the problems in the structure of criteria such as the HDI. The major problem here is the ways that the results are used. Perhaps reflecting the nature of the United Nations, the end result of HDI survey is a national ranking: in 2004, Norway ranks first and Sierra Leone 177th, etc. The HPI ranking is almost an inversion of the HDI ranking, but not exactly, as the criteria for the two indices differ. In short, the United Nations' barometer measures the relative/aggregate well-being of a nation. Two problems arise from this. First, such a barometer is likely to be a source of international competition rather than serving as a means to draw attention to problems: a higher ranking makes a nation feel secure and a lower ranking may generate a sense of crisis. Similar rankings can be found in many facets of contemporary life; ranking is easy for many people to understand, but it tends to mask or occlude many other aspects of life. The HDI ranking, for example, serves to conceal the composition of specific criteria such that, while Japan ranks ninth on the scale of empowerment of women, in one of the criteria on this scale, 'entry into industry in the capacity of executive officer', it ranks among the lowest countries.

The second problem of a national ranking is that it may conceal the ill-being of other social units. For example, the HDI ranking does not indicate the ill-being of an ethnic minority within a nation, or of groups that live beyond national boundaries, such as the Hmong mentioned earlier. Of course, the UN and World Bank are interested in problems such as poverty among ethnic minorities and conduct research to ascertain its extent. But general barometers such as the HDI only indicate the composite problems of national units.

Additionally, such general barometers do not identify specific patterns of ill-being. I have suggested that ill-being can be identified through its patterns. It is even possible to obtain the necessary and sufficient conditions of ill-being from the analysis of how particular patterns spread. But these patterns cannot be derived from a general index.

For example, level of education, one of the indices incorporated in the HDI, can only be partially measured in terms of school attendance. Arguably the content of knowledge taught at each level of an education system is more important than attendance figures. Needless to say, general knowledge levels are closely related to factors such as adequate school buildings, the implementation of a proper education system, school attendance rates, and so on. In short, there are limits to measures that focus only on the quantitative aspects of education. This is not to say that such measures are useless, but to emphasize that these limits must be addressed.

We have now formed an approximate image of the data required for our purpose: first, we need to collect data that relates to ill-being for each nation. Those data include suicides, murders, domestic violence, child abuse, abuse of the elderly, homelessness, etc. Second, such data needs to be not only on a national-basis, but also according to other units, with particular weight on regions, ethnicity, sex and class/caste. Third, we need to re-examine data that reveal inconsistencies between objective reality and social perceptions. The need to re-examine the 'validity' and 'credibility' of these criteria is often discussed, yet such re-examination is typically unsatisfactory under the current environment, which prefers homogenizing, international rankings.

Practical motivation

More than any other area of sociology, the sociology of well-being and ill-being is driven by practical motivations, as it should be. It particularly relates to cells 2 and 4 in Figure 1.2. Sociology, as mentioned, directly relates to cell 4: the researcher searches for the gap between accident and inevitability, to separate 'infinite responsibility' and 'irresponsibility.. The activist, on the other hand, is fed with this knowledge, and sets out to reduce ill-being. These two perspectives, however, are destined to differ. While both aim at 'practical applications', the former is required to make theoretical and empirical judgments about missed opportunities while the latter is required to provide judgment criteria on the effectiveness of specific measures for reducing the effects of ill-being. Let me give an example.

The government of Vietnam has designated August 10th as 'Defoliant Victims' Day'. It was the day, forty-three years ago in 1961, on which the US military first employed the defoliant Agent Orange (dioxin) for military purposes in Vietnam. At the time it was claimed by Ngo Dinh Diem that 'these chemicals would cause no harm whatsoever to human health' (Dai 2000: 15–16). Far from this irresponsible claim, 150,000 children are now suffering as second and third generation victims. I have visited the Peace Village in both Ho Chi Minh City and Hanoi. The sight of the children, particularly in Tu Du Hospital at Ho Chi Minh City, was heart-rending: a child with swollen head and bulging eyes due to chicken pox, a child without an arm, another without a leg, one without an eye, a child with a deformed head, another whose skin has become very dark, one whose legs are permanently bent, one whose mouth has been split, and so on.

One of the NGOs supporting those children is the Vietnamese Association for Victims of Agent Orange/Dioxin (VAVA). I met Dr Nhan, a former Welfare Minister and now the Deputy President of the organization. VAVA is currently fighting two lawsuits in New York against the American manufacturers of Agent Orange—one demanding compensation for the victims and the other demanding restitution of the environment polluted by the product. Dr Nhan, also an eye doctor, asked me to pass the following message to the Japanese people: it is obvious that those children are affected by the defoliant used by the US military, but they need more scientists and doctors to prove the fact; please spread the facts and turn Japanese citizens' minds to this problem; they want petitions circulated and collected through the internet to support their court cases; and, he said gingerly, they need monetary support as they are still poor.

The Vietnamese government is not involved in the lawsuits. Also, they are not suing the US government, politicians or military strategists. I asked Dr Nhan why. Surely, in addition to the manufacturer, the US military (and the South-Vietnamese government–known as a 'US puppet') who decided to use the defoliant, is certainly responsible for its after-effects. Why does VAVA not accuse them?

'I understand what you are saying. Everyone asks the question', Dr Nhan replied with a grin. 'We do not, because, suppose we sue the American government and demand compensation. If we win, what would happen? The compensation money will come from American taxpayers. Naturally, the American people would not be happy about it. If that happens, even if we win, we will turn the American people against us, which is not what we want. We NGOs want to fight hand-in-hand with the American people. On the other hand, the manufacturers reaped enormous profits from the sale. All we want is to spend some of those profits on compensation for the victims and cleaning up the polluted environment'.

As seen in this example, citizen's movements for the reduction of ill-being entail specific viewpoints and considerations. In contrast, when sociology attempts to contribute to practical outcomes, it does not mean that sociologists should share the same perspectives and actions as those movements.

Sociology should, first of all, devote itself to studying the social diffusion and psychological depth of ill-being. Second, it should engage in the study of missed opportunities. And lastly, it should consider what needs to be done to reduce ill-being. Sociology addresses all of these dimensions through its practice. The most important role of sociological research, however, is to initiate changes in the image (perception) people have of the facts, incidents and states of ill-being.

Postscript

I have discussed the object of the sociology of well-being and ill-being, and the roles for sociology in this field. In this discussion I have made frequent reference to the Vietnam War. There are several reason for this: the Vietnam War was the largest-scale war fought in Asia since WWII. There is an abundance of excellent novels, films, criticisms, photographs and journalistic accounts on the subject. Yet, sociological studies on the war are virtually non-existent. Sociology rarely even mentions it. In Japan at the time there were citizens' associations such as *Beheiren* (Peace for Vietnam Citizens' Association) and its close associate, the supporters of American deserters, and some sociologists were involved in those activities (Sekitani and Sakamoto 1998). However, their work had little lasting influence, if any, in sociological studies. Were there no objects of study for sociology despite the great amount of ill-being caused by the war? As indicated, I think there were. Considering that sociological theories and concepts are refined through application to the empirical-historical world, this situation appears to be unbalanced. It is not too much to say that sociology has to date largely been content with the 'Procrustean bed'. Sociology may have discussed ordinary people's 'privatization' of problems, but it has done little to de-privatize and deconstruct their images and imaginations. In a way, this is a confession that sociology itself has become 'internalized'. The radical nature of the sociology of well-being and ill-being begins by combating this situation. To do this I consider the Vietnam War as a strategically powerful field to begin with.

Adorno considered Auschwitz the field he must always return to, and Nussbaum has built her argument on the basis of the poor women in India. Our sociology of well-being and ill-being, at least in this paper, has considered the Vietnam War as its spiritual base. There is no discrepancy between placing a spiritual base on a historical event and pursuing universality in the study. On the contrary, it creates a synergy with a healthy tension.

The kind of human ill-being which was the focus of the Frankfurt school, such as Adorno and Horkheimer, was 'barbarous civilization'. Why have human beings, instead of stepping into a truly humane state, fallen into a new barbarous state? The 'new barbarism' here directly refers to the Holocaust (Adorno 1966). As long as the 'new barbarous state' is deeply connected to anti-Semitism, it connotes an historically specific element. However, if it is viewed only as a problem of anti-Semitism, the incidents in progress in Palestine cannot be explained. Why is it that the 'new barbarism' has become part of the universal problem of human being? For Adorno, civilization and barbarism go hand-in-hand as a dialectical whole. The 'new barbarism' seems to remain alive and well in the twenty-first century.

It goes without saying that ill-being is not confined to incidents and conditions related to the Vietnam War. The ill-being of humanity, which we have defined as satisfying the three elements in the phrase 'killing many innocent people', is all around us as small-scale ill-being. Starting our investigation with those small-scale incidents of ill-being does not in any way blunt the cutting-edge of the sociology of well-being and ill-being.

2
An Axiomatic Approach to the Disadvantage Index

Hiroshi Hamada

Introduction: Human well-being and the liberal paradox

If a scientific investigation of 'human well-being' were possible in sociology, what form would such an attempt take? Whatever this might turn out to be, the first step must be to provide a clear definition of 'human well-being'. Although defining this term is an easily recognizable necessity, it is easier said than done. The difficulty arises from the fact that a close examination of the term 'human well-being'—one of the phrases in Kwansei Gakuin University's COE program, 'The Study of "Social Research for the Enhancement of Human Well-being"'—shows it to be somewhat clumsy. This clumsiness does not stem from the fact that the word 'well-being' sounds rather formal and removed from our daily experience of well-being, nor is it simply a question of what is the correct technical term for expressing the state referred to as well-being.

Well-being is unarguably a formal term, however, if we were to substitute more everyday terms, such as 'happiness', this would not, in fact, remove the clumsiness attached to 'human well-being'. This is because the awkwardness is inherent in the very 'combination' of 'human' and 'well-being': there are elements in these two concepts which seem to be fundamentally mutually exclusive. To put it bluntly, 'modest personal happiness' seems disproportionate to the grand idea of 'consistent choices directed towards achieving a better social state'.

The 'happiness' we feel in our everyday lives usually refers to a state of mind and to events that are too minor to be grasped in terms of 'humanity' at large or to be discussed in academic terms. A glass of beer after work, the comfort of knowing on our day off work that we can sleep in, and so on, make us feel happy, but as to whether these things are 'human' well-being, we would have to say that they are not. The scientific (sociological) investigation of 'human well-being' is not about searching for ways to make each person happy. Most people, naturally, would rather be happy than unhappy. However, each person has a different perception of happiness, and it is doubtful that a universally applicable 'prescription for happiness' exists.

Let us consider, then, how we can arrive at human well-being—or, in other words, social well-being—by starting from the individual's perception of well-being. It is to be expected that there will be individual differences on the question of what constitutes a state of well-being but we can at least say that individuals desire to be in a state of well-being. When a person comparing state x with state y feels that x is more desirable, that person is happier in state x than in state y.[1] It follows that a social state which is desirable for the individual, rather than a state which is not, can always be said to lead to 'well-being'. Defining 'What is a state of well-being for the individual?' is precisely the same as defining the desirability felt by each person in society towards a variety of social states. In terms of welfare economics, this is defining 'individual preference'.[2]

Let us think of 'deriving social preferences from a set of individual preferences' in the more limited sense of 'starting from personal well-being to arrive at human well-being'. This does not indicate that we aim to progress from satisfying personal well-being to satisfying human well-being. The problem at hand is whether or not we can socially determine (through certain specific processes) the order of desirability of individual social states. This reference to socially determining does not necessarily mean collating common factors from a variety of individual choices. Nor does it mean determining social choices by a majority vote. If rules such as majority decision satisfy the prescriptive conditions, we may apply these rules; however, the suggestion is not that we should decide everyone's well-being by majority vote.

Our goal at present is to determine social well-being on the basis of personal well-being, using one method or another. Speaking from the viewpoint of formal procedures, under specific conditions we designate function f (collective choice rule), which assigns one social preference relation R to the set of options $R_1, R_2, \dots, R_n$, which make up the individual preference order for n individuals. In other words, our task is to find the function, from amongst the infinite number of functions found in $R = f(R_1, R_2, \dots, R_n)$, which satisfies certain conditions.

According to Sen's theorem, known as the 'liberal paradox', it is logically impossible to derive a social decision function from combinations of individual preferences under the following three conditions: an unrestricted domain; the Pareto principle; and liberalism (Sen [1970] 2000: 14). Let us take a brief look at these conditions.

'Unrestricted domain' demands that the domain of collective choice rule f includes all logically possible combinations of personal order. This is a reasonable demand, as individual preferences should be all-inclusive.

The 'Pareto principle' considers that if all members of society prefer social state y to social state x, then y should also be seen as the desirable social preference. This is a principle which deems matters judged to be good by all individuals as also being judged to be good by society: a condition that seems extremely natural (often too weak) as a condition for social arrangements.[3] To be precise, this means that $\forall i, (xP_i y) \Rightarrow xPy$ holds for every pair of alternatives x and y in the social state set X.

Finally, it is liberalism that guarantees the minor freedoms or happiness of the individual. To be exact, there is at least one pair of alternatives for each individual i and when it comes to making social choices the individual has the power to decide how to order these. In other words the following holds:

$$\exists x, y \in X, [xP_i y \Rightarrow xPy] \wedge [yP_i x \Rightarrow yPx]$$

There is no social decision function which would satisfy all of these three conditions. A social decision function is a collective choice rule f, the range of which is restricted to those preference relations R, each of which generates a choice function $C(S, R)$ over the whole set of alternatives X (Sen [1970] 2000: 52).[4] This theorem logically confirms the intuition I referred to at the beginning of this essay: '"small personal happiness" and "consistent choices in relation to a better social state" cannot coexist'.

Although not in as precise a form as Sen's 'liberal paradox', in the context of the history of philosophy, Saburō Ichii has claimed that 'happy feelings' are by nature subjective matters for each individual and he expressed serious doubts about the possibilities of measuring the feelings of total happiness in any given society, or of objectively comparing the total happiness in different societies (Ichii 1971: 102). Sen's 'liberal paradox', whilst being confined to specific types as an aggregate of 'well-being', can be viewed as backing up Ichii's intuition. Ichii changed the issue of enhancing 'well-being', pointing out that the degree of concentration of suffering commonly experienced by vast numbers of people at specific times might be more important than the degree of dispersal of 'happiness' experienced by various people (Ichii 1971: 139). If Ichii's claim has a persuasive power beyond rhetoric, this could be because it refers to the asymmetrical nature of the ultimate states of 'well-being' and 'ill-being'. The meaning of this is as follows. Being able to define ill-being and suffering on the basis of individual choices in no way differs from the formal definition of well-being. However, there should be considerably less need to acknowledge liberal choices in the case of ill-being than in the case of well-being. This is because well-being and subjective good feelings are relative, meaning that if a person's desires are continually satisfied, that person will eventually cease to feel the same good feelings (Ichii 1971: 139). This is the empirical basis for the law of diminishing marginal utility. This is why it is extremely difficult to specify the ultimate goal of constant attempts to increase the well-being of the majority of members of a particular society. In other words, we could say that it is difficult to define the ultimate state of well-being.

It is to be expected that there will be the same relativity in ill-being as there is in well-being. If a person continues to experience what is objectively the same consistent level of ill-being, subjectively, their suffering would be likely to decrease. One may argue that defining the ultimate state of ill-being is just as difficult as defining that of well-being. In the case of ill-being, however, we can see that many people encounter death on the path leading to its ultimate state (or the ultimate destination). Conversely, we can conjecture that it is difficult to discern these types of common elements in the process of seeking the ultimate state of well-being. Consequently, the necessity for requiring liberal conditions, namely, that each individual i have at least one pair of alternative choices (x, y) and the power to decide how he/she will order these social choices, can be seen as being weaker with regard to choices concerning ill-being.

Sen's poverty measure and Takayama's revisions

To the best of my knowledge, there is practically no research which uses an axiomatic approach in constructing an index for measuring the levels of ill-being for society as a whole. There does exist, however, an established body of research in economics which regards poverty as one dimension of ill-being. Let us take a brief look at this research in order to examine the possibility of defining a measurement of social ill-being, using a poverty measure.

Sen attempted to combine both poverty and inequality with a view to measuring them—despite the fact that these two concepts whilst being mutually related are also different from one another. Sen proposed several desirable axioms as poverty measures and showed that the measurements derived in this way become the function which includes the Gini Coefficient as independent variable (Sen 1976). These results are still regarded as the standard for axiomatic research into poverty measures. Takayama Noriyuki subsequently pointed out several problems with Sen's poverty measure and made some improvements (Takayama 1979). Let us briefly confirm just what Sen's poverty measure and Takayama's revisions are (the following notation is based on Takayama 1979).

Definition: poverty line

This is a basic value which regards income falling below it as belonging to the impoverished classes. The question of how we define the poverty line in a given society is an important issue which needs to be debated, but in this work it is regarded as a given parameter. We assign the value z to the poverty line throughout the following discussion.

Definition: head count ratio

The proportion of members of a society who belong to the impoverished classes (in relation to the whole). If we assign m for the number of poor people and n for the total number of people in a society, then the head count ratio H becomes $H = m/n$. $S(x)$ expresses the set of people possessing incomes which fall below a given income value x. The number of elements included within $S(z)$, the set of poor people, is m. $|S(z)| = m$.

Definition: income gap

We use the individual income gap g_i to express the gap between the income y_i of individual i and the poverty line z. $g_i = z - y_i$.

Definition: income gap ratio

We total the individual income gap for the poor and express the value compared to the combined incomes of the poor as income gap ratio Q.

$$Q = \sum_{i \in S(z)} \frac{g_i}{mz}$$

Head count ratio of the poor H and income gap ratio Q are widely used in empirical research, but they suffer from the failing that they are unresponsive to income distributions for the poor. Because the poverty head count ratio H, literally, merely counts the number of poor, it is insensitive to disparities between relatively affluent people amongst the poor, who are only just below the poverty line, and those who fall well below the poverty line. In a word, head count ratio H is insensitive to the degree of poverty. Meanwhile, income gap ratio Q is insensitive to head count ratio H, failing to react at all to backward shifts in income fluctuations inside the impoverished classes.

Sen clearly expressed, in the form of axioms, the multiple conditions which the poverty measure ought to satisfy and developed formulae for the measurements which satisfied these conditions. He designates the poverty measure, which ought to be derived from the axioms, as P_s. Sen assumes that poverty measure P_s is the standardized sum of the weighted income gap as[5]

$$P_s = A \sum_{i \in S(z)} v_i \cdot g_i \tag{1}$$

For the purposes of standardization, A is a constant and v_i is weight. Without loss of generality we assume that an individual income satisfies

$$y_1 \leq y_2 \leq \cdots \leq y_m = z \leq \cdots \leq y_n .$$

Axiom M: monotonic welfare

Suppose that for every income vector y, strict preference $>$ is complete on the set of personal welfare function values $\{W_i(y)\}$. The same type of relation is defined for the set of personal incomes also, and

$$y_i > y_j \Rightarrow W_i(y) > W_j(y)$$

holds for every i and j.

In other words, monotonicity requires that decreases in the income of the poor must increase the poverty measure. We apply the following axiom to weight.

Axiom R: ordinal rank weights
The weight v_i regarding the income gap g_i is the same as the ranks between the poor. $v_i = m + 1 - i$.

Axiom N: normalized poverty value
When all the poor have the same income, the following holds.

$$P_s = HQ$$

We are able to specify constant A and weight v_i from the axioms.

Theorem: Sen's poverty measure
When the numbers of poor are sufficiently high, the poverty measure P_s, which satisfies axioms R, M and N is

$$P_s = H(Q + (1 - Q)\, G_w).$$

G_w here is the Gini Coefficient of the impoverished classes.

Proof
See (Sen 1976).

Takayama has pointed out two flaws in Sen's poverty measure and has proposed an alternative measurement in order to deal with these problems (Takayama 1979). Takayama's critique contains important issues, for sociology, and the measurement which he proposes possesses the desirable quality of satisfying the decomposability as to subgroups. The problems with Sen's poverty measure P_s, as pointed out by Takayama, are as follows. The first is that Axiom R completely ignores information regarding those people above the poverty line. The distribution of the impoverished classes is exactly the same but when, for example, we attempt to measure the lives of the people found above the poverty line, and are confronted by two widely divergent lifestyles of the two societies, the problems with Axiom R become abundantly clear. If the affluent class found in one society were to be overwhelmingly extravagant when compared with that in the other society, then the poverty measure in the former would assume a relatively higher value compared to the latter, but Sen's poverty measure P_s is unresponsive to this difference. Takayama's proposal, in effect, requires the poverty measure to take a sociological perspective, which is capable of seeing poverty as an experience of relative deprivation. Put simply, Sen's poverty measure P_s is insensitive to the 'relativity' of poverty.

The second problem is that Axiom N is arbitrary in the sense that it fails to rationalize completely the Gini Coefficient as an inequality index of overall income distribution. This is quite a difficult specification to understand but, in essence, it means that if we amend the axiom slightly we can deduce the Gini Coefficient as a unique inequality index for overall income distribution.

Firstly, we define the income gap q_i on the basis of difference from the total mean μ_0.

$$q_i = \mu_0 - y_i.$$

We assign

$$I = B \sum_{i \in S(y_n)} w_i \cdot q_i + C$$

to income inequality index I, for every income vector. B and C are constants for the purpose of standardization and w_i is a non-negative weight. Here we define weight as rank in society as a whole, in order to introduce relativity into the index. In other words, we revise axiom R in the way set out below.

*Axiom R**
The weight of the income gap w_i is equal to the rank of individual i in the total population.

$$w_i = n + 1 - i$$

We also revise Axiom N in the following manner.

*Axiom N**
If every member of society were to have the same income, then we would have $I = 0$ and when the most affluent people monopolize all income this would be $I = 1 - 1/n$.

Theorem: Takayama's axiomatic construction of the Gini Coefficient
The unique inequality index which satisfies axioms M, R* and N* is the Gini Coefficient.

Proof
This is proven by elementary algebra similar to Sen's poverty measure theorem (see Takayama 1979: 750–1).

Takayama introduces the new concept of 'censored income distribution' in order to revise the poverty measure on the basis of the above results.

Definition: censored income distribution
We call the income profile which corresponds to poverty line z and which satisfies the following conditions

$$y(z) = (y_1, y_2, \ldots, y_m = z, \ldots, y_n)$$

$$\text{where } y_1 \leq y_2 \leq \ldots \leq y_m = \ldots = y_n$$

the censored income distribution.

In short, censored income distribution is the type of distribution in which people's income above the poverty line z all becomes z. For every censored income distribution profile y (z), Takayama's poverty measure P satisfies

$$P = D \sum_{i \in S(y_n)} w_i \cdot (\mu - y_i) + E$$

D and E are constants, for the sake of standardization; w_i is a non-negative weight and μ is the mean of the censored income distribution. The axiom for standardization regarding poverty measure P is as follows.

Axiom N2
If no one falls below the poverty line, then $P = 0$. If the income of a poor person is zero, then the poverty measure is equal to the head count ratio ($P = H$).

Theorem: Takayama's poverty measure
The only poverty measure which satisfies axioms M, R* and N2 is the Gini Coefficient G_p of the censored income distribution.

Proof
This can be proven via elementary calculations (see Takayama 1979: 753–4).

The convenient feature of poverty measure P (Gini Coefficient G_p of the censored income distribution) is that, as a result of the lack of overlap between the impoverished classes and other classes, it is easy to analyze. We can now divide society into two: a poor group (people falling below the poverty line) and an affluent group (people sitting above the poverty line). We can express situations in which there is no overlap as

$$G = G_{\mu} + \left(p_1^2 \frac{\mu_1}{\mu} G_1 + p_2^2 \frac{\mu_2}{\mu} G_2\right)$$

and cases in which there is a general division into m individual subgroups as[6]

$$G = G_{\mu} + \sum_{i=1}^{m} p_i^2 \frac{\mu_i}{\mu} G_i$$

In this formula G_{μ} is the total Gini Coefficient for situations in which income is equally distributed (the subgroup mean per person only) between all the subgroups (Bhattacharya and Mahalanobis 1967; Aoki 1979; Konishi 2002). When we analyze the Gini Coefficient G_p of the censored income distribution on the basis of this analytical formula, then the following holds.

$$G_p = G_{\mu} + \left(p_1^2 \frac{\mu_1}{\mu} G_1 + p_2^2 \frac{\mu_2}{\mu} G_2\right)$$

$$= \frac{1}{2n^2\mu} (z - \mu_i)\, m\, (n - m) + p_1^2 \frac{\mu_1}{\mu} G_1$$

$$= p_1 \left(1 - \frac{\mu_1}{\mu}\right) + p_1^2 \frac{\mu_1}{\mu} G_1 \qquad (2)$$

Notwithstanding the fact that Takayama's poverty measure, in terms of calculation formalities, is the same as the Gini Coefficient (strictly speaking, a simplified version of it), we are mindful of the fact that it is always the degree of poverty that is being measured. Takayama's poverty measure, or in other words the Gini Coefficient of the censored income distribution, is, intuitively speaking, the degree of inequality of the whole society, which has ignored the gap between the classes above the poverty line.

Disadvantage index construction: an axiomatic approach

In the previous section we have briefly identified the construction and advantages of a poverty measure but there are, inevitably—from our perspective of wishing to measure society's ill-being—some deficiencies (not primarily deficiencies in the poverty measure itself). These stem from the fact that although poverty may well be one dimension in the construction of ill-being, we cannot represent the total degree of ill-being solely in terms of the degree of poverty. We, surely, ought to be able to estimate the degree of poverty more comprehensively—quite aside from income—by considering various dimensions such as the level of health, degree of lifestyle security, employment conditions (school conditions) and comfort of dwellings.

If we were able to adapt the poverty measure to these multiple dimensions, then our objectives might be largely achievable. To this end we need to expand the Gini Coefficient to be able to define it in relation to the data for *m* dimensions. Below I attempt to express, using formulae, an expanded concept of the poverty measure—and in view of the fact that it measures disadvantage, I will, for the present, call it a disadvantage index.

Let us now say that there are *m* types of resources which we can use to create a more desirable state for an individual's life. Some examples of the resources being considered here include income, education, health, and network capital (friendship relations).

Definition: resource vector

We assume that *m* types of resources can be measured by positive real numbers. Then a personal resource vector $x = (x_1, x_2, \ldots, x_m)$ can be expressed as a point on Cartesian product of *m* sets of positive real numbers,

$$R^+ \times R^+ \times \cdots \times R^+.$$

Definition: resource vector value

Each individual can transform his own resource vector to a utility (real number). There are infinite numbers of this type of function *f*: $R^+ \times R^+ \times \cdots \times R^+ \rightarrow R^+$. We call the real number, dependent variable of the function, the resource vector value.

Below, for simplification, I use the Cobb-Douglass function as a mathematically natural function. The resource vector value $x = (x_1, x_2, \ldots, x_m)$ is

$$f(x) = a \prod_{i=1}^{m} x_i^{\alpha_i} \qquad \text{where } 0 < \alpha_i < 1, \ \sum_{i=1}^{m} \alpha_i = 1$$

(*a* is constant). The reasons for using the Cobb-Douglass function here are: its desirable qualities as a utility function and its ease of use.

It satisfies the law of diminishing marginal utility since its first and second derivative are

$$\frac{\partial f(x)}{\partial x_i} = a\alpha_i x_i^{-1+\alpha_i} \prod_{j \in N \setminus \{i\}} x_j^{\alpha_j} > 0,$$

$$\frac{\partial^2 f(x)}{\partial x_i^2} = a(-1+\alpha_i)x_i^{-2+\alpha_i} \prod_{j \in N \setminus \{i\}} x_j^{\alpha_j} < 0,$$

With $N = \{1, 2, \ldots, n\}$we express the set excluding only i as $N \setminus \{i\} = \{1, 2, \ldots, i-1, i+1, \ldots, n\}$. The assumption that the sum of exponential is 1 implies that the utility is fixed with regard to scale (when total resources increase b times, then utility also increases b times). Simultaneously we can express the disparity between resources in terms of which contribute most to utility by the power exponent.

Furthermore, the functional approach proposed by Sen practically assumes that in the context of our discussion, the function which changes the resource vector into utility differs between individuals (Sen [1985] 1988). We can use constant a in the Cobb-Douglass function to express this type of disparity in ability to change resources between individuals. In cases where the utility function differs between individuals we say that a_j ($j = 1, 2, \ldots, n$). Naturally, we can get the same results by defining separately for each individual the index for all coordinates (alternatively, results expressing even more detailed disparities). However, for the present, what is needed is an acknowledgement of the assumption that we can change the resource vector real number value, using certain functions.

According to the definition, we can express the respective vectors for two individuals as

$$x = (x_1, x_2, \ldots, x_m), y = (y_1, y_2, \ldots, y_m)$$

(All the coordinates include scores, amongst other things, for level of income and health and the degree of lifestyle security.) We define the distance between individuals using the absolute value of the differences in the utility function

$$d(x, y) = |f(x) - f(y)|$$

We call y_i and y_j the resource vectors for individuals i and j respectively.

$$y_i = (y_{i1}, y_{i2}, \ldots, y_{im}), y_j = (y_{j1}, y_{j2}, \ldots, y_{jm})$$

If we denote $\bar{y}$ the mean utility, then the utility Gini Coefficient is defined as

$$G = \frac{1}{2\bar{y}n^2} \sum_{i=1}^{n} \sum_{j=1}^{n} | f(y_i) - f(y_j) |$$

Moreover, in order to define the disadvantage index we must define the censored income distribution. To do this we must apply the concepts appropriate to the income poverty line in relation to utility. We call this the disadvantage boundary.

Definition: disadvantage boundary
We call the standard value which regards any resource vector values lower than itself as being in a disadvantage environment, the disadvantage boundary value. We call degree points in the Cartesian product of *m* sets of real numbers whose value is below the disadvantage value, the disadvantage boundary. If we express the disadvantage boundary value as *z* and the disadvantage boundary set as *Z*, then this can be shown as

$$Z = \{x \in R^+ \times R^+ \times \cdots \times R^+ \mid f(x) \leq z\}$$

We are alert to the fact that there are individuals with different resource vectors, even where they share the same utility. We define the 'censored utility distribution', which corresponds to the 'censored income distribution' as follows.

Definition: censored utility distribution
We call the utility distribution which corresponds to disadvantage boundary value z and which satisfies the following qualities

$$y(i) = (f(y_1), f(y_2), \ldots, f(y_m) = z, \ldots, f(y_n))$$

$$\text{where } (f(y_1) \leq f(y_2) \leq \cdots \leq f(y_m) = f(y_n))$$

the censored utility distribution. In other words, censored utility distribution is a utility distribution which has adjusted the utility of resource vectors, with a value greater than *z* so that they all become *z*.

Definition: head count ratio

I call the proportion of the whole of all members of society, whose resource vector utility falls below disadvantage boundary value z, the head count ratio, just as in the case of the poverty measure. If we make the number of disadvantaged people m and the total number of people in the whole society n, then head count ratio H is $H = m/n$.

We express the set of people possessing a resource vector with a utility of below z as $S(z)$. The number of elements included in the set of disadvantaged people $S(z)$ is m. $|\, S(z) \,| = m$.

Definition: resource value gap

The disparity between the utility $f(y_i)$ of the resource vector y_i of individual i and disadvantage boundary value z is expressed using the individual resource gap g_i. $g_i = z - f(y_i)$.

We express disadvantage index D, which is defined in terms of the utility of the resource vector,

$$D = A \sum_{i \in C} w_i \cdot (\mu - f(y_i)) + E \tag{4}$$

in relation to censored utility distribution profile $y(z)$. In this formula, we assume that A and E are constants, in the interests of standardization; w_i is a non-negative weight; μ is the mean of the censored utility distribution; C is the set of individuals included in the censored utility distribution; $f(y_i)$ is the utility of the resource vector of individual i $y_i = (y_{i1}, y_{i2}, \ldots, y_{im})$; and is transformed into proper value for the censored utility distribution. I revise Axiom M in the following way, in response to the view that changes a resource vector into utility.

Axiom M: monotonic welfare*

We define a complete and strict preference on the basis of the individual's welfare function value set $\{Wi\ (y)\}$, for every utility profile y. These same relations are also defined on the utility set. Then for every i and j the following holds.

$$y_i > y_j \Rightarrow W_i(y) > W_j(y)$$

Next we determine the standardized axiom for disadvantage index D, in the following manner.

*Axiom N2**

In the event that no one falls into the disadvantaged people set $S(z)$, $D = 0$. Also, if the utility for disadvantaged people is a total of zero, then the disadvantage index D is equal to the head count ratio ($D = H$).

*Axiom R2**

The weight w_i attached to the resource value gap is equal to the rank of individual i in the total population. $w_i = n + 1 - i$. However, the rank to which I refer here is the rank of the resource value (utility).

Theorem 1: disadvantage index

The unique disadvantage index which satisfies axioms M, R2* and N2* is the Gini Coefficient G_n of the censored utility distribution.

Proof

Consider the extreme case in which no one falls into the group of disadvantaged people $S(z)$. In this case, the mean of the censored utility distribution μ becomes equivalent to z. From (4) we have

$$D = A \sum_{i \in C} w_i \cdot (z - z) + E$$

$$= E$$

And also from Axiom N2* we get $D = 0$. Therefore, we can show that $E = 0$. If we substitute the weight from Axiom R2*, then we can write (4) as

$$D = A \sum_{i \in C} (n + 1 - i)(\mu - f(y_i)) \tag{5}$$

from $E = 0$. Next, we will consider the case in which the utility of disadvantaged people is zero. In this case the mean of the censored utility distribution μ becomes $\mu = z(n - m)/n$. It is also,

$$\sum_{i \in C} i \cdot f(y_i) = \sum_{i=m+1}^{n} i \cdot f(y_i) = \sum_{i=m+1}^{n} i \cdot z = \frac{\mu n(n + m + 1)}{2}$$

From this and (5) we see that

$$D = A \sum_{i \in C} (n + 1 - i)(\mu - f(y_i))$$

$$= A\left(\frac{-\mu n(n+1)}{2} + \sum_{i\in C} i \cdot f(y_i)\right) = A\,\frac{\mu m n}{2}$$

If the utilities of disadvantaged people are all zero, then $D = H$ from Axiom N2*. Thus

$$D = A\,\frac{\mu m n}{2},\quad D = \frac{m}{n} \Rightarrow A = \frac{2}{\mu n^2}$$

If we substitute the value of constant A for (5), then

$$D = \frac{2}{\mu n^2} \sum_{i\in C} (n+1-i)\,(\mu - f(y_i))$$

$$= \frac{2}{\mu n^2}\left(n(n+1)\mu - \frac{(n+1)n\mu}{2}\right) - \frac{2}{\mu n^2} \sum_{i\in C} (n+1-i)\, f(y_i)$$

$$= 1 + \frac{1}{n} - \frac{2}{\mu n^2} \sum_{i\in C} (n+1-i)\, f(y_i)$$

We can write the Gini Coefficient G_n of the censored utility distribution as

$$G_n = 1 + \frac{1}{n} - \frac{2}{\mu n^2} \sum_{i\in C}^{n} (n+1-i)\, f(y_i)$$

Therefore we have shown that $D = G_n$. The disadvantage index, defined in relation to the m dimension resource vector utility, satisfies all of the above-mentioned Axioms M, R2* and N2*.

Disadvantage index: computational analysis

I will confirm the nature of the disadvantage index, defined in Part 3, by means of computation. We previously assumed that we could measure all m varieties of resources with positive real numbers. In this we use a lognormal distribution, with a non-negative real value. As is widely known, income and assets are subject to a lognormal distribution.

Assumption 1: assumption regarding the distribution of each resource
We assume that each component of an m dimensional resource vector (the value of each coordinate) respectively follows a lognormal distribution. When $x = (x_1, x_2, \ldots, x_m)$, we express each dimension using random variables $X_1, X_2, \ldots, X_m$, then

$$X_1 \sim \Lambda(\mu_1, \sigma_1^2), X_2 \sim \Lambda(\mu_2, \sigma_2^2), \ldots, X_m \sim \Lambda(\mu_m, \sigma_m^2)$$

Theorem 2: lognormal utility distribution
We define the utility for each person using the Cobb-Douglass function. If we express this using random variables, then

$$U = a \prod_{i=1}^{m} X_i^{\alpha_i} \quad \text{where } 0 < \alpha_i < 1, \sum_{i=1}^{m} \alpha_i = 1$$

In this case, the utility distribution for each individual under Assumption 1 follows a lognormal distribution. In other words,

$$U \sim \Lambda\left(\log a + \sum_{j=1}^{m} \alpha_j \mu_j, \sum_{j=1}^{m} \alpha_j \sigma_j^2\right)$$

Proof
This is clear from the nature of the lognormal distribution (Aitchison and Brown 1957: 11).

When the members of society possess the resource vectors which satisfy Assumption 1, the disadvantage index value of that society is the Gini Coefficient of the censored utility distribution, as shown in Theorem 2. If we accept Assumption 1, then—on the basis of Theorem 2—our analysis of the disadvantage index is, ultimately, limited to analyses in which utility follows a lognormal distribution. I introduce the following lemma in order to clarify the analytical framework.

Lemma 1: mean of censored utility distribution
Suppose that utility distribution follows a probability distribution which has a finite mean. In this case, the mean of censored utility corresponding to disadvantage boundary value z is

$$\alpha = \mu_1 p_1 + z(1 - p_1),$$

where p_1 is the share of population represented by the disadvantaged (people whose utility falls below the disadvantage boundary level) and μ_1 is the mean utility of the disadvantaged classes.

Proof

Generally the mean can be expressed by a convex combination. If we assign $f(t)$ to the probability density function of the utility distribution, then the total mean of utility is the sum of the impoverished classes' mean utility

$$\mu_1 = \int_0^z t \cdot \frac{f(t)}{p_1}\, dt$$

and the weight (population share) of the mean utility of the other classes. Since the members of those classes apart from the disadvantaged possess, according to the definition of censored utility distribution, a utility for all members of z, the mean of any density function will be z. If we assign p_1 to the population share of the disadvantaged classes, then the following holds.

$$\alpha = \mu_1 p_1 + z\,(1 - p_1)$$

Lemma 2: decomposition of the disadvantage index for a lognormal distribution

When utility is subject to the lognormal distribution $\Lambda\ (\mu,\ \sigma^2)$, we can decompose the disadvantage index D, which corresponds to disadvantage boundary value z, as

$$D = p_1\left(1 - \frac{\mu_1}{\alpha}\right) + \frac{1}{2\alpha}\left(\int_0^z \int_0^z |x - y|\, f(x)\, f(y)\, dxdy\right),$$

where α is the mean of censored utility distribution shown in Lemma 1; μ_1 the mean utility of the disadvantaged classes; and p_1 is the population share made up by the disadvantaged classes.

Proof

From equation (2) and the mean of the censored utility distribution,

$$D = p_1\left(1 - \frac{\mu_1}{\alpha}\right) + p_1^2\left(\frac{\mu_1}{\alpha}\right) G_1.$$

The Gini Coefficient G_1 for the utility of the disadvantaged classes is

$$G_1 = \frac{1}{2\mu_1} \int_0^z \int_0^z |x-y| \frac{f(x)}{p_1} \frac{f(y)}{p_1} \, dxdy$$

$$= \frac{1}{2\mu_1 p_1^2} \int_0^z \int_0^z |x-y| \, f(x) \, f(y) \, dxdy.$$

Substitute this for D, we have

$$G_1 = p_1 \left(1 - \frac{\mu_1}{\alpha}\right) + \frac{1}{2\alpha} \int_0^z \int_0^z |x-y| \, f(x) \, f(y) \, dxdy \qquad (6)$$

We cannot solve the integral equation of the second term in formula (6) because the upper limit is a finite value. We thus analyze the disadvantage index using numerical calculations, following the steps set out below.

1. Create random numbers which obey a lognormal distribution with the parameters μ_i, σ_i ($i = 1, 2, \ldots, m$), as m dimensional vectors of n individuals. We assume that each dimension is independent to each other in the sense of probability.
2. Calculate utility on the basis of the Cobb-Douglass function and construct a utility vector. The length (the total number of constituent elements) of the utility vector is n.
3. Create a censored utility vector which corresponds to disadvantage boundary value z, based on the utility vector drawn up in 2.
4. Calculate the Gini Coefficient of the censored utility distribution drawn up in 3.
5. Repeat steps 1 to 4 and calculate the mean. The number of further repetitions and the sample size n employ a mix which keeps the mean of error down to 1/100.

We use *Mathematica* to calculate the above series of procedures. We fix dimensions of resource vector for 3. Table 2.1 and Table 2.2 show the changes in the disadvantage index, corresponding to changes of the parameter of the first dimension.

From the calculated results we can predict what will probably happen: if the conditions for other parameters are equal in Assumption 1, then the disadvantage index will increase along with increases in parameter σ; and the disadvantage index will decrease along with increases in μ.

Table 2.1: The disadvantage index where $\mu_1 = \mu_2 = \mu_3 = 0.5$, $\sigma_2 = \sigma_3 = 2$, $\alpha_1 = \alpha_2 = \alpha_3 = 1/3$

	$\sigma_1 = 1.0$	$\sigma_1 = 1.2$	$\sigma_1 = 1.4$	$\sigma_1 = 1.6$	$\sigma_1 = 1.8$	$\sigma_1 = 2.0$
z=1	0.1137	0.1208	0.1238	0.1296	0.1376	0.1370
z=2	0.1141	0.1170	0.1237	0.1260	0.1330	0.1339
z=3	0.1134	0.1203	0.1225	0.1250	0.1331	0.1409
z=4	0.1133	0.1179	0.1236	0.1259	0.1331	0.1382
z=5	0.1148	0.1169	0.1233	0.1284	0.1347	0.1395

Sample size: n = 100, number of repetitions = 100

Table 2.2: The disadvantage index where $\mu_2 = \mu_3 = 0.5$, $\sigma_1 = \sigma_2 = \sigma_3 = 2$, $\alpha_1 = \alpha_2 = \alpha_3 = 1/3$

	$\mu_1 = 0.0$	$\mu_1 = 0.2$	$\mu_1 = 0.4$	$\mu_1 = 0.6$	$\mu_1 = 0.8$	$\mu_1 = 1.0$
z=1	0.1674	0.1544	0.1391	0.1327	0.1248	0.1162
z=2	0.1628	0.1533	0.1423	0.1322	0.1209	0.1114
z=3	0.1643	0.1523	0.1442	0.1329	0.1256	0.1127
z=4	0.1678	0.1525	0.1438	0.1358	0.1210	0.1167
z=5	0.1639	0.1532	0.1449	0.1303	0.1228	0.1154

Conclusion

In this work, I have produced formulae for an index measuring the degree of social ill-being – the disadvantage index, by applying the poverty measure proposed by Sen and revised by Takayama. One of the points of caution when actually analyzing the data is that each component of an *m* dimensional resource vector must be something contributing to either the individual's ascendancy or welfare. It is also desirable for these respective dimensions to be non-negative real numbers.

There is another method for measuring social well-being/ill-being which I have not mentioned in this work because I have limited the discussion to the construction of an axiomatic index. This other method is practical statistics. We can mention, in support of it being a more orthodox methodology, its synthesis of the numerous variables which contribute (or are thought to contribute) to well-being/ill-being into a comprehensive index, via principle components analysis. This method, for example, measures average life span, average income, GNP, per capita GNP, average health levels and so on for each society. It then extracts the first components with the highest eigenvalue (contribution rate), on the basis of the PCA, and finally determines the rank of each society on the basis of these first component scores. It is difficult to introduce information regarding the relativity of well-being/ill-being in each society when comparing various societies using main component analysis, but this is not the main defect of this approach: it is, rather, the frequent use of mean values and totals for each variable. Henceforth, we need also to take into account conformity with this type of metrical approach.

In order to make the focus of the discussion more diffuse, I have in this work, intentionally, not discussed the following issues, which I would now like to acknowledge in concluding. Firstly, what are the very resources which contribute to personal utility? Secondly, there is the question of how one determines the disadvantage boundary value, the first condition we consider in order to calculate the disadvantage index. Thirdly, I have advanced the Cobb-Douglass function as a function for converting the resource vector into its value but what is also needed, perhaps, are attempts to adduce from axioms which types of functions are appropriate.

3

Violence in Modern Society: Towards Social Research for the Enhancement of Human Happiness[1]

Masahiro Ogino

Prologue

I will begin with the story of a friend, K. K owned a bar which she managed by herself near the apartment where I was living. It was a quiet part of town, and near the train stations, so it was frequently quite empty. At such times, she would occasionally ring me, and I would go to her empty bar and listen to her story.

She once asked my advice on how to attract people to the bar. At the time, she would have had over 20 years' experience in the hospitality industry. I didn't think I was in any position to advise her, but I made some suggestions about how to attend to customers on the basis of my experiences as a professor, for whom my students were customers.

Naturally, these vague suggestions did not result in an immediate influx of customers. Days continued to pass without anyone entering the bar. I visited regularly as her only customer. One day, she began to talk about herself. 'Professor (she always referred to me so), do you know about the discriminated villages? I'm from there.'

She said that in elementary school she had been regarded as the leader of a juvenile delinquent group. An occasional customer, who claimed to have been K's classmate, said, 'Back then I couldn't speak to her, I was that scared of her.'

Soon K found that the police were looking for her on a charge of theft. Returning home and telling her father, she was handed a 10,000 yen note and told 'Run away at once.' She escaped to the busy downtown area of Osaka and entered the bar industry. She was 12 years old.

Later she moved to Tokyo, dreaming of becoming a songwriter, working in bars as she wrote lyrics that did not sell. One day someone told her that he would introduce her to a famous songwriter, Y, who would help her make her debut as a songwriter. She handed over 2.5 million yen as commission. But it was a scam. There was no debut. She lost the money. She then attempted suicide, taking sleeping pills. When she didn't die, she decided to return to Osaka.

In Osaka, she opened a bar. She said, 'I hate gangs, but somehow they like me.' She dated a gangster for a while. It seemed inevitable, fated. Later she married, divorced, and opened another bar, the one I knew. When I started going to it, she was married a second time, to a public servant. K hardly spoke about him or her previous husband. She had an elementary-school-age daughter who was fathered by another man (neither of her husbands).

K's business gradually improved. Various people came to the bar, mostly those in the hospitality industry, laborers, and people without a fixed job. One of them was a gangster, T. As a rule, the bar did not serve gangs, but being a childhood friend, T sometimes came on his own to drink. One day, when I asked K how T was, she answered 'He killed himself.' This is but one example of how I would sometimes learn of the 'sudden death' of a customer in the bar.

Then the great Hanshin-Awaji Earthquake struck. K's shop and the building it was in were totally destroyed and I lost contact for a while. Half a year later she contacted me. She had opened a pub in a neighboring town. Unlike the last bar, she was now close to a railway station and had more customers. According to K, they were 'mostly office workers.' The first time I visited her there, one customer was vehemently discussing anti-discrimination education. When he left, K complained, 'I don't like him. He was sacked from his workplace because of trouble with a woman.'

K had divorced again and had a new boyfriend. He was a childhood friend and an ex-gangster, with no fixed job. When I had first met him, before the earthquake, he was telling, a little proudly, about how he was learning calligraphy. He was giving a lengthy lecture on how to hold chopsticks, saying that elementary school teachers cannot even teach the way to hold chopsticks. Later, as K's new 'partner', he once said, 'Yakuza are the weakest people. They want to boast because they are timid.' After K opened the pub, he would frequently get very drunk in other places and K would go to pick him up. He was eventually arrested for violating the Firearms and Swords Control Law and received a prison sentence. He was also involved with drugs. K's only daughter entered senior high school but quit soon after, becoming involved in drugs under his influence. K continued to run the pub, seemingly indifferent.

One day when I hadn't visited the pub for a while, I happened to meet K on her bicycle. She said that she wanted to talk and asked me to meet her at a coffee shop in an hour, after she finished some business. I was waiting at the designated coffee shop when she arrived. She appeared to be fine. The pub had been successful, she said, but she had collapsed 6 months earlier. Tests revealed that she had cancer. She was admitted to hospital for a while but had now been discharged, and the doctor had told her that she could do as she wished. She spoke a little excitedly. She said that she had undergone radiation treatment and took off her hat. She had lost her hair from the treatment.

K then began to talk about her new 'job' in a so-called 'pyramid selling' scheme. She had already started selling shampoos and soaps. She talked passionately, in the persuasive tones typical of pyramid scheme sellers, about how rational the organization was and how the efforts of its members generated profits. However, since there wouldn't be any immediate windfall, she was considering setting up a subcontract building cleaning business, and asked my opinion. I pointed out that a cleaning business could become difficult, since workers would need to be employed. In that case, she murmured, she had no choice but to run a pub. She then asked to borrow some money, with her jewelry as security. I agreed. Finally, K added, 'I don't know how long I'll live but I can't die now. I have to make money for my daughter and partner.'

A while later K came to my house with shampoos and other goods. She was advertising the effectiveness of the shampoo to my wife, but then she began to play with our young child. A little abruptly she said, 'There's a difference from birth. There are children like this, who are loved so much, and others who suffer at the hands of their parents.' She added, 'Around me, I see people who are always at the pachinko parlor and don't look after their kids.' K later bought picture books for my child, and contacted me about the opening of her new shop. Since our conversation at the coffee shop, she had not once mentioned the borrowed money. I could not make it to the opening of her shop, but my wife rang her after a short while and it seemed to be doing well. K died a week later.

Personal ethics

An ethical life

There are several distinct characteristics in K's ethics. The first is that she did not bemoan the situation she was in, but acted on the basis of how well she could deal with and live with that situation. One cannot choose where one is born. One cannot know in advance whether they will be born into a rich or poor family, whether they are born in Japan or another country. If we call this situation, where a choice cannot be made beforehand, 'fate', then K knew how to deal with fate.

While in elementary school, K was seen as being the center of a juvenile delinquent group. About this she would say, 'I never ran from that.' K never glamorized her experiences unnecessarily or shifted the cause of her failure onto someone or something else. She 'never ran'. K had probably always covered for her 'mates'. If she had been 'accused of theft', it may well have been a false charge.

Those who know how to deal with fate have a strong will to survive. K once attempted suicide, which suggests that for a time, at least, she lost her will to live. This followed immediately from her losing her dream of becoming a songwriter, and might be explained by saying that at this stage K was not yet closely connected with her fate. However, it is more important to note that the suicide attempt also shows K's strong character of non-dependence on others. Yet, although staunchly independent, she never refused those who depended on her. Her last 'partner' had revealed that he was in some respects a weak person; witness, for example, his amphetamine addiction. K accepted people as they were. According to K, for example, although her partner was dependent on her in some ways, there was more to him than that. Once, when things became rough in the area where they were living, he became the mediator and resolved the situation. She had respected him ever since. K may have felt that his 'failures' in other respects were not his fault, but she did not express such excuses.

Although fiercely independent and typically preferring a steady life, at one point K tried to get rich quickly through pyramid selling. This seems to oppose her ethics, but was perhaps a response to the inevitability of her death. She appears to have wanted to build a foundation for her daughter and partner before she died. But her usual steady practicality shone through in the end, as she opened a new shop before she died.

Although K must have wavered many times, when various 'incidents' arose in her life, she invariably sought some way to manage them, even while accepting them as her fate. After K's illness and death, while feeling a strong respect for her ethical life, I also had a strong irrational feeling. It was partly sparked by K's observation that 'people are never born equally' a few months before her death.

Sociological issues and renewal of methods

There are two main reasons for this lengthy focus on the life of one particular person. One concerns the methodology of social survey. This concern has two main parts: an issue related to ethics in a broad sense and one about the expression of surveyed data. Some sociologists have begun to suggest that it might be best if 'surveys' did not exist, arguing that they probably do not contribute to 'happiness' in any way. Others have argued that surveys lead to surveillance. In any case, there is certainly a need to fundamentally reconsider all aspects of what it means for sociologists to conduct surveys.

However, despite criticisms, there has as yet been no new attempt to update the empirical study of sociology. This paper aims to provide a starting point for one promising new direction, and it starts with K.

Starting with a single person implies two things. First, it signifies that 'surveying' does not involve special and exceptional activities, and nor is there a special situation required for this act to develop. Conversation and communication have an aspect of a survey in that they are employed to collect information, which is then utilized in daily life. In this sense, a survey is not a special act. Surveys exist only as an extension of daily conversation, and do not always happen intentionally. K was a friend, and was not the subject of an intentional survey—at least not initially. However, listening to her story is in itself a kind of survey, and if this develops into intentional sociological research, the act itself remains the same. Individual researchers invariably typologize reality and form heuristic hypotheses based upon their real experience in daily life. They must do this, whatever method is employed, whether questionnaire or interview, for example. For social surveys, the 'need to build rapport' is often talked about. As surveys exist only in daily life, however, this strategy of 'building rapport with the subject of survey' cannot be plausibly advocated.

Second, beginning with K's story reveals the kind of situation from which sociological research begins. While it is impossible to conclusively answer the question 'what is happiness?'—the sort of question which is constantly asked but has no answer—one thing is certain; the question is directly connected to the death of human beings. Some deaths give the impression that life has been fulfilled, and some deaths come suddenly, like K's. It is the latter which necessitates sociological research. If her death had not been sudden, I would not have thought to write about K. We feel sadness and regret towards a person's death and question how the death occurred. If there is any meaning at all for the existence of sociology, it lies in the effort to answer this question. This begins with questioning the meaning of death around us, and not only of family or friends. Meaning should be sought by questioning the unreasonable deaths in one's own society.

Hence I begin this approach to a new sociological methodology with the story of my friend K. The philosophical, methodological and ethical issues of social survey will be discussed in detail in another publication. This paper will focus on the second reason for presenting K's story.

K's episode hints at the central sociological issue that should be tackled at this moment. Sociology, to date, has typically attributed the unhappinesses of life to the stratified social structure. One prominent mode of this approach is to attribute the individual's fate to their position in the class system of a supposedly equal society. Bourdieu's 'reproduction theory' is a typical example (Bourdieu and Passeron 1970). Bourdieu argues that people are equipped with a unique 'habitus' of the class in which they were born. They behave according to it and cannot behave otherwise. He claims that society has a predetermined fate ready for each person who is born, a fate which must be accepted.[2] This claim is typically interpreted heuristically to mean that people do not step out of the path fate has laid for them. From this perspective it is unthinkable for the common people (*classe populaire*), to climb the social ladder. This may be unfortunate, but it cannot be helped. Fate is unfortunate.

Those who do not accept their fate and attempt to pioneer a new life, most typically end in failure. Many novels and movies present stories in which people attempt to overcome fate but end up failing. Such stories frequently revolve around the exposure of a crime committed by a character with an unhappy past. The sociologist Munesuke Mita, published a paper titled 'Manazashi no jigoku (Hell in his eyes)', which explores the background of a 19 year old—we'll call him N—who committed a double murder, attempting to trace the circumstances leading to the murder (Mita 1979).

Sociological theories such as reproduction theory and Mita's 'manazashi theory' do not, however, explain the irrationality I felt at K's death. At the base of reproduction theory is a fatalistic worldview: fate cannot be altered. If fate cannot be changed, then there is no need for sociologists to reconfirm the 'reality' of this unchangeable fate. 'Manazashi theory' generates a different question: why that particular person, of all those who exist in similar social conditions and circumstances, committed murder, for example.

In the first place, my feeling was evoked by the fact that K fell ill and died while continuing her fight against fate. I am not suggesting that her life was unfortunate. That is not for me to judge. There are, however, several factors in K's life that sociologists might focus on. For example, we might note her academic background—quitting elementary school—and that there were deviants around her, such as her ex-gangster partner. But K herself was not a deviant. My feeling of irrationality cannot be wholly explained within the framework of social strata reproduction.

Difference in sociology

Raymond Aron pointed out that the words 'social', 'sociology' and 'socialism' are new, born from the mid eighteenth to nineteenth centuries (Aron 1969: 1). Specifically, as an adjective, the word 'social' means 'of society', and as a noun it means 'something of society'; but this provides little clarification about what 'social' actually means.

In fact, 'social' has many meanings, both affirmative and negative. As an adjective, it can be used to refer to things that have a 'social'—rather than individual or particular—significance, such as a social movement to correct inequality, or to be 'socially' recognized, as most clearly evident in much sociological terminology (such as social status). It has a broad and holistic meaning, as can be seen in its relationship to 'socialism', but it is also a particular and generic term for certain social policies and social services, such as social insurance and social welfare.

At the same time, it is frequently used with negative connotations when referring to the problems of society. In both Japan and France, for example, the domestic sections of the daily newspapers report numerous incidents of murder and fraud. In this context, 'social' is used as an obscene word describing the dark part of human nature.

The word 'social' expresses various aspects of human life which deviate from the code and are not contained by the system.

The ambiguity of the word 'social' is suggestive of the nature of sociology itself. Many sociologists aim to discover social issues and reveal the structures which cause them to be issues. The prerequisite for this sort of sociology is 'difference'. The starting point is to identify various differences not yet recognized in society, or to which appropriate measures have not yet been applied by society, and to regard them as social issues. The potential subjects of such surveys include a vast array of deviate behavior, exclusion and discrimination (Ogino 2001). This approach follows a logic that tries to draw difference into identity, believing it good for difference to gain some sort of identity and acceptance in society.

Reproduction theory, mentioned previously, is one among many in sociology that follow this logic. But to analyze the negative aspect of the 'social'—that side that indicates that human beings are also characterized by something that is not contained within the system—a different sociological theory is required. Such a theory must grasp society not from the perspective of socially constructed differences, but from a position in which social class or stratum does not exist in the first place. To examine that which does not belong to the system, a totally different approach is necessary.

This approach has its initial germ in Durkheim's conceptualization of *anomie*. In the latter half of the nineteenth century Durkheim perceived that the traditional class structure of French society had dissolved and a new situation was spreading in which only desire expanded limitlessly (Durkheim [1897/]1981: 281). According to Durkheim, this happens in a society where there is a 'developed industry' and equality is valued.[3] In reality, the only places where symptoms of anomie appeared at the time were in large cities such as Paris. However, the conceptualization of anomie was especially significant for pointing out that social life could not be properly understood simply in terms of the class structure. It is necessary to begin the examination not from the perspective of difference but from one that regards social difference as nothing. An example of this perspective can be seen in Canetti's concept of the 'crowd'. For Canetti (1966), the crowd refers to a phenomenon in which the individual differences of human beings disappear into one mass. The crowd appears suddenly out of nowhere, and can disappear just as suddenly. There is no essential basis for the appearance of a crowd. Its essence is its baseless nature, its fundamental uncertainty.

Returning to K, then: If we attempt to understand human being from a perspective in which social difference is invalid, it is necessary to regard K as a free being, and not as an indistinguishable constituent of a particular social category, whose life course was determined by her membership in that category. K was free. Her freedom was secured because she knew how to deal with fate.

Violence

Human freedom is not unlimited. Among other things, freedom is violated by what we can call an 'incident'. The degree of violence of an incident increases in proportion to the degree to which it violates someone's freedom. From this perspective, cancer would have been the most violent incident in K's life.

Modern society's freedom to maintain social order is also limited by incidents, while its efforts to construct a new global order create new incidents. This is nowhere better typified than by the terrorist destruction of the World Trade Center Buildings in New York City on 9 September 2001. '9/11' was socially recognized as a global incident and various global-scale countermeasures were instituted with the aim of preventing similar terrorist attacks. Some of these counter-measures eventually developed into an incident in which a Western military alliance, led by US and UK forces, invaded Iraq and overthrew the Hussein administration.

Incidents have several characteristics. First, they occur suddenly. Immediately after the incident at least, it seems to have happened accidentally. It is an unforeseeable situation, and those who become directly involved have no idea that they will be the victim of an incident until it happens. Various analyses will be carried out to find the cause of the incident, but this will only happen retrospectively. Second, an incident gives the impression that its victims are chosen by 'random sampling'. Emphasis is placed on the unluckiness of the victims, who are in the wrong place at the wrong time.

There is still little sociological research analyzing incidents with full recognition of these characteristics. The focus of research into such incidents tends to be limited to the assailant, such as a murderer, and only the unfortunate fate of the assailant is highlighted. Novelists, critics and sociologists, as well TV audiences and newspaper readers try to find the assailant's motive, as if they are prosecutors and judges. The victims of the incident are typically ignored. As previously mentioned, in the case of the 19 year old double-murderer,

N, Munesuke Mita examined the circumstances which presumably led to the crime. But he showed very little interest in the backgrounds of the victims (a night security guard and a taxi driver). We cannot have a full account of an incident if we do not analyze the victims as well. N and his victims did not know each other. The victims presumably could not have imagined that they would be killed by an unknown youth. It was a sudden death. Their stories are not told by novelists or sociologists, and they are soon forgotten.[4]

The following article from the *Asahi Newspaper*, regarding 'crimes without motives', is rather interesting in considering the characteristics of incidents.

> This year, crimes committed by mentally ill persons and deviates stood out. The stabbing of US Ambassador Reischauer, which resulted in the resignation of the National Public Safety Commission Chairman; the Mitaka City tragedy of a female prosecutor's family, where the eldest son brutally murdered his younger brother; the random, serial assaults by a youth which terrified residents in the Jōsai Area in Tokyo; the random killing of a young woman in Nerima; and then this stabbing of a chief judge. There were also many other murder and stabbing incidents caused by 'irritation' and 'displeasure'. According to Tokyo Metropolitan Police statistics, 20% of the criminal offences were committed by people with mental illnesses. Crimes without reasonable reasons. This year, these incidents have troubled us and forced us to think.
>
> The young, random assailant of the Jōsai Area was caught on the 26th, nearly two whole years since the first incident last spring. The mother of one victim, who received brutal injuries to his lower abdomen, voices her concern about her 12 year-old son's future. She says, 'Rather than this being an issue for the police, I feel that it is the responsibility of the whole society which leaves these perverts at large.'
>
> Inspector Akiba of the Metropolitan Police, section manager in the investigation team for this incident, says, 'I have been in investigations for nearly 20 years, but it's the first time I was faced with such a difficult incident. I went to the schools but could find no leads. Even the teachers, who see students everyday, don't notice anything. Someone who is usually normal changes in an instant and this is difficult to discover. Crimes by deviates will become a big issue of crime prevention and police investigation.'
>
> Until now, in most incidents the offenders could be traced from people known to the victims. However, psychopathic crimes are

> usually random or coincidental. With the problem of perverts on the loose, crime investigation has reached a crucial turn.
>
> One day, towards the end of the year, in the waiting room of the Tokyo Metropolitan Government's Life Rehabilitation Center, at Ueno, on the banks of Shinobazu Pond, a mother stands dejectedly, holding a baby. 'She told us that she ran away from her unbearable, alcoholic husband. This is one of the better cases. We've had a man suddenly take off his clothes, draw a knife from his belly band and attack, right in the middle of an interview', Takeichi Machida, manager of the consultation section, says and sighs.

This newspaper article is from the evening paper of 27 December 1964. Incidentally, the incident analyzed by Mita occurred in 1968. 'Crimes caused by trivial reasons' and 'random or collateral crimes' were on the rise, and, as the article pointed out, the characteristics of the criminals were changing. The article is 40 years old, but the characteristics described are similar to those seen in recent youth crimes. The article also has foresight, in referring to the family of the victim. Is there a source, in the 1960s, for incidents with similar characteristics to the current, various incidents? Or are crimes without motives not connected to a particular historical condition? At the least, it can be said that the more chances there are for encounters with strangers, the greater the potential for random crimes.

Incidents and casualties

Some incidents produce far more victims than crimes such as murder. A typical example is war. Nothing shows the violent nature of incidents as vividly as war. The application of science and technology to the development of military weapons not only produces a mass of victims but the damage also extends to those who are not soldiers. The atomic bombs dropped on Hiroshima and Nagasaki clearly illustrates this characteristic. For the people of Hiroshima and Nagasaki, the atomic bomb and the fact that Japan was at war had no immediate connection. The flash and sound of the atomic bomb was an incident which came without warning, overwhelming the class structure which existed among the people of Hiroshima and reducing it to nothing.

In the case of the Vietnam War, the border between the soldiers and the civilians was further obscured. Helped by the fact that it was a long-lasting war, the battlefields (or potential battlefields) of Vietnam were divided into several different spaces. For one, there were big cities like Saigon. Then there were the rural villages, separated into an area under the control of the South Vietnamese Army, an area under the control of the National Liberation Front of Vietnam (Vietcong), and a mixed control area (where the South Vietnamese Army and the Vietcong competed). The damage to the people was different depending on where they lived (Honda 1981). Naturally, battles were executed based on geopolitical decisions. However, peasants do not live according to such decisions. To them, the chances of having their house burnt down or being sprayed with defoliant were largely incidental.

Of course, wartime civilians anticipate the damage from war. They dig air-raid shelters and prepare for war damage. But the damage caused by an atomic bomb or defoliant goes far beyond their projections. Moreover, weapons such as the atomic bomb, defoliant, and the depleted uranium shells used in the Gulf War have another common characteristic: they leave after-effects. They not only immediately affect the victims, but also bring about long-term diseases and the slow deaths of victims, as well as causing defects in the fetuses of direct victims.

Unforeseeable damages create uncertainty (while some risk is predictable, uncertainty is that part which is beyond prediction). Uncertainty gives war an incidental dimension. This uncertainty, which is always a factor in modern wars, has not yet been adequately considered. Western social theories have instead emphasized the point that order is installed through violence such as war.[5]

In a sociological study of the Holocaust, Zygmunt Bauman argues that over the course of the history of civilization, the execution of violence has become separated from moral consideration and is increasingly controlled by the principle of rationality (Bauman 1992). He claims that the Holocaust was a product of a rationalized bureaucracy typical of modern society, that proceeded through the widespread adherence of the populace to the principles of such bureaucracy. In contrast, screen-writer Claude Lanzmann argues that the Holocaust cannot be attributed to such structural factors but was a sudden 'extermination operation' which began without warning. For Lanzmann, the Holocaust refuses all 'historical explanations'. He says:

> Up to now, all works on the Holocaust have tried to illustrate this event as having occurred naturally, with the help of history and chronologies… The extinction of European Jews cannot be deduced logically or mathematically from such presupposed systems. Between

> the various conditions which enabled the extermination and the extermination itself, the fact of extermination, there is a severance, a gap, a leap, a deep abyss. (Lanzmann 1995: 4)

Alongside the Holocaust, numerous mass murders in the twentieth century have the character of an incident. When considering violence in the twentieth century, one should not look towards the violent nature structurally contained within modern society as Bauman did, but start from the point that an order is constructed through a seemingly accidental incident which suddenly occurs.

Here we must consider another way in which uncertainty may be characteristic of an incident. Where there is an undetermined power relationship between two parties, conflict may arise. If, for example, the weaker party refuses to acknowledge the other's dominance, a war situation may arise. In this sense, Hobbes was not wrong to argue that in the 'natural state' all men are equal, and are therefore in a state of war. In other words, a war starts between two powers that do not recognize each other's sovereignty. So why does one party attempt to conquer the other? Lévi-Strauss comments in a little known paper, 'War and commerce among the Indians of South America' (Lévi-Strauss 1943), that 'a business transaction indicates that the possibility of war has been dissolved peacefully, and a war is the result of a transaction unfortunately gone wrong.' Lévi-Strauss sees only a very fine line between war and exchange.

Lévi-Strauss was dealing with the society of South American Indians, and the extent to which this applies directly to the issue of violence in modern society is open to debate. However, it is worth examining his idea that contact with others results either in war or trade. In modern society, trade means commodity exchange, while Lévi-Strauss was describing gift exchange. Returning to the Vietnam War from this perspective, the Cold War was clearly the backdrop. The conflict was ideological: whether to build an equal society on market principles, or to build an equal society on non-market principles. The USA aimed towards building a market-governed society in East and South-East Asia, where 'equality' would be realized through monetary exchange. When this objective was threatened, the bombing of Vietnam began. In this sense there was only a fine line between exchange (to allow commodity exchange) and war (to invite battle by not allowing commodity exchange).

Let us now consider some of the issues to be resolved by modern sociology. First there is a theoretical question regarding the relationship between the introduction of a market economy and violence. Social issues appear as various incidents arise from the penetration and expansion of a market economy based on the principal of 'equal' exchange. These social issues can no longer be attributed to social divisions or class, as discussed above. Therefore new questions must be answered, such as: What sort of antagonism and conflict are generated by an attempt for commodity exchange between two parties? What conditions create violence? Does violence disappear as the market economy's penetration deepens?

Second, there is the empirical question of where and when the introduction of the market economy has generated violence. This paper will focus particularly on the second, empirical issues.

Issues unique to time

The specific events discussed so far in this paper are concentrated around the 1960s. This is not coincidental. The 1960s was a significant transformation period for the world and for Japan. The Vietnam War arose in the context of the Cold War between the USA and the USSR. Asia was pulled into the war: from Vietnam, obviously, to the Korean and Hong Kong soldiers supporting the US forces, to the US support bases in Japan, particularly Okinawa, and finally Thailand, where US soldiers spent their furloughs. Although some claim that 'globalization' emerged after the Cold War, a close relationship between Asia and the rest of the world developed through this war.

Although there were movements such as Beheiren (the Federation of Citizens for Peace in Vietnam) in the 1960s, from the Japanese perspective, the Vietnam War was a peripheral event, somebody else's problem. Okinawa was still occupied by US forces. Economically, it was a high growth period, and with the rapid penetration of the market economy the Japanese people's lifestyle (food, clothing and housing) was rapidly and dramatically changing. At the same time, the Japanese population became more mobile. Coal mines in North East Japan and Kyūshū closed down and a large number of workers moved to the Tokyo and Kansai areas. The young murderer, N, came to Tokyo as part of a group employment program after finishing junior high school. He had tried to finish senior high school while working, but failed.

Less remembered than the Vietnam War, is the pollution issue in Minamata at the time. Minamata Disease was caused by the discharge of methyl mercury into the Shiranui Sea by a company called Chisso. Methyl mercury is a by-product of manufacturing acetaldehyde, a material for plasticizer. The dumping continued until 1968, when the manufacture of acetaldehyde was stopped because the chemical industry had switched to oil for its raw material. From the 'sympathy money agreement' in 1959, in which Chisso compensated a number of patients, until 1968 when the government recognized that Minamata Disease was caused by industrial pollution, the issue was considered 'finished' (according to the Minamata Disease Patient Assessment Board) at the government administrative level. We should not draw connections between Vietnam and Minamata lightly, but there are similarities between these two serious incidents.

In both, immense damage was caused by the achievements of the chemical industry. A lasting sequela was left by the use of defoliant in the Vietnam War. In a corner of a Hanoi hospital, patients who were exposed as fetuses are still being treated today. Although the Vietnam War supposedly ended in 1975, after 30 years, new victims continue to be born.

The defoliant used as a chemical weapon, was originally developed as an agricultural chemical and contained dioxin, an organochlorine compound. Dioxin is an inevitable byproduct in the manufacturing process of agricultural chemicals, but also occurs from burning waste compounds. The Chisso Minamata Factory was the first in Japan to succeed in the industrial manufacture of polyvinyl chloride in 1941 (Ui 1985: 101). In the 1950s, the market was overwhelmingly dominated by Chisso. The disposal of polyvinyl chloride is today regarded as the main culprit in dioxin generation.

Even after the government recognized that Minamata Disease was pollution-induced, Chisso did not immediately accept responsibility. In 1971, Ken'ichi Shimada, then president of Chisso, reportedly said:

> Since October 1959, we have employed a method that does not discharge any mercury-containing waste water into the sea... Therefore, this renewed demand for compensation was like having an old wound reopened, so to speak.[6]

But in fact Chisso continued to discharge factory waste water until 1968, when a decision was made to halt acetaldehyde production. Yet Chisso persisted with its denial, in 1972, distributing a booklet to its employees titled '15 years of the Minamata Disease issue'. The booklet claims that the Minamata Disease was not caused by factory waste water, but maybe by some new agricultural chemical, which had begun to be used in the Minamata area. Nevertheless, the

1973 decision in the Minamata Disease lawsuit was in favor of the plaintiffs, the victims. Direct negotiation started between Shimada and the patients at the Tokyo head office of Chisso. Here Shimada reportedly would begin by saying 'I would like to apologize deeply', and then, 'Patients keep appearing one after another and our company has reached its financial capability limit. In fact, we will be in serious trouble if we're unable to pay even the previously determined compensation', in an attempt to change the terms of the agreement to the company's advantage (Ishimure 1974: 152).

In the Minamata Byō Kōshōkan (Minamata Disease Evidence Museum) founded by Sōshisha, a support organization for the victims, various products are exhibited which use Chisso products as their raw material. They were developed during Japan's high economic growth period and illustrate how Chisso contributed to the growth of the Japanese economy. In the 1960s, great changes occurred across Japanese society. In short, it was an era which saw the rapid commercialization of food, clothing and housing. The synthetic materials developed by Chisso played a significant role.

What was happening in the 1960s?

The principles of the market economy were rapidly penetrating East and South-East Asia, spreading at different speeds in different places and at various social levels, such as community and family, at the same time causing friction. The market economy creates two associated phenomena: 'dislocation' and 'division'. These are interlinked, and each has the potential to induce violence.

In the case of Minamata, Mr. S said:

> We'd catch the fish, but no one would eat. They wouldn't buy. Even the Fishing Co-op, not anymore. The shops in the shopping arcade closed their doors, not one shop sold fish. Not just here. Of course in Minamata, but all along the coast no one went out to fish. Because no one ate fish. Ourselves, we didn't eat it either. So, you see, how do you live on fishing? It was an awful situation. We just couldn't survive. Even myself, my joints began to ache, and I was unsteady on the boat. It was awful. The terrible effects were appearing to myself too... Everyone knew about the fish caught in the bay, so we thought, if we bring in fish caught in the open sea, they'll buy, they'll eat. Of course, they did... We brought it (fish from the open sea) in and began to sell. But then, we'd never had to ask people to buy our fish, we'd never done

> that before. Before, everyone would come and ask to buy the fish we caught, and we never had to say, please buy our fish. We didn't have any experience of selling like that. So you see, there was no way we could make a profit.[7]

When rumor spread about the strange disease and fish from the Shiranui Sea could no longer be sold, some fishermen began to sell the fish themselves on the market. However, this did not go well. Mr. S said, '(My father) would get drunk, and just start to give away all the (fish on sale).' He appears to have treated monetary exchange as no different from gift exchange, accepting that an imbalance would be generated between the exchangees. Mr. S moved to Kitakyūshū in 1960 with his wife and two children and became an office worker. Similarly, many fishermen left Minamata after 1960 to work in Osaka or Nagoya.

Devices (for example, factories) which advance capitalism cause various types of dislocations. To begin with, the industries peripheral to capitalistic production such as agriculture, forestry, fishery and various self-employed businesses are dismantled, dislocating the workers in those industries. In the 1960s in Japan, there was also a string of mine closures. The extraction of mineral resources leads to the accumulation of capital, but mine development had built its own type of 'society' with unique management. Many mines provided everything from schools to entertainment facilities to enable mine workers and their families to live in mining towns. With the closure of the mines, though, workers and their families had to move out of the company towns and start life again at a new location. Conflict and violence frequently arise in the newly settled places, maybe caused by dislocation.

With dislocation comes division. This was also evident in the Minamata case. Mr. S emphasized the following point.

> Destruction of the local community...worse than environmental destruction or the destruction of nature, this was most painful, the destruction of human beings themselves. The Minamata Disease was just that. Moreover...moreover, for instance, one household, a family, would be divided in two. You know why, don't you? Back then families used to cook and eat a whole pot full of fish together. Often with neighbors. We ate lots of contaminated fish, from the same pot. But then, when the Minamata Disease certification system was set up, we gathered the courage to apply, and received medical check-ups. Then

> it goes to the certification committee, and the children are certified but not the parents. Withheld and rejected. Or, the parents are certified but not the children. It was all like this. There were families where all members were certified, six or seven, in the same area. Though I won't name them. Like that, the government administration started to be discriminatory. Everyone had the symptoms, but not everyone received certification. Assessment withheld. Assessment rejected. Those who were withheld—some even applied five or six times—still withheld. Even when the symptoms were evident, the national government wouldn't allow the committee to give certification. Rejected at the certification stage.
>
> In the past, when there were purse nets, about 30 people would be around one net. There were many like that here. Everyone helped each other and shared with each other in life. But with the Minamata Disease, human relationships were torn apart. Among fellow patients. The community disintegrated. It was terrible. No more conversation. Human relationships destroyed. Alas. Even among blood relatives, this happened.

This statement is a clear example of the ways that capitalism leads to the division of human relationships. It also shows the fundamental issue of Minamata Disease. Non-ethical capitalistic production divides families and communities. This can be clearly seen in the area affected by the Minamata Disease, and is an 'incident' which occurs where capitalistic production takes place. Eventually, however, Mr. S returned to Minamata to attempt to rebuild the local community. Neither Mr. S, nor Minamata, simply surrendered to the division (I intend to discuss this point in detail in another paper).

Fixation towards equality

Money mediates exchange. As a rule, this exchange takes place between strangers. Adam Smith says, 'If, for example, among a race of hunters, it usually takes twice the amount of labor to kill a beaver than it does to kill a deer, one beaver should naturally be exchanged for two deer' (Smith [1776/]1978: 80). One prerequisite for this condition is that the two hunters do not know each other. This implies that, in a family group, monetary exchange is excluded except where it has a strong sense of gift, such as giving pocket money to children. In the pre-capitalist society of Minamata, in addition to the immediate family, a 'boss' fisherman maintained family-like relationship with the fishermen below him. Similarly, money is normally not involved in relationships based on 'friendship' or 'love'. In the 1960s, though, as marketism began to penetrate, with its principle of realizing equal exchange through money, money began to mercilessly invade relationships which had not previously involved money. This invasion itself is a violent incident, and triggers a further chain reaction of various kinds of violence (for example, family conflict).

The penetration of marketism accompanied by violence in Japan resulted in the birth of a society in which the extent of marketism was like no other. An affluent society had been realized, where starvation barely existed. The convenience store is symbolic of this. In the center of major cities around the world, some shops are open 24 hours, but in Japan in many places convenience stores are even abundant in the residential areas of cities and towns.

The convenience store is a 'transparent space' equipped with fulfillment, odorlessness and safety. Fulfillment is that the convenience store can supply goods necessary for daily life and that one will not starve if there is a convenience store. Although it sells food, it is clean, sterile, and has no odor. Whereas former fish and fruit shops were filled with smells owing to the nature of their goods, in the convenience store the smell of foodstuffs is eliminated. Plastic packaging (a product of the chemical industry) plays a big role here, wrapping all of the food, such as 'boxed lunches', and most of the other products as well. Safety is secured. In some respects it may appears to be a space for 'healing'. It may feel as though the brightly illuminated convenience store is the only safe place in a residential area. It gives the impression that an absolutely perfect utopia-like space has appeared there.

Marketism, which was created through violence, generated the space called the convenience store. It is also a victory for synthetic materials produced by the chemical industry, once led by Chisso. Organic chemistry plays a big role in exterminating 'pests' and 'weeds' to build a spotless space. Many of the goods on the shelves of the convenience store are products of organic chemistry. We have discussed Chisso paying compensation to some Minamata Disease sufferers in 1959, and then hiding the fact that it continued to discharge waste water containing organic mercury into the Shiranui Sea until 1968. This is an inexcusable crime; but the acetaldehyde and vinyl chloride that Chisso produced throughout those years laid the foundations for today's transparent spaces.

When marketism begins to take over in this way, equal exchange becomes obvious, and some begin to feel violence if it is breached even to a small extent. The emergence of the litigious society as can be seen in the USA is one way for a society to deal with this. Japan seems to have developed a different way. For example, there is a phenomenon called 'withdrawal', in which (typically young) people withdraw into the relative security of their homes and private spaces. Youths who are experiencing withdrawal are reportedly not reluctant, however, to go to a convenience store. In the transparent space of the convenience store, the only kind of interpersonal relationship acceptable is monetary exchange. (Those withdrawn youths are also obsessive about cleanliness.)

Epilogue—A will to give

Finally, back to K's story. K complained that 'There's a difference from birth.' Sociologists tend to attribute this 'difference' to something like the reproduction theory, which assumes the existence of a stratified social structure. However, this paper hypothesizes that a society with a principle of marketism organizes order through incidents. Incidents happen in a transparent space seemingly removed from violence and where the principle of equality works, not in a stratified social structure. The principle of equality governs relationships between strangers, a typical example of which is the exchange of goods. The principle of equality works between strangers on the assumption of uncertainty (the principle of marketism approves and encourages exchanges with unknown persons, presupposing some degree of uncertainty due to not knowing, and always holds the possibility of violence. Of course, violence takes many forms).

Certainly, there is a violence which in spite of resistance cannot be overcome, such as a random killing or an incurable disease. Disparity within a capitalist society should be measured by whether one has the will to stand up against all kinds of violence, including those which cannot be resisted. This will to face up to violence is related to the will to give. The will to give is only about giving, no return is expected. Having the will to give, where one gives and receives from others without fearing an encounter with violence, and not becoming buried in the superficial world of equality achieved through the exchange of goods, enables the overcoming of an encountered incident. The attitude which most lacks the will to give is withdrawal into one's home, shopping only at convenience stores. The people that K referred to 'who are always at the pachinko parlor and don't look after their kids' also lack a will to give. These 'parents' spend only for themselves, and are hardly different than the socially withdrawn youths. K, however, did not refuse anyone who depended on her. She had a strong will to give. Sociologists must seriously consider how to persuade people towards giving.

4
Nietzsche and the Height of Happiness

Kojiro Miyahara

Introduction

At the end of the eighteenth century Jeremy Bentham clearly articulated the central principle of utilitarianism, coining the motto 'the greatest happiness of the greatest number'. On this view, the ideal shape of society is the one that maximizes individual happiness. From a quantitative perspective, then, the 'total happiness' in a society can be calculated by adding up the happiness of each individual member.[1]

When I first encountered the idea of 'the greatest happiness of the greatest number' I was impressed. It seemed a simple, well designed, and morally excellent principle. However, a question gradually arose, which I came to think of in terms of 'daifuku (great fortune) rice cakes'. Bentham's principle comes down to the idea that 'it is good to distribute as many rice cakes to as many people as possible'. Yet, happiness is not a homogeneous thing like rice cakes. It is an experience which cannot be measured quantitatively. It differs from person to person, and even for the same person, it differs according to the time and occasion. It seems misdirected to count such a wide variety of experiences in a single uniform way to calculate a 'total happiness'. Of course, at the beginning of the twenty-first century, 'the greatest happiness of the greatest number' is not widely accepted in its simple forms. There have been many attempts to refine and qualify the concept, which have produced many variations of the phrase. Among these attempts, though, the core idea of being able to quantitatively measure happiness remains as popular as ever.

In contrast, in this paper I examine the 'quality' of happiness, which cannot be quantified. I will conduct this exploration from a Nietzschean perspective, which seems to be the polar opposite of Bentham's. In the process, I will consider how this Nietzschean perspective sheds light on the issue of happiness in an 'advanced' society such as today's Japan.

Nietzsche's 'sociology of knowledge'

From the Nietzschean perspective, there is a qualitative distinction between high and low forms of happiness. The background of this distinction lies in the historical experience of 'masters' (conquerors) and 'slaves' (the conquered). Today this experience is becoming forgotten, but the quality of happiness cannot be discussed from a Nietzschean perspective without referring to masters and slaves. For Nietzsche, the master's happiness is the 'high' form of happiness and the slave's is the 'low' form of happiness.

Typically, the term 'height' tends to evoke quantitative differences. It can be measured by large or small values in a scale, such as 'body height' or 'high income'. But Nietzsche's high/low distinction is not quantifiable. As a person's 'height of social status' in pre-modern society could not be interpreted with quantities such as income, assets, educational qualifications or relative standing in examination scores, likewise, the 'height of happiness' is a very qualitative distinction.

Nietzsche asks '*whom* the happiness is for'. The qualitative experience of happiness differs for different people, but as we have seen, Nietzsche distinguished two main types: the master and the slave. A similar approach can be found in the sociology of knowledge, emphasizing that the very experience of 'happiness' differs depending on a person's actual mode of existence (social, historical, physiological, mental, etc). Contemporary culture is significantly based upon presuppositions of an abstract concept of 'human being' that imagines a homogenized happiness for all. In fact, in 'advanced' societies today there are no masters or slaves. These different social types have disappeared, and the majority of the middle-class citizens have indeed become increasingly homogenized. Nevertheless, Nietzsche reminds us, a master and a slave survive inside each of us. He further observes, as will be later described, that a third type, the 'young child', is starting to emerge. He argues: 'Indeed, our body is but a social structure composed of many souls' (Nietzsche 1885–86: 37). The Nietzschean individual is not one but many. The distinct status types of the past are now moved into and internalized by each individual. The question can thus be reframed as, 'happiness for which one *within* myself'? From this perspective, the object of a Nietzschean sociology of knowledge shifts from the external society to the society within the individual.

Happiness of the master, happiness of the slave

Nietzsche refers to a 'happiness of high tension' in *Beyond Good and Evil* which he formulates in terms of the 'master and slave' morality. The 'master' Nietzsche identifies is neither the 'aristocrat class' nor the 'social winners' that we might imagine today. Its central image originated with the ancient Greeks before Socrates, from the overwhelming conquerors who did not doubt their own power and virtue. 'It was the noble races which left behind the concept of the "barbarian" in all their tracks, wherever they went', including the 'Roman, Arab, German, Japanese nobility, Homeric heroes, Scandinavian Vikings' (Nietzsche 1887: 42). The 'master', in this context, means a noble barbarian.

According to Nietzsche, these noble and creative people had 'the feeling of plenitude, of power, which seeks to overflow, the *happiness of high tension*, the consciousness of a wealth which would fain give and bestow' (Nietzsche 1885–86: 270, emphasis added). They were 'complete men, overloaded with power and thus *necessarily* active, they must not separate action from happiness. They considered being active necessarily associated with happiness' (Nietzsche 1887: 38–9).

But did those who were conquered, whose heads were pressed down, who sunk into resignation as they cursed their fate, and worked everyday in hard labor, have no opportunities to feel happiness? Yes, they did. The slaves could enjoy the 'happiness of the slave'. Nietzsche regarded the happiness of the 'powerless, the oppressed, those festering with poisonous and hostile feelings' to be totally different from the 'happiness of the master'. For the slave, 'happiness comes out essentially as a narcotic, an anesthetic, quiet, peace, "Sabbath", relaxing the soul, stretching one's limbs, in short, as something *passive*' (Nietzsche 1887: 38–9). The 'happiness of the slave' is not characterized by an active high tension but rather a passive low slack.

The slave, faced with his self as he is, sighs. 'I wish I could be someone else!"—that's what this glance sighs." But there is no hope here. I am who I am. How could I detach myself from myself? And yet *I've had enough of myself*!' (Nietzsche 1887: 154 emphasis added). Thus he tries to turn his eyes and distract himself from himself. Lying down and dozing. Sleeping. Becoming intoxicated on alcohol and other drugs. Forgetting himself in gambling and entertainment. Seeking every kind of pleasure that provides a moment of respite and allows him to forget himself. Seeking sympathy and rescue. A prominent method for forgetting oneself that has developed in the most 'advanced' societies is through an excessive attachment to working life—the so-called workaholic—which is frequently combined with age-old methods of indulging in passions such as hatred, jealousy and revenge.

In contrast, the happiness of the master is derived from the effort to secure and enjoy his or her existence. It stems from a continual awareness of one's own power in the midst of an activity characterized by tension, especially a war. To the question 'What is happiness? Nietzsche responds: 'The feeling that power *increases*—that resistance is overcome.—*Not* contentment, but more power; *not* peace at any price, but war; *not* virtue, but efficiency (virtue in the Renaissance sense, *virtu,* virtue free of moral acid)' (Nietzsche 1888: 166). One cannot directly strive for this happiness. It is merely an accompaniment to the activity. 'Do I then strive after *happiness*? I strive after my *work*!' (Nietzsche 1883–85: 333). This 'work' is, of course, not labor for a livelihood, but an activity with public value. The policing described by H. Arendt is a prime example. The happiness of the master is an experience derived from a creative 'activity'.

According to Nietzsche, certain happiness is felt to be 'high' because it reverberates with the happiness of a mentally and physically 'high' person, of past conquerors, of those overflowing with pride and vitality. The 'high person' preceded 'high happiness' in history. The same can be said of 'low happiness'. In what one finds 'happiness' is itself defined by the actual existence (social, historical, physiological, mental, etc) of particular persons.

A brief reflection on my personal experiences may help to shed some light on these distinctions and to locate them in a more contemporary context. I have felt happy, for example, when engrossed in a difficult task. The pleasure of creating something new, the feeling of fulfillment as one's whole being comes together as one focused actor, the exaltation of breaking limits, the elation of receiving praise, and gratitude for being entrusted with a 'task' are some of the factors. The tensions that accompany these sensations arise at least in part from the corresponding risk of failure. Happiness containing such tension is felt as 'high happiness'. Alternatively, I also feel happy when I am idle and free from immediate obligations or worries. On the first morning of a long weekend, I awake and doze off, half-watching the TV while lying back in bed. The relaxation of knowing that nothing needs to be done, the comfort of stretching out, and the security of knowing that everybody is doing the same are some of the factors. This happiness is a release of tension and is felt as 'low happiness'.

When I experience 'high happiness' the master within me feels happy. Inversely, when I experience 'low happiness', the slave inside me is happy. That I can experience both 'high happiness' and 'low happiness' depending on the particular context of daily life and the seasons of the lifetime indicates the presence of both the master and slave within me. This experience is not unique to me. According to Nietzsche, modern men are more or less 'the blending of the blood of masters and slaves' (Nietzsche 1885–86: 275). This remains true for the majority of people in modern societies today.

This is not to say that high happiness is 'real happiness'. Nor am I saying that low happiness is only a 'false happiness'. There is a strong tendency in contemporary society to dichotomize experiences into real and false (or normal and abnormal) when the quality of the experience cannot be expressed quantitatively. Consider the dichotomy used in talking about the quality of love. In modern discourse, love between opposite sexes and between singles is regarded as 'real', while love between the same sex and adultery is regarded as 'false'. In ancient Greece, however, this particular distinction did not exist. For them, the question was whether the love was 'noble or vulgar', 'high love or low love' (Foucault 1984).

Our society distinguishes between high and low quality of clothing, meals, and hotel service, for example. But we do not speak of a person's actions and experiences as high and low. Instead we speak of them as real and false. A 'real love' and a 'false love', a 'real happiness' and 'false happiness'. When 'high and low' become the question, things instantly become awkward. Today it is deemed rude to say 'low love' or 'low happiness'. Everyone is equal, so there shouldn't be high or low forms of love and happiness. That is how we feel, what we have been taught, how we have been socialized. The Nietzschean approach does not allow this escape into the real/false dichotomy. To say it plainly, 'high happiness' is real happiness for masters and 'low happiness' is real happiness for slaves. A brief exploration of Nietzsche's view of history will help to explain how this perspective on happiness came about.

Happiness for the 'Last Man'

In Europe, the end of the ancient regime saw the downfall of master-type men and the rise of slave-type men to power. The slaves' *ressentiment* towards the masters had crystallized as Christian morality—the 'slave revolt in morality' had succeeded. The Renaissance was a large-scale counter-movement against this; the master-type man was momentarily revived. In the end, though, through the Reformation and the modern political and social revolutions, the slave-type men prevailed. Modern society abolished the social types master and slave, while normalizing the dominance of the slave as a pattern for human societies. Nietzsche saw this trend occurring in the masses (the middle class) of Europe at the end of the nineteenth century. He characterizes this historical development as the emergence of the 'last man' (in *Thus Spoke Zarathustra*).

On his first attempt at preaching in the town square, Zarathustra begins with a depiction of the 'the most despicable man', at the polar opposite to the *übermensch* (overman).

> Lo! I show you the *last man.*
>
> "What is love? What is creation? What is longing? What is a star?"—so asks the last man, and blinks.
>
> The earth has become small, and on it hops the last man, who makes everything small. His species is ineradicable as the flea; the last man lives longest.
>
> "We have discovered happiness"—say the last men, and they blink.
>
> They have left the regions where it is hard to live; for they need warmth. One still loves one's neighbor and rubs against him; for one needs warmth.
>
> Turning ill and being distrustful, they consider sinful: they walk warily. He is a fool who still stumbles over stones or men!
>
> A little poison now and then: that makes for pleasant dreams. And much poison at the end for a pleasant death.
>
> One still works, for work is a pastime. But one is careful lest the pastime should hurt one.
>
> One no longer becomes poor or rich; both are too burdensome. Who still wants to rule? Who still wants to obey? Both are too burdensome.

> No shepherd, and one herd! Everyone wants the same; everyone *is* the same: he who has other sentiments goes voluntarily into the madhouse.
>
> "Formerly all the world was insane,"—say the subtlest of them, and they blink.
>
> They are clever and know all that has happened: so there is no end to their derision. People still quarrel, but are soon reconciled—otherwise it upsets their stomachs.
>
> They have their little pleasures for the day, and their little pleasures for the night, but they have a regard for health.
>
> "We have discovered happiness,"—say the last men, and they blink... (Nietzsche 1883–85: 24–5)

Nietzsche's prediction of the emergence of the 'last men' appears in many ways to have been realized. It depicts with surprising accuracy the dominant way of living of middle-class citizens in present-day Japan—the majority of the population, myself included.

Men and women live longer than they ever have (Miyahara 2004). We avoid the cold (and increasingly, in recent times, the heat) and pain by all means, and endlessly seek ease, peace of mind and comfort. This extends as well to human relationships, and various considerations ('kindnesses' to prevent hurting and being hurt) are employed to avoid pain and injury. Every kind of anesthetic is on the market, and dazzling (but safe) entertainment has become a major industry. The awareness of equality among peers is stronger than ever, with people always checking each other's (status) movement. In an atmosphere where ruling or being ruled is both considered too bothersome, there is a strong tendency to exclude those who are different. Subjected to a longer than ever period of education and exposed to a copious amount of 'information' through the mass media and internet, anyone can know what is happening on the other side of the globe. Ordinary people have seemingly well-informed opinions and are 'sophisticated' in an unprecedented fashion. There is no religion or beliefs held in common, but 'health' is special. The only sin is to damage one's health...

Comfort, ease, security, leisure, rest, and anesthetic. This happiness obviously belongs to the 'happiness of the slave'. No wonder: the 'last men' are the 'herd without a shepherd', the slaves who purged the masters. 'The greatest happiness of the greatest number' is a persuasive maxim among such slaves without masters. Since the happiness of the slaves without masters is regarded as the basic homogenous unit of happiness—the 'slack' happiness that accompanies a release from tension—the thoughtless manipulation of counting up the 'total happiness' in society no longer seems thoughtless.

'Painless civilization' and happiness

Nietzsche's depiction of the 'last man' in the 1880s predicted key features of our time very well. Yet there is a subtle difference which should be acknowledged. Compared to the 'last men', we are not confident that we are happy.[2] We are more affluent, comfortable, at ease, equal and long-lived than ever before in the history of humankind, but we are not quite sure if we are really happy. Quite a few Japanese people feel that it was better in the past, when they were still in a 'developing country'. It has become a defining characteristic of consumerist society that many people are seeking further pleasures, stimulation and penance, and wandering about in search of 'happiness'.

Under these circumstances, many voices have arisen preaching the way to 'real happiness'. Among them, I want to discuss Masahiro Morioka's (2003) *Painless Civilization Theory*. Its critical posture towards modern civilization, especially its interpretation of the 'self-domestication' of man, resonates with Nietzsche's critique of the 'last man'.

Compared to wild animals, domesticated animals have a distinctive set of characteristics. They live in a man-made environment, food is supplied automatically, they are protected from natural threats, their breeding is controlled, breed improvement results, and there is an evident change in body form. All of these characteristics are applicable to human beings, who have domesticated themselves, as well (Obara 1995). Morioka adds 'management of death' and 'voluntary constraint' to this list before asking about the meaning of self-domestication in civilization. In what Marioka calls the 'painless civilization', 'desires of the body strip the joy of life. This is the deepest meaning of self-domestication, and it is the most fundamental problem progressing in our civilization' (Morioka 2003: 18).

'Desires of the body' are the desires to 'seek comfort and avoid pain'. They attempt to maintain the *status quo*, to stabilize, and to multiply if there is a chance, to manage a living, life and nature by sacrificing others. Furthermore, while keeping 'the current "framework" of one's own comfort', it seeks further comfort, ease and leisure. At the radical end of this is the 'preventative pain-killing' movement, which aims to eliminate all kinds of pain through genetic engineering and the abortion of those fetuses identified as 'defective' or at-risk through antenatal diagnosis. The desires that radiate from the bodies of the countless masses of people become a rushing torrent that swallows individuals. Morioka calls this the 'painless currents'.

> The desire to live at ease, to lead a stable life, to live without experiencing real pain, to let nothing go once it is obtained, to expand without reforming oneself. Such 'desires of the body' are strengthened in conversations between people, in thoughts and in institutions, and are woven together to become a torrent and a swell, gathering a great force which cannot be controlled by an individual's power. It moves people, channels a way for society, flows into, out of people's body, and penetrates human thought and behavior. (Morioka 2003: 117–18)

Naturally, there are counterarguments—notably for our purposes, one that observes that this is still not a universal condition or experience in the world. For one thing, even in affluent Japan, there are people who continue to suffer from illness and poverty. In Africa and Asia, every kind of suffering and pain imaginable—including poverty, famine, war and epidemics—are continuously reproduced. One will argue that the painless civilization critique may have a certain—widespread but not universal—validity in 'advanced' societies like Japan, but it does not apply to 'developing' regions. Yet a quick glance at the headlines of global politics will suffice to reveal that where the pain has not yet been alleviated, efforts to do so are of the highest priority. Such moves are not simply awaited, but are desired and increasingly demanded by the inhabitants of the developing world. And such demands are compelling for the inhabitants of the de-hierarchized and egalitarian painless societies. Hence, in spite of the merit of this particular critique, we continue to devote all available means towards further removing pain from this world. It seems that, at the end of this road, the quest for the painless civilization engulfs all of humankind.

> In time the population will become constant, the global environment controlled, productivity increased, and those [who remain] of the world's poverty class supplied with a bare minimum of food and medical care to survive for the time being. As they too will be provided with goods and money, and tools for removing pain, sooner or later in the pain-eliminating society there will be no poverty as a class of people. As the elites who lead the way towards a painless modern society feel

> that it is unpleasant to see the existence of the homeless, the poor and people who cannot see the doctor, they will make the effort to either pull the people of the poor class into the middle class or preventatively remove their existence. In this way, most of the people of an advanced painless society will be sufficiently supplied with goods, money and pain removal tools, and as a result they will be invaded to the core by the pathology of pain elimination. (Morioka 2003: 348–9)

Such a situation would be welcomed by Nietzsche's 'last men'. In the 'advanced' societies of today, though, quite a few people suffer uneasiness or emptiness about this sort of happiness. They try every way to be rid of these feelings, but their efforts simply stimulate the 'desires of the body'. Seeking every kind of healing, diversion and 'spiritual fulfillment', the 'painless currents' are multiplied.

So what is the 'joy of life'? Morioka says, "There are times when, faced with unmanageable suffering and struggling in it, my inner self is demolished and transformed into a new unforeseen self. The unexpected joy felt then is the 'joy of life'" (Morioka 2003: 18). Morioka's claim that life is a 'function which works to demolish and surpass the "framework" which supports my current self (such as job, status, income, family, and others)' explicitly draws on Nietzsche's claim that 'life is a body which tries to surpass and escape the body' (Morioka 2003: 21).

This 'joy of life' is not the same as the fulfillment gained from the success of a difficult enterprise or a victory over a strong counterpart. It is also different from the excitement brought about by adultery, juvenile delinquency and subcultural adventures. As long as we do not break the existing frame of daily living (job, status, income, family, and others), the 'joy of life' will not be realized. The 'joy of life' is an utmost happiness which arises from the bottom of self-existence when we live life fully around the 'central axis for my being', which is 'to be myself'. It is not a comparison with others, but about finding that 'point on which I can deeply affirm my whole life, … in those last, final moments of my life' (Morioka 2003: 168). As I understand it, the most important thing is to live with active power, to 'go forward to the limit of what I can achieve' (Deleuze 1962: 93).

Yet, every day, the swells of the 'painless currents' engulf us. The more we resist, the more ferociously the currents swirl, feeding on the energy of our resistance. With traps and cunning, it invades every corner of our society, each cell of our body. Nevertheless, Morioka declares war against this painless civilization.

> Warriors, advance to the city center where the desires of the body swirl. Advance to the technological center that controls this society. You will skillfully invade the central section, tempt the painless civilization using your body as a weapon, when the core part is at last inserted, cover it by your whole body, suck it dry, seal it, and lock it in so that it will never again escape outside. (Morioka 2003: 436)

Fundamentally I sympathize with Morioka's criticism of contemporary society, but feel an incongruity with his ascetic monk-like moralistic idealism.[3] Ultimately, what Morioka appears to be doing is strictly distinguishing 'real love' (unconditional love) from 'false love' (conditional love), and 'real happiness' from 'false happiness'. Contrary to Nietzsche, he seems to be reinvigorating the conventional hostility between the real and false, and equating this to the fight between good and evil in order to reignite the 'slave revolt in morality'.

Nietzsche also had an ascetic tendency. Yet he made a continuous effort to laugh away his inner "monk", often succeeding. For Nietzsche, both the low and the high forms of happiness are 'real'—but the latter is 'higher'. Both conditional and unconditional love are 'real'—but the latter is 'higher'. This 'height' was often equated with 'beauty', such that in his masterpiece *Thus Spoke Zarathustra*, good and evil, truth and falsehood, are transformed into the issue of 'beauty and ugliness'. Whereas 'good' must prosecute 'bad' and 'true' must accuse 'false', 'beauty' never condemns 'ugliness'. Rather it laughs at ugliness and entices ugliness towards itself, towards beauty.

The best of Nietzsche's work contained laughter and dance. 'And lost be the day to us in which a measure has not been danced. And false be every truth which has not had laughter along with it!' 'Everything heavy shall become light, everybody a dancer, and every spirit a bird: and verily, that is my Alpha and Omega!' (Nietzsche 1883–85: 119, 158). Laughter and dance, agility of the body, a birdman rather than a superman, these are the essence of Nietzsche's responses to his society. While rejecting the ascetic extremes of Morioka's painless civilization critique, we can nevertheless learn a lot from the best of Nietzsche.

Happiness of the young child

The best Nietzsche had another image of 'happiness', quite distinct from the happiness of the master and happiness of the slave. This was the 'happiness of the young child'.

Jesus reportedly said: 'Unless you become as young children, you will not enter the kingdom of heaven.' This was the source of

Nietzsche's 'young child', signifying innocence and purity, a holy existence. We must be clear, however, about what Nietzsche meant by 'innocence' and 'purity'. Regardless of Jesus' intention, 'innocence' and 'purity' typically indicate a condition which is uncontaminated by moralistic evils such as sexual desire or the desire to rule others. This association is so-well enshrined that when Freud observed the existence of 'infantile sexuality', he was widely condemned by many who believed the suggestion too appalling to even mention. According to nineteenth century bourgeois standards, young children must not have sexual desire; they must not have a desire to rule others, nor any egoistical desires.

Such a response is typical of what Nietzsche regards as the pathology of Christian morality and its modern derivative: bourgeois mentality. For Nietzsche, like Freud, there is nothing wrong or dirty about sexual desire itself. For those who are mentally and physically healthy, for those with a life full of energy, for those who bear the future, sexual desire is 'innocent and free', providing the 'happiness of paradise on earth', 'all the future's thanks-overflow to the present', 'the great cordial', 'the reverently saved wine of wines', 'the great symbolic happiness of a higher happiness and highest hope' (Nietzsche 1883–85: 76–8). Indeed, what is dirty or debased is the mentality that regards sexual desire as dirty or debased. Similarly, neither a desire to rule others nor egoistical desires are bad or dirty in themselves. Without these, there would be no vigor to life. Innocence and purity exist in the very midst of a vigorous life.

Young children are innocent. Food that is good is good. Food that tastes bad is bad. What they like, they like, what they dislike, they dislike. What is beautiful is beautiful and what is dirty is dirty. This simplicity is what is innocent and pure. It is not because they do not have sexual desire, the desire to rule others or egoistical desires. It is because these are openly expressed, without pretence or perversion. Nietzsche does see something sacred in the nature of young children, but it is not the holiness perceived by common morality.

Nietzsche appears to regard the young child as the highest form of human existence. In the well-known episode of the 'Three Metamorphoses', he discusses the molting and transformation from 'camel' to 'lion' to 'young child'. The camel's motto is 'You shall!' The camel obediently follows commands from his God or traditional authority, and hurries along the way with as heavy a load as possible. The camel transforms into a lion, though, upon reaching a desert. The lion's motto is 'I will!' He fiercely fights against the God or authority that he had respected and obeyed for a long time (Nietzsche

1883–85: 40). But the lion is still not enough. Although the 'sacred No' overthrows the old values, it cannot create new values. For that, a further transformation is necessary, from the lion to the young child. The 'sacred No' must be transformed to the 'sacred Yes'. The young child's motto is 'I am'.

> The child is innocence and forgetting, a new beginning, a game, a self-rolling wheel, a first movement, a sacred Yes.
>
> For the game of creation, my brothers, a sacred Yes is needed: the spirit now wills *his own* will; the world's outcast now conquers *his own* world. (Nietzsche 1883–85: 40)

The 'Three Metamorphoses' show the developmental stages of human beings. Only after the camel-like apprentice stage can a man become a master. The models for the Nietzschean master, the noble barbarians, were in fact these masters: lions. They break the old, oppressive rules of the small community and extend out to the wide oceans and continents. Yet, there was an exceptional, ultimate place which exceeded the master. That is the young child. Characterized by 'innocence', 'forgetting', a 'new beginning', 'play', 'self-rolling wheel', 'first movement', and most of all immersing itself in the 'play of creativity' for the 'sacred Yes', the young child is actually the most mature man.[4]

A mature and complete man becomes like a child. 'The maturity of man—that means, to have reacquired the seriousness that one had as a child at play' (Nietzsche 1885–86: 108). This intuition of Nietzsche may be unexpectedly close to common sense. 'A truly matured person is one who plays well.' He does what he likes, lives how he likes, does not criticize others, does not condemn himself, and enjoys the 'play of creativity' at any time, anywhere. He plays 'beyond good and evil', like the monk Ryōkan who played ball with children.[5] Nietzsche called this sort of mature person the 'young child'.

A young child will transform their own 'here and now' into a playground, whether it be on a crowded, peak-hour train, a dirty side street, a sweltering hot day or in pouring rain. It transforms all of existence into its playthings: clothes, food, birds and clouds, words and facial expressions, itself and other people. Playing, it will laugh off and dance over anything, however unpleasant it may be. This 'happiness of the young child' is different to the 'happiness of the master'. One could say it is a much higher form of 'happiness itself'.

Height of happiness

Summarizing the discussion so far: Nietzsche discerned three qualitatively distinct forms of happiness by asking 'happiness for *whom*?' First is the 'happiness of the slave', the happiness where comfort and rest are passively received. Second is the 'happiness of the master', the 'happiness of battle and conquest', a joyous engagement in activities where battles and challenges must be fought and the self, the other or something else is conquered. Third is the 'happiness of the young child', the 'happiness of play and creativity'.

As we have seen, for Nietzsche, an individual is in fact a 'community of numerous souls'. Early modern man emerged from a 'blending of the blood of masters and slaves'. Taking this a step further, we (late-)moderns can further consider ourselves to each be a 'community of the master, slave and young child'. Inside me (and each of us) lives a slave, a master and a young child. I can therefore experience each of the three sorts of happiness, depending upon the time and occasion, and my stage of life. Also, because of this, I feel the 'happiness of battle and conquest' as a 'high happiness', the 'happiness of comfort and rest' as a 'low happiness', and the 'happiness of play and creativity' as an especially high form of 'happiness itself'.

It is worth repeating that the 'height' of these three modes of happiness cannot be quantified. Those who imagine a bar chart when they hear 'height' would picture the master's happiness as 'greater' than the slave's happiness and the young child's happiness as 'greater' than the master's. Such people cannot qualitatively sense the 'height', because like the 'last men', the master within them is dying.

If the master within dies, the young child within will not awaken. The Nietzschean young child awakens only when the master has rid himself of any negative or oppositional feelings towards the slave. We are not discussing a literal baby, but a young child who as a mature man has overcome denial and confrontation. The happiness of this young child is so high as to nullify the highs and lows of experience. In other words, the sense of 'height' is necessary to abolish itself. To achieve the 'happiness itself' of the young child, we must not let our inner master die.

In retrospect, it appears that the advocates of the 'greatest happiness of the greatest number' mistook the slaves' 'low happiness' for happiness itself. But the master inside us requires the 'high happiness' of battle and conquest, while the young child within awakens to the 'happiness itself' of 'play and creativity', indifferent to high and low.

Modern society and happiness

To conclude, I will sketch out the implications of this discussion for contemporary society. At the beginning of the twenty-first century, the 'happiness of comfort and rest' is considerably widespread among the middle-class citizens who make up the vast majority in the 'advanced' societies, including Japan. An unprecedented amount of rice cakes of happiness are supplied to this group almost automatically. In contrast, 'battle and conquest' can only be enjoyed by a steadily decreasing group of elites. Some sport players, entrepreneurs, leaders (and prospective leaders) in various fields have goals which rouse them. They have opponents to fight and conquer. The rest, the majority, have no objectives beyond 'living an average life'. The eras of 'Wealth and Military Strength' (a government slogan in late nineteenth century Japan), 'Advancement in Life' and 'Economic Power' have long gone. These 'grand narratives' which once mobilized individuals have disappeared, and society will no longer provide individuals with an aim in life.

The lack of a goal to strive for is intolerable for the master inside each person. There seems no longer any need to fight, as food, shelter and clothing are available in excess, with little need to exert oneself. But without engaging in at least an inner battle, the 'happiness of the master' cannot be achieved. A sense of unease grows. Strangely, under these circumstances, people may start to envy those who do *not* have easy access to 'comfort and rest'. People with disabilities, minority groups of various kinds, other 'unfortunate people' and the 'socially vulnerable' begin to appear somehow as fortunate for having a cause that they must fight. The stories of their 'heroic lives' appear to be sensational—and people rush to the bookstores to vicariously share the experience. At the same time, however, these 'last men' will not easily give up their own 'comfort and rest' or their petty sense of superiority for being 'whole of limb' (Akasaka 2001).

It has been nearly ten years since the Aum Shinri Cult incident, arguably a manifestation of such uneasiness. Shōkō Asahara, the blind guru, was a living model of a 'heroic life', and thus attracted many 'fortunate' people. At the time of the incident, I read through many testaments of the executives of the cult who had been arrested. One account which left a strong impression recalled the high school days of a young executive, who later expressed deep regret in court. He wrote that, as a student of a prestigious school famous for its university entry rates, he could not bear the apathetic faces of the commuting office workers on the train. Seeing nothing to hope for in such a future, he did not enroll in university, but instead joined the Aum Shinri Cult. In the end, as we know, this proved to be a misguided approach to seeking the great aim of his life in 'battle and conquest'. Shinji Miyadai, a sociologist, placed the daily life of 'blumer and sailorsuit girls' at the opposite end of social-spectrum to the Aum Shinri Cult incident (Miyadai 1998). (The term 'blumers and sailorsuit girls' comes from a social phenomenon where high school girls' school uniforms, with sailor-collared-dresses, and sporting uniforms, including sports shorts called 'blumers', became sexual fetishes for some males.) The girls themselves became items to be bought and sold. The latter is called *enjo kōsai* (assisted dating).[6] While youths attracted to the Aum Shinri Cult were fascinated by its doomsday theory, the 'blumers and sailorsuit girls' were becoming the latest social adaptation. These girls, who drift around the city and receive money through *enjo kōsai*, appear to be highly adept at the task of living happily without aim. Miyadai claims that they have acquired the wisdom of 'living sweetly through the endless everydays'.

At present (in 2004), the majority of Japanese youths can neither devote themselves to a doomsday cult nor 'live sweetly through the endless everydays'. They live with an incomplete happiness and unhappiness. The fundamental problem remains unresolved—they have no goal in life that challenges their entire existence. Our 'painless' civilization's primary approach to resolving this unease is to further realize the mode of being that Nietzsche called the 'last man'. We continue to strive for a society where people work moderately and play moderately, where people are health-conscious and avoid conflict in human relationships and soaks up the 'happiness of comfort and rest', and we marginalize or exclude those who express doubts about this lifestyle. But such a society is unsustainable for the modern offspring of the 'blending of the blood of masters and slaves'. We require a society in which the 'happiness of battle and conquest' can be experienced. This must be taken into account when considering the ideal manner of work, education and social welfare in contemporary society. Making life comfortable, pleasant and safe is not sufficient. It is necessary to create a society in which each person can have something to fight for, an object to conquer; a society in which the 'happiness of the master' can be enjoyed.

Only amidst this 'happiness of the master' can the 'happiness of the young child' awaken. When the 'happiness of battle and conquest' is widespread, the 'happiness of play and creativity' can be felt in every corner of the society. Is this not the society which our present 'advanced' society should aim for? One clue for achieving this might be found among the energetic women of modern society. Some women have a talent for creating small playgrounds around themselves. Shops selling pretty accessories have appeared in abundance. Although only slightly different to 'comfort and rest', this is nevertheless an example of how to live happily through 'play and creativity'. Men, in their own way, now have much to learn from such women. We must prepare the societal environment to allow still more people to enjoy the 'play of creativity'.

Undoubtedly, as much assistance as possible must be given to 'developing' societies, where people continue to suffer from famine, war and epidemic, in order to raise their standards of living to align with the 'advanced' societies. At the same time, 'advanced' societies should create a new form of happiness that is appropriate for the continuing 'advancement' of society. This is the unique task facing our 'mature society'.[7]

5
Language and Well-being: Three Basic Essentials of Linguistic Rights[1]

Nobutaka Kamei

Introduction

Language is inseparable from social life. The status of a language in society, particularly if conferred by a state's linguistic policy, has a crucial influence on the language users' well-being. In recent years, there is a growing demand for recognition of linguistic rights—or the linguistic human rights of minorities—which, alongside calls for multilingualism has attracted a great deal of attention. Debates about linguistic rights—about what rights must be guaranteed to individuals and/or communities and on what grounds—however, often revolve around abstract ideals, while insufficient consideration is given to the perspective of the language users' pursuit of well-being. This paper attempts to formulate a universal notion of the rights to pursue well-being and propose a vision for workable linguistic policy. By analyzing several multilingual situations in terms of the pursuit of well-being, three absolutely essential linguistic rights are derived: (1) the right to acquire and use a language without physical suffering (biological condition); (2) the right to access a variety of resources via a language (developmental condition); and (3) the right to demand a greater choice of languages when the first two conditions are met (cultural condition). The notion of linguistic rights must be elaborated through actual attempts to resolve the real-life pain and deprivation suffered by language users, rather than through any intellectual or emotive pursuit of utopian dreams. This paper presents models for linguistic policies that should be adopted by every country (nation-state) in the world and strongly urges that sign languages be given official language status.

Language and the pursuit of well-being

Language is a biological feature of human beings. It is also a cultural behavior, inseparable from social life. *Homo loquens* (the talking man) has been the most likely alternative while modern humans are defined as *Homo sapiens* (the intelligent man) (Fry 1977). Language is one of the most remarkable features acquired by humans through evolution. The fact that some language is used in every human society is sufficient evidence to conclude that linguistic ability is a universal human faculty (Pinker 1995). The ability to use any particular language, however, is a socially acquired cultural attribute. There are approximately 6,000 languages in the world—a remarkable diversity. Human languages can be broadly divided into two categories; spoken languages and sign languages. Every human individual acquires one or more languages suitable to his/her physical abilities and social environment and employ(s) it/them in everyday life. Language is one of the most important cultural traits that one learns, and it plays an important role throughout a human life.

Due to its centrality in human life, the status of a language in society, particularly in terms of state linguistic policies, is of crucial importance for the individuals' well-being. According to Masuda (1978), no country in history has fully escaped some degree of social disquiet relating to language, and many have experienced political conflicts that might rightly be described as language wars. People have always been concerned about the standing of their language in their society.

In recent years, as traffic in capital, labor and information across state borders has become an everyday matter for a significant proportion of the global population, encounters between users of different languages continue to increase sharply. Thus, it is probably safe to say that the present demands for language parity/recognition are presently stronger than ever before. A nation-state requires one or more working languages to run the state bureaucracy, etc. If it claims to be democratic, its recognition of the particular working language/s has a direct impact on its citizens' suffrage. To secure social rights, its education/language policy must be conducive to the pursuit of well-being.

How can a nation-state ensure equity for users of diverse languages, while satisfying its own institutional needs for a certain working language or languages? This is an issue of great significance for the pursuit of well-being.

Two episodes involving multilingualism and well-being

How should people pursue well-being in a society where multiple languages are used?

Generally, the idea of multilingualism has become popular, especially among intellectuals. Its principle is the official acceptance of more than one language and suitable policies to support their use. The reality, however, is not that simple. I will discuss two recent incidents involving multiple language use and people's pursuit of well-being.

Are the people's voices elitist?[2]

In Ghana, West Africa, where 41 African languages are used, the only official language has been English since its colonial days. In 2002, the new government announced that all school education would be conducted in English. While intellectuals were strongly opposed, the general public welcomed the policy (Yokozeki 2004)

According to Yokozeki, the intellectuals' opposition was based on arguments about the effectiveness of teaching children in their native languages and the importance of recognizing and respecting their native cultures and traditions. However, the public expressed a strong desire for the high quality education that English symbolized for them. The government responded to the public's demand. Until then, education in Ghana had been provided, depending on the demands of the times, in English in some periods and in several native languages in others. Today, it appears that the people are pinning their hopes on English, rather than multilingualism.

Why the Japanese government refuses to recognize Sign Language

In 2004, the Japanese government and non-government organizations met to discuss various international treaties and other issues. Among the issues discussed was whether to officially recognize Sign

Language. The government rejected the suggestion, comparing it to the issue of minority ethnic languages. The representative of an organization of the Deaf countered that Deaf people are Japanese, of the same ethnic group, and called for Sign Language to be recognized as language (Japanese Deaf News 2004).

As I will discuss in more detail later, from a linguistic point of view, it is generally agreed that the sign languages used by Deaf people are natural languages with their own grammar and vocabulary system. The Japanese government's position is, from a scientific perspective, a sophism. Perhaps for political reasons it is reluctant to implement multilingualism due to anticipated financial or electoral costs. Either way, this bigoted stance denies the linguistic needs of the Deaf who are native Japanese citizens and permanent residents.

Multilingualism aims at enabling users of any language to pursue their well-being. These two cases, however, illustrate that the idealistic multilingualism does not necessarily achieve people's pursuit of well-being. We must not apply the abstract ideals of multilingualism to actual situations but, instead, draw out a realistic notion of the rights and strategies to achieve it, while focusing closely on the experiences of users of different languages and their ideas of well-being. It is from such a perspective that this paper aims to redefine linguistic rights.

Origin of Linguistic Rights

Universal Declaration of Linguistic Rights

In June 1996, participants in the World Conference on Linguistic Rights in Barcelona, Spain, adopted the Universal Declaration of Linguistic Rights that opened with the following words.

> The institutions and non-governmental organizations, signatories to the present Universal Declaration of Linguistic Rights, meeting in Barcelona from 6 to 9 June 1996, … In the belief that a Universal Declaration of Linguistic Rights is required in order to correct linguistic imbalances with a view to ensuring the respect and full development of all languages and establishing the principles for a just and equitable linguistic peace throughout the world as a key factor in the maintenance of harmonious social relations; HEREBY DECLARE … (World Conference on Linguistic Rights 1996)

Celebrating that all languages are equal, the declaration as a whole was dedicated particularly to the calls for the rights to use and develop minority languages to support users of these languages in their pursuit of well-being. This document perhaps best represents the idealistic form of multilingualism.

Although the origins of the idea of rights relating to language dates back at least to Article 2 of the 1948 Universal Declaration of Human Rights,[3] it was not until the 1980s that it began to be asserted as an inalienable human right and discussions were initiated to clearly designate in concrete terms what concepts such as 'linguistic rights' or 'linguistic human rights' included (Fukuchi 1999). The Universal Declaration of Linguistic Rights was epoch-making as it clearly articulated the terms, principles and ideas of these rights. However, it does not have the status of an international law, having been made by non-government organizations with no official participation by national governments.[4]

What are linguistic rights?

Many propositions and resolutions have been formulated concerning linguistic rights. The Universal Declaration of Linguistic Rights has 52 articles, stipulating in great detail a person's rights concerning almost any linguistic activity in which one could possibly engage, from government services, education and research, to publishing, computer software and even shopping receipts. They can be summarized in two key categories (Gengoken Kenkyukai 1999).

1. The right to identify oneself with the language of one's community, learn it at school and use it in public institutions.
2. The right to learn the official language of one's own region.

For convenience I will refer to the former as 'the right to the language of one's community' and the latter as 'the right to the official language'. It must be noted that linguistic rights originally include both of the two directions: the right to the language of one's particular community and the right to the official language. Similarly, the Linguistic Society of America issued a Statement on Language Rights in 1996, which includes both categories, pointing to the two opposite directions.

The direction of discussions of linguistic rights

Although the declaration of linguistic rights includes both of the categories outlined above, such rights have not always been discussed in these terms. In general, the rights that point to separation have been given greater emphasis. Skutnabb-Kangas, a leading advocate of linguistic rights, was one of the first to draw attention to these rights.

I analyze the direction of discussion of linguistic rights from her writings (Skutnabb-Kangas 2003; Phillipson and Skutnabb-Kangas 1995).

First, linguistic rights are discussed as inalienable human rights. In other words, every language is considered to inherently demand unconditional acceptance rather than on some other ground and, therefore, all languages are entitled to unreserved recognition by governments. Second, discussions tend to favor arguments for maintenance of minority languages. When a minority language is near-extinction, it is seen as a crisis. In view of its importance for the relevant culture, the right to respect and use the language is strongly promoted.

As advocates of linguistic rights more-or-less follow these lines, we can assume that these form a typical standpoint on linguistic rights. The researchers who have introduced the concept of linguistic rights to Japan also tend to emphasize the importance of the right to the language of one's community over and above the right to the official language (Gengoken Kenkyūkai 1999).

Shortcomings in linguistic rights discussions and this paper's approach

Discussions of linguistic rights are undoubtedly based on democratic ideals. They are not, however, entirely free of defects.

First, they are not examined from the perspective of the language users' pursuit of well-being. They are treated as inalienable rights without consideration of what specific rights must be guaranteed for the pursuit of well-being. Debates, therefore, produce a plethora of unattainable demands. Second, the perspectives of scholars favoring language diversity permeate the arguments, as in the tendency to place the right to the language of one's community before the right to the official language. Third, great attention is paid to protecting the 'mother tongue', while little attention is given to cases such as Deaf people who are socially impeded from acquiring and using their sign language. Finally, societies with great language diversity are not considered; in many African countries, for example, between tens and hundreds of languages are used. It is utterly unrealistic to insist that all of those languages should be recognized as official languages.

Discussions on linguistic rights to date have centered mainly on European or North American contexts, where two or, at most, a few languages are used. The scope of the discussions has thus been too narrow to develop a comprehensive and realistic notion of linguistic human rights. As a consequence, the Universal Declaration of

Linguistic Rights enshrined unrealistic ideals, which effectively hindered its principles from being adopted in international treaties. The argument that linguistic rights arise naturally where a language is used has some merit in ideal terms, but it is not compelling enough to move policy-makers in the vast majority of countries to open a way for its language users to pursue their well-being.

To overcome their shortcomings, this paper aims to draw out a universal notion of the rights to pursue well-being and present a vision for practical linguistic policies. I will analyze a number of cases involving language and well-being, from which I hope to identify the fundamentals of linguistic rights. By focusing particularly on cases of African countries and the use of Sign Language by the Deaf, which the debate has thus far failed to adequately address, I will outline a comprehensive picture of the rights related to language. From the vantage point thus attained, I hope to find clues to answer the questions raised by the two cases outlined above.[5]

Situations involving language and well-being

Divorcing language maintenance from linguistic rights

Before commencing my analysis, I need to establish that discussions of linguistic rights should be separated from issues concerning the maintenance of minority languages, and should focus primarily on the language users' pursuit of well-being. As mentioned above, many advocates of linguistic rights argue for the maintenance of minority languages. Hence, the two issues are often discussed as one. As a result, the overall rights of language users lose focus.

In sociolinguistics, three categories of orientations underlying linguistic policies are recognized (Ruiz 1984; Nakagawa 1996).

1. Language-as-problem: minority languages are recognized as a hindrance to the social unity of a nation-state.
2. Language-as-right: language is regarded as a user's right.
3. Language-as-resource: the existence of a language is regarded as a resource with value in-itself.

Obviously the issues concerning the pursuit of well-being are primarily associated with orientation (2). From the general thrust of the debate about linguistic rights, it might appear that orientations (2) and (3)—language-as-right and language-as-resource—are separatist and decentralist while orientation (1)—language-as-problem—is assimilationist and centralist. But as the Universal Declaration of

Linguistic Rights indicates, linguistic rights include both separatist and assimilationist orientations. So the concept of linguistic rights, orientation (2), is deeply related not only to (3) but also to (1).

Orientations (1) and (3) both approached language in terms of operational advantages and disadvantages, rather than in terms of the users' pursuit of well-being. To the extent that they are concerned with well-being, orientation (1) assumes the perspective of rulers, while orientation (3) assumes the scholars' perspective. Both positions disregard the well-being of language users.

Language users may well exploit either or both orientations (1) and (3) in their argument for the right to use a language in pursuit of well-being. In the debates about linguistic rights, however, orientation (3) is more often treated by scholars as being concerned with the language user's rights. This kind of view expects the language users to regard their language and identity positively in order to save minority language from extinction and sustain it in the future. As long as researchers continue to advance this sort of inverted argument, their discussions will increasingly digress from concerns about the well-being of the users.

This is not to deny that research concerning linguistic cultures may at times contribute to the rights of language users. This paper, however, will not address orientation (3) on the perspective of linguistic rights, as its aim is to discuss linguistic well-being from the perspective of language users.

Multilingualism and apartheid

As explained at the outset, multilingualism and the language user's well-being are often discussed as direct correlatives. But is this justified?

I define multilingualism as the standpoint that acknowledges positive value in the use of multiple languages, guaranteeing and promoting such use in linguistic policies and programs (Miura 1997). Multilingualism is less a set of abstract values than a notion of policy direction. It is thus largely instrumental in incorporating language users' rights into actual policies. Calling for the use of multiple languages in all aspects of everyday life, the Universal Declaration of Linguistic Rights is undoubtedly the most significant formal expression of multilingualism.

In principle, I support multilingualism, as I will explain later. However my reservation is that it is not necessarily the best way to increase language options. We must fully assess the affinity of multilingualism with segregationist views before introducing multiple languages to a social system. Through an examination of the research into the history of the education/language policy of the Republic of South Africa (Mine 1996; Hyslop 1999), I will attempt to derive the basic essentials of linguistic rights.

The Republic of South Africa achieved notoriety in modern history as one of the last countries to abolish racial discrimination policies, or apartheid. The general election of 1994 was the first in the country's history to involve all races, marking the official end of apartheid.

What was the education/language policy of the South African apartheid regime? Did the white government deny the blacks their tribal languages and contrive their extinction? In fact, they did the opposite. South Africa's apartheid regime thoroughly committed itself to educating its black population in their native languages. The government ensured that the respective indigenous languages were adopted and used in the schools for black children, by employing black teachers and allowing local leaders to participate in running the schools.

Offering education to black people in their own languages has emotive appeal, but in fact it was no more than a clever tool of racial segregation.[6] The black population was excluded from the state's formal education system until the white government introduced the policy called 'Bantu education' for black youth. The policy did not aim to promote higher education for blacks, or their participation in the society as equals to the whites, but primarily to carry out crime control and secondly to expand the labor force in such a way that it would not threaten the privileges of the whites. This new policy abolished the missionary-run education for black children, resulting in even fewer opportunities for them to be educated in English.

The associated linguistic policy was likewise a product of various political intentions. The white government gave black residents land and a degree of autonomy. The pockets of land given were, however, too barren and/or small to be useful. By calling the lands 'Bantustans' and regarding them as independent states, the government made black South Africans foreigners in their own country. The Bantu education was designed to create an illusion of ethnic self-determination through the use of indigenous languages, control the people's awareness of identity and thus confine their political ambitions within the boundaries of the Bantustans. Providing education in tribal languages was also calculated to undermine the unity of the blacks.

The South African liberation movements defied the constraints of this linguistic segregation policy and continued to tell the world of their plight, anger and claims for human rights, until at long last, with international support, they succeeded in ending the apartheid regime.

This is certainly not the only case in history where multilingualism was employed by a system to hinder people's pursuit of well-being. Hence, before implementing multilingualist policies, careful consideration must be given as to how they would work, what they would bring about, and how they might be used for political and economic purposes. In particular, we must ensure that such policies will not result in depriving a certain language community of its political and economic resources. Linguistic policies must be formulated with the primary purpose of ensuring every individual the right to access various resources through language. This corresponds with the principles of the pursuit of well-being upon which the notion of human development is grounded (Haq 1995), and must always be included in linguistic rights as a basic essential, regardless of geographical or historical context.

Linguistic rights of the Deaf

The linguistic rights of the Deaf, to date, have been largely overlooked in discussions of linguistic rights. As the Deaf have different grounds for such rights than the users of spoken languages, we might expect to find different fundamental linguistic rights.

If our aim is to incorporate the fundamental right of access to resources in the simplest form of policy, we will probably find that this condition is only satisfied when every resident is guaranteed the opportunity to be educated in an official language. If the official language is a spoken language, though, a full range of necessary conditions for the pursuit of well-being will be denied to residents who are Deaf users of Sign Language.

Historically, sign languages were naturally invented within groups of Deaf people and are transmitted from one generation to the next.[7] It is not a collection of gestures but a natural language with its own grammar and lexicon. Sign languages—as natural languages—differ from place to place. A Deaf child who learns his/her local sign language by observing Deaf people in the region use it as naturally as a hearing child learns his/her local spoken language. However, Deaf children are often raised by hearing parents, which makes it difficult to experience a sign language within the family. Typically, Deaf children meet fellow Deaf people outside of the home environment and learn Sign Language from non-family members. As acquisition, transmission and diffusion of sign languages occur autonomously among Deaf people, they have their own distributions, dynamics and histories unrelated to those of spoken languages. The language database *Ethnologue* (2006) indicates that there are 119 sign languages used around the world.[8] Sign languages are undeniably natural languages constituting human linguistic cultures. Every country and region has Deaf people, who constitute a minority community of residents.[9]

Since the end of the nineteenth century, however, educators have often prioritized making Deaf students learn a spoken language, rather than the sign language they naturally acquired among Deaf peers. This strategy continues today, particularly in industrialized countries such as Japan and Germany. Oralism, the method that expects a Deaf person to use a spoken language which s/he doesn't normally hear by reading lips of other speakers, brings him/her a great deal of physical suffering. It is such a difficult communication method for the Deaf that they can at best become barely competent in understanding what the other says. Many schools for the Deaf banned sign language on the grounds that it would impede the students' acquisition of the oral method. This left a great number of Deaf people feeling hurt, oppressed or angry about being forced to use the spoken language. Some Deaf people choose to live as members of signing community after graduating schools for hearing children, while their parents expected them to become members of a speech community and had chosen oral method for the education.[10]

Today, organizations of the Deaf around the world are strongly pressing for Deaf people to be educated in their own sign languages and to be facilitated to participate in society as signing citizens. In July 2003, the World Congress of the Deaf was held in Montreal, Canada. Participants from all over the world passed a resolution that distinctly proclaimed the linguistic rights of the Deaf.

> Opposing the violation of the linguistic and human rights of Deaf people still common worldwide and reaffirming that Deaf children have a right to bilingual education in their indigenous sign and written languages. (World Federation of the Deaf 2003)

Some of the movements seeking reform in education for the Deaf began to use 'linguistic rights' as their key phrase (Zenkoku Rōji o Motsu Oya no Kai 2004). This new perspective joined the debate about linguistic rights, which until then had only been concerned with spoken languages. Nevertheless, we must acknowledge the fact that the linguistic rights of the Deaf can hardly be dealt with as an extension of the debate about spoken language rights. The Deaf are distinguished from communities of minority spoken language users in that it is extremely difficult to assimilate them into the community of the majority language users.

When minority spoken languages are discussed, emphasis is primarily given to the right to use the language of one's own community, thus tending towards a separatist orientation. This in itself is testimony to how easy it is for language users to be assimilated into the majority community. Depending on their particular circumstances, such language users can choose to exercise their rights to the official language and participate in the dominant community.

In contrast, Deaf people cannot readily choose to be assimilated into the majority, because of his/her physical/sensory constraints. Actually, sign languages are highly independent of the mainstream and are not easily sent to extinction by the pressure of spoken languages. Universally Deaf people have been maintaining their signed languages even under the oppression of oral methods by hearing teachers and parents. This aspect may be regarded as one of their 'advantages' in the standpoint of the maintenance of minority culture. But in other aspects the situation is not so favorable. Deaf people, whether they like it or not, have to consider their rights from the standpoint of different language users with little opportunity to be assimilated into the majority speech community.[11]

What must be done to protect Deaf people's rights to access a variety of resources? No matter how well the Deaf are guaranteed education in the official spoken language, it does not provide access to all resources as their physical and sensory constraints still make acquisition and use of the language difficult, if not impossible. It may even bring them physical pain. Only sign language can be naturally acquired and used by the Deaf without strain.[12]

The acquisition and use of a language without suffering physical pain must be included as a fundamental linguistic right. This has never been denied to the majority of people, who can hear and grow up in an environment where a spoken language is used. In contrast, the Deaf have been repeatedly deprived of this most basic right and barred from access to resources in many aspects of life. As it involves the process of language acquisition of the person as a biological being, this must be pronounced as one of the most fundamental issues in discussions about linguistic rights.

Well-being via the two fundamental rights

I have so far derived two essential fundamentals of linguistic rights; acquisition and use of a language without physical pain, and access to resources by using a language. If these are satisfied, can people achieve well-being? My answer to this question is a qualified 'yes': they can achieve their linguistic well-being to a certain extent. I will explain in terms of spoken and sign language respectively.

First, in terms of spoken languages, let us return to the case outlined earlier: the linguistic education policy in Ghana (Case 1). This case reveals the honest feeling of the people when the two essential rights are about to be met. The Ghanaians are hoping that acquisition and use of English will provide their (hearing) children a good education and access to other resources, such as higher education and job opportunities. They support the government policy in the belief that it will fulfill their expectations. Regardless of the ideals, in other words, the people believe that education in their indigenous languages has never achieved the desired outcomes. People elsewhere have also shown a similar preference for education in an official language of European origin (Yoneda 2004).

This phenomenon has often been interpreted as a form of linguistic discrimination in which a dominant language such as English, with its political and economic power, represses minor languages to extinction. Such a view, however, seems to treat the Africans (and others) as passive people. We need an alternative view that understands such people to be simply pursuing well-being on their own initiative in the linguistic situations that they are in. A similar phenomenon is found among the Deaf in Africa. The following discussion is based on my long-term fieldwork in Africa (Kamei 2002–2006, 2003a, 2003b, 2004).

Education for the Deaf in Africa was gradually established after the countries achieved independence in the 1950s or '60s. The African-American Dr. Andrew Foster (1925–87), Deaf himself, and the Christian Mission for the Deaf that he founded, made a great contribution to the development of education for the Deaf.

At a time when developed countries were concentrating their education for the Deaf on the acquisition of spoken languages, Foster and his colleagues pioneered a view that stressed the importance of sign language and put it into practice in Africa. They trained Deaf youth from all parts of Africa and employed them as teachers to educate the Deaf in sign language. His movement established 31 schools in 13 countries; hence, Foster is called the 'Father of Deaf Education in Africa'.

Foster was born in the United States. He used ASL (American Sign Language) as the basis of his work, and helped to spread it across the African continent. Today, Deaf people in many parts of Africa use sign languages derived from ASL. Some researchers are critical of Foster for adopting ASL rather than the local sign languages that otherwise might have developed in their respective parts of Africa (Schmaling 2001, 2003).[13]

Nonetheless, Foster is highly admired by Deaf people in every part of Africa. I have never met anyone who has a bad word to say about him. Those who were taught by Foster and worked with him are proud of the experience. Foster has become a legend and a role model for the Deaf in Africa. His life and activities are repeatedly told in sign language folklore, long after his death.

Deaf people in Africa feel fortunate to have access to education through sign language. The respect they express for Foster reflects the level of well-being they have achieved as a result of this education.

The cases above show that a certain level of well-being may be achievable when the two fundamental linguistic rights are met, and that the means to achieve it is not necessarily multilingualism. They provide a real picture of our contemporaries pursuing well-being. It is ironic that advocates of multilingualism outside of these communities are not exactly happy about this picture.

Where does multilingualism fit?

Above, I said that 'a certain level of well-being' is achievable when the two fundamental linguistic essentials are met. By 'certain level' I acknowledged that the two fundamentals are not sufficient. If the situation allows, nothing is more effective than reducing the factors that could hinder people from the pursuit of well-being. Therefore I will put forward the third fundamental linguistic right: the entitlement to greater choice of languages.

Are people meekly prepared to use any language if it is physically possible to acquire it and its use provides access to resources? It would certainly save time and effort for some language users if many language choices are available resources, allowing them to use the language they're familiar with. This view cannot be ignored as it has been observed that even in Africa, where a great diversity of languages is used, it is the local languages used by people in everyday life that most help their development (Miyamoto 1998).

In a society where multiple languages are part of the culture—closely associated with its history, religion and value system—linguistic policies that ignore this fact would almost certainly be met with resistance. It is safe to assume that policies that reflect the diversity of linguistic cultures would be more efficient and less liable to emotional friction in providing access to resources.

In fact, this third fundamental right has always been recognized in the debates about linguistic rights. Nonetheless, from the perspective outlined in this paper, there are three points to note.

First, the argument for the right to sign language rests on different grounds than the argument for cultural rights. The linguistic rights of the Deaf are grounded in their rights for freedom from being forced to use a language that causes them physical pain in its acquisition and use. It is impossible to discuss this in the same light as the right to choose a language derived from cultural diversity.

Second, if linguistic policy is to reflect diversity, we must not forget that sign language is also a multilingual world. No less than the abundant variations of cultures based on spoken language, the world of sign languages include a great number of languages and corresponding cultures. In a significant number of countries, more than one sign language is used. Although the educational work by Foster and his colleagues did not record any such cases, it has been reported that when a school for the Deaf attempted to introduce a new sign language from abroad it was met with strong opposition from the local Deaf population (Kamei 2004). Multiculturalism and multilingualism must expand their horizons beyond spoken language to the diverse world of sign languages and their cultures.

Third, we must not be hasty in institutionalizing ill-considered multilingualism. Without suitable access to resources, the introduction of multiple languages to social systems, especially education, may result in forms of linguistic segregation that echo the South African apartheid policy, regardless of its intent. People would probably be more tempted to choose the major language that provides easy access to resources than forced multilingualism that does not benefit them.

This fundamental right to allow multiple language choices is an important one in cultural and emotional terms. Yet it must be dealt with cautiously. What is clear at least is that it should not be considered ahead of the other two fundamentals, which are essential to linguistic well-being.

Linguistic policy based on fundamental rights

Three fundamental linguistic rights

The three fundamental linguistic rights presented in this paper are:

1. the right to acquire and use a language without physical pain (biological right);
2. the right of access to resources by using a language (developmental right); and
3. with the first two rights met, the right to seek an increased choice of languages (cultural right).

In the light of these three fundamentals, most of the arguments about linguistic rights in terms of multilingualism have focused on European spoken languages and have failed to address issues beyond the 'cultural right' (3). We must not ignore the fact that some of our contemporaries suffer intolerable pain and deprivation related to language, even though linguistic problems derived from cultural and historical backgrounds are certainly important.

Even in Europe and America, many linguistic problems involve access to resources, such as inequity between classes and in employment opportunities, as reported in Canada and Belgium (Masuda 1978). Although linguistic problems are typically discussed in terms of the politics of cultural and individual identity, what is required now is more objective analyses of developmental rights (2).

Minimal model of linguistic policy

It would certainly be ideal if we could adopt a policy that affirms all of the languages in existence. But there are at present more than 6,000 human languages in use. In some countries, such as Cameroon and Nigeria, for example, there are in excess of 200 different language communities. The stark reality is that a state that adopts a multiple-linguistic policy incurs large expenditure. Canada, for example, reportedly spends 500 million Canadian dollars (422.6 million USD) per annum to maintain its dual language system (Namita 1998).

Since the ideal is thus obviously impossible, we must focus on achieving 'a certain level' of linguistic well-being through a practical policy focused on (1) biological and (2) developmental rights.

What is urgently needed is recognition of a sign language as an official language. This does not mean to make learning the sign language compulsory for the whole population but it does mean creating a system that makes it possible for the Deaf to: communicate via sign language at any public institution, to study the sign language at educational institutions ranging from kindergartens to universities, and to access sign interpreting services when necessary at workplaces, service providers and public events. This may not sound like a very tall order, but in fact, the environment in Japan and many other countries has not been conducive to the Deaf performing these activities. A number of other countries, however, have already designated their local sign language as an official language of the state. Accordingly, the Deaf community and linguists in Japan are beginning to pursue similar policies from the government (Takada 2004; Yonekawa 2002).

The next step is to guarantee the entire population the opportunity to be educated in the official spoken or sign language. UNESCO has been campaigning since 1990 for 'Education for All'. The policy recommendation of this paper claims that governments should provide all Deaf children the opportunity to be educated in an official sign language as well as all hearing children in the official spoken language.

I propose a policy model, in which the state designates at least one official spoken and sign language each, and protects them as working and educational languages, by investing in the required research and development of teaching materials in both languages. It must also establish a system to ensure the use of both of these languages in all public institutions, which, in turn, requires adequate training and provision of teachers and interpreters for people to access public services and other essential resources in either of the two languages. I call this 'a minimal model of linguistic policy' (Figure 5.1), which details the very least that the government is expected to do to fulfill the two fundamental rights (1) and (2).

From this perspective, the Japanese government was clearly mistaken in its response discussed in Case 2. Lacking understanding of the importance of biological right (1), which is fundamental to a person as language user, it avoided the issue by using the confusions in multilingualism debates and ignoring the developmental rights (2) of the Deaf. The Japanese government currently does not meet this minimal standard for supporting its people's pursuit of well-being.

Towards responsible multilingualism

This minimal model barely meets the essential conditions (1) and (2), and is thus certainly not optimal. It would be best if the cultural and historical backgrounds of every region were taken into consideration and as many alternative languages as possible made available. A system with increased language choice to meet condition (3) is

Figure 5.1: The minimal model of linguistic policy

One spoken language + one sign language

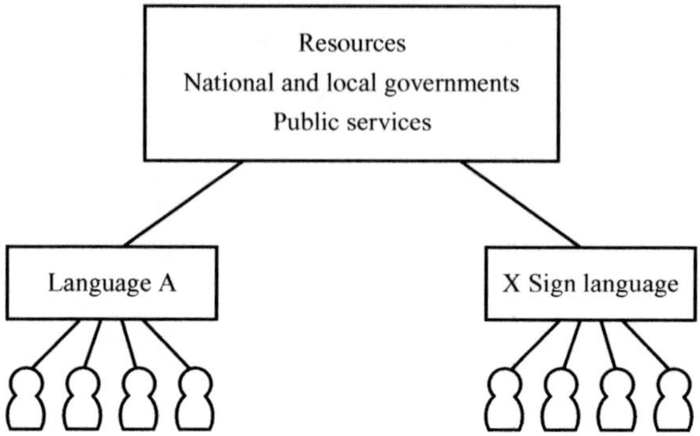

The state designates one spoken language and one sign language as its official languages and ensures all residents access to either language of their choice. This model represents the minimal policy that the state must implement to meet biological and developmental linguistic rights.

Figure 5.2: The optional model of linguistic policy

Multiple spoken languages + multiple sign languages

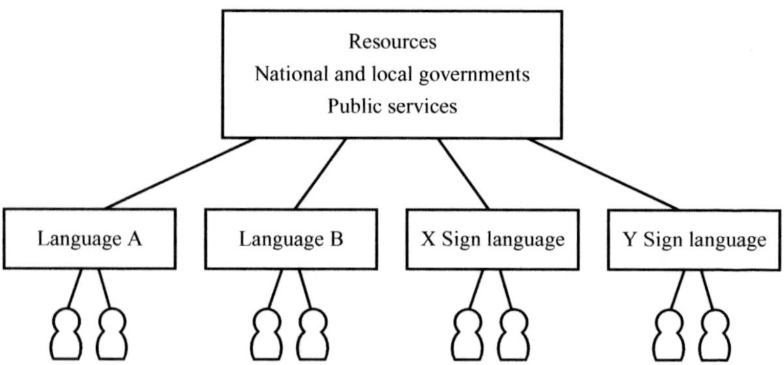

Taking cultural linguistic rights into consideration, the government offers as many language options as it can. What is important here is: (a) that if the government is to adopt a multilingual approach to spoken languages, it must do the same to sign languages; and (b) multilingual policy that does not provide access to resources is irresponsible and should not be adopted.

represented by what I call the 'optional model of linguistic policy' (Figure 5.2). This indicates that the minimal model is not restrictive, but rather is open to multilingualism.

But two important points must now be added to the multilingualism debate. First, if a linguistic policy is to be open to more than one spoken language, it must also be open to multiple sign languages. As mentioned, the fact that there are many sign languages around the world must be respected. Multilingualism must protect the cultural diversity of the Deaf as well as the hearing if it is to be fair and open to both groups of people.

Second, a multilingual policy that does not provide access to resources is irresponsible and should not be adopted. It will produce some form of apartheid. People are sensitive about their own conceptions of well-being and will not support a system that does not respect these.

Conclusion

Through consideration of three fundamental linguistic rights, I have presented a vision for a linguistic policy: a minimal model that lays a path to responsible multilingualism.

From an idealistic perspective, this may seem a backwards step. It may also draw criticism from those who are concerned about the danger of forced assimilation to official languages. But I would ask such critics if it is better to continue to allow the absence of government policies in respect to people's pursuit of linguistic well-being? In the current situation, where resources are distributed solely according to the needs/demands of the majority, a realistic program for a broader pursuit of well-being must be seen as a priority.

The concept of linguistic rights must be elaborated through actual attempts to resolve the real-life pain and deprivation suffered by language users rather than through an intellectualist pursuit of utopian dreams of multilingualism. The intellectualist/idealist argument is too weak to move governments. In contrast, a narrower argument focused on the urgency of providing the minimal essentials necessary for the people to pursue linguistic well-being and that allows for the phased implementation of 'higher' objectives may lead to a realistic resolution of the problems faced by minority language users. In short, it seems that linguistic rights need to be addressed from a scientific rather than idealistic perspective. Only then will more radical and effective discussions be possible.

6
On Facts: Towards a Folklore of Happiness and Unhappiness

Yoshiyuki Yama

Since its beginning in Japan, folklore has tended to focus on happiness and unhappiness within traditional village communities. In particular, both the stories and the research surrounding them focus on a member of the village community who experiences happiness and unhappiness through some particular encounter. This is the single most important issue of folklore. As a narrative, folklore depends upon the informant's faith in the world being in fact as it is in the stories—and hence, such stories are only meaningful to those who share this faith-based world-view. In other words, folklore can only be internally understood; and this has led to criticism, including accusations of nationalist interpretations. This paper examines the formation of the facts behind folklore and their relationship (in Japan) with nationalism, traced back to the nativist (*kokugaku*) thought of the Edo Period. If this approach can overcome the nationalist tendencies of folklore, it might lead to the re-creation of folklore based on a dichotomy of happiness and unhappiness.

Abode of happiness and unhappiness

In 1934, Kunio Yanagita and others launched a *sanson chōsa* (rural survey), marking the beginning of systematic research in the field of folklore. The statement of purpose for this work was presented in the *Kyōdo Kenkyū Saishū Techō* (Local Research Data-Gathering Manual), which describes the key points of data gathering as follows.

> What ideals does the survey's subject hold in his daily life in order to be respected as a member of the village, to have a happy family and to lead an irreproachable life? What kind of education has he undertaken and what kind of skills has he endeavored to acquire in order to attain these ideals?
>
> Who do the villagers trust and turn to for leadership? What are the things that the village expects its members to do for the community?
>
> What sanctions are enforced against violators?
>
> Who do the villagers call upon for help when they try to avoid calamities that they consider incapable of avoiding (overcoming) by their own efforts alone?
>
> Does the village immediately try to adapt to changing times, or does it try to protect and hold on to traditions? Or has it been modifying existing rules to move with the tide of the times? What experiences has it had as a result? (Yanagita et al. 1934/1998: 1–2)

These questions concisely summarize the primary foci of the field of folklore studies in its early days. The first question is particularly important for showing that 'happiness' in traditional rural communities was a matter of interest to folklorists. Its particular reference to 'a happy family' is also worth noting, for it demonstrates that a 'family' was considered to be the basis for the enjoyment of/and endeavors to attain 'happiness'. This emphasis is further evident in other questions that started with 'family origin' and ended with 'stories by a happy person or family'.

The folklorist's interest in 'happiness' is clearly evident in the survey's questionnaire when it asks about 'the rise and fall of a family'. These questions indicate a firm perception that not only 'happiness' but also 'unhappiness' arise at the family level, and indicate that folklore studies have been based on that perception since its inception. In this sense, the schematization of 'the rise and fall of a family' can be seen as an 'event' that heralded the birth of a 'folklore of happiness and unhappiness'.

Two of the published reports of the survey focus solely on this question about the rise and fall of the family: Hajime Shuzui's *Ie no Seisui nitsuite* (1936) (About the Rise and Fall of a Family) and Tokuzo Ōmachi's *Ie no Seisui* (1937) (Rise and Fall of a Family).

Shuzui explained the significance of research into the rise and fall of families by saying that 'the problem of wealth disparity in rural communities was woven with village class composition as the woof and the rise and fall of the family as the warp'. He thus recognized the family as a clue to understanding the problem of wealth disparity, arguing that it 'would provide useful information for solving the same problem in a wider and more complex society'. To this end he classified the survey data into six 'causes for the rise and fall of a family' (Shuzui 1936/1984: 96–7).

These six causes can be summarized as: (1) the decline of old-established families due to infiltration by new culture, (2) the introduction of lavish lifestyles, vanity and debts relating to participation in political movements, (3) village affairs such as joining a mutual aid financing association or becoming a guarantor for other people's debts, (4) the deaths of work horses, labor shortages, etc. due to natural disasters such as floods or fires, (5) extravagance, indulgence and laziness such as drinking, womanizing, gambling, etc, and (6) popular beliefs regarding the decline and fall of a family.

There are several interesting points here. First, although the report was titled the 'rise and fall' of a family, it focused almost exclusively on the decline of a family, i.e. 'unhappiness'. On this point, Shuzui states, 'I wanted to address the question of what internal forces sustain a family in contrast to these causes for family decline, but did not have sufficient data to do so'. He left the issue to be addressed in the future.

Nevertheless, he observed, 'In this rural survey, we posed questions about the rise and fall of a family and collected answers from villagers. I have merely reorganized the answers about family decline as required to compile this report. Therefore, many important facts may have been overlooked, and the report may appear to place a disproportionate emphasis on superficial information. However, I consider that simply reporting the villagers' answers is worthwhile, for it at least reveals a certain outlook on life held by them' (Shuzui 1936/1984: 97). In other words, his approach highlights the villagers' perception of the 'facts' surrounding happiness and unhappiness, rather than merely the researchers' perception of them.

What is more interesting is that the villagers' perception of 'facts' is divided into two main groups. For example, the report provides relatively detailed explanations and examples of the first five of the causal categories, while for the sixth category it only lists examples, with no explanation other than: 'Popular beliefs about decline and fall of a family. Various folk sayings and popular beliefs are being practiced. However, I will simply present a few cases collected in the survey this time' (Shuzui 1936/1984: 103).

The difference in his approach is explicable by the observation that the answers in the first five categories were 'rational' enough for Shuzui to understand and explain in terms of his own views, whereas he considered the latter group of answers to be 'irrational'; that is, they were not explicable in the same terms.

Ōmachi's (1937) report appears to be simply a revision of Shuzui's, with some additional examples. However, his attitude to the two types of answers seems markedly different. For example, in an introductory statement to the case studies of 'popular beliefs regarding the decline and fall of a family' Ōmachi states that 'in villages with many cows and horses, the rise and fall of a family is often linked to the breeding performance of their livestock'. After presenting some cases, he goes on to state:

> In this village, however, it is said that if two or three horses died in one year in a family, that family would always suffer misfortunes. They do not regard the death of a horse as a mere economic loss but as a sign of impending decline of some sort in the family fortunes.
>
> Thus, our search for the causes of the decline and fall of a family has gone through physical, social and rational factors and finally arrived at mental, intangible and superstitious factors. (Ōmachi 1937: 25)

This statement suggests that, rather than treating 'mental, intangible and superstitious factors' and 'physical, social and rational factors' as two distinct types, he was focusing on the continuum of these factors in the villagers' perceptions. At the same time, the statement, 'finally arrived at mental, intangible and superstitious factors', reveals a shift in emphasis. At least, it is apparent that both sets of factors are recognized as having equal value. In other words, it establishes that the villagers' perceptions of 'facts' regarding happiness and unhappiness straddle two dimensions—the physical, social and rational and the mental, intangible and superstitious.

This positional shift was influenced by systematic accounts of Yanagita's folklorist philosophy and methodology. Yanagita describes the classification of collected data as follows.

> Our eyes are at work from the start and can do the job from afar. A tremendous amount of research data can be collected with our eyes,

> including on communities, housing, clothing, etc. Next, we work our ears. To do so, we need to go close to our subject. Mental information is more difficult to obtain. I have been saying jokingly that the first category can be called 'traveler's research' because a passing traveler can collect such information. Similarly, I call the second category 'lodger's research' and the third category 'countryman's research'. (Yanagita 1934/1998: 98)

In particular, he states that 'the third category contains so-called folk beliefs, which can be understood only by fellow country people, and that is where I locate the fundamental importance of folklore research' (Yanagita 1934/1998: 99). Accordingly, he classified the collected data into three categories: (1) Tangible Culture, (2) Language and Arts, and (3) Mental Phenomena—with detailed research items for each category. 'So-called folk beliefs, which can only be understood by fellow country people' is one of the 'mental phenomena' of the third category. For Yanagita, such 'mental phenomena' was understood to be 'the fundamental importance of folklore research'. Thus, developing an understanding of 'mental phenomena' became the ultimate challenge for folklore research.

This observation shifted the folklorists' focus of attention from 'physical, social and rational factors' to 'mental, intangible and superstitious factors' in the search for the 'facts' concerning happiness and unhappiness. Such 'facts' were understood to inhere in specific individuals. But the process of establishing 'mental phenomena' as conceptual 'facts' was burdened by the limitation that they could only be 'understood by fellow country people'.

This limitation came to be seen as definitive of folklore and became a target for criticism, especially in relation to nationalism. As Kenji Satō points out, 'a new paradigm for folklore will not emerge' if folklore is only understandable by 'fellow countrymen', where these are restricted to 'people from the same home town' (Satō 2002: 313). The potential academic development of folklore certainly depends on whether or not this limitation can be overcome. However, the relationship between this specific concept of 'facts' and the claim that they 'can only be understood by fellow countrymen' has yet to be examined in detail. Although this constraint certainly defines the nature and limitations of folklore, as many critics have pointed out, it appears unlikely that this specific conception of 'facts' is itself restricted to this context.

In order to fully understand this conception of 'facts', we need to consider carefully how they came about, what was adopted and what was discarded in the process of the formation of folklore as a field of academic study. In other words, I am attempting to deconstruct folklore through an examination of this specific concept of 'facts'. This task is unavoidable if we are to formulate a new approach for folklore, focused on happiness and unhappiness.

I shall begin my examination of this specific concept of 'facts' by reviewing various ways that 'facts' have been perceived by modern sociology.

The fact of multiple facts

Generally speaking, when a question is asked about a 'fact', the question is not about the concept of a 'fact' itself. As in a crime investigation, the search for facts proceeds on the assumption that 'facts' really do exist. In other contexts, however, the concept of 'fact' itself is questioned. In sociology, in the wake of ethnomethodology and constructionism, it is not only common, but increasingly understood to be necessary to question the very existence of 'facts'. This can also be seen in the popularity of 'meta-history' in historical studies, the problem of representation highlighted by the critique of, for example, Orientalism, and concerns about history textbooks that present only the 'liberal view of history'. In all of these cases, the question arises: 'what is a fact?'

Hideo Hama is among those who pursue this question, with special concern for the potential of 'the sociology of history'. According to Hama, Garfinkel calls a logical conclusion derived from congruence theory the 'pluralism of worlds' (by comparing Shütz' congruence theory to Parsons' correspondence theory). Hama argues that, according to congruence theory, the object is a product of the individual observer's perception, and there is no privileged observer that can truly determine what the object is. On this basis, he maintains that congruence theory leads to a 'pluralism of histories' (Hama 2000: 194–5). Hama uses Kurosawa's film, *Rashōmon* (based on Akutagawa Ryūnosuke's short story *Yabu no Naka*)as an example of such historical pluralism.

> In *Rashōmon*, three individuals talk about an incident (a man's death) from their own recollections. The three stories they tell are vastly different from each other. A thief says that he killed the man after fighting fairly for the man's wife. The man's wife says she stabbed him with a knife in frenzy after he abandoned her. The dead man says, through a medium, that he killed himself with the knife when he

> learned that his wife had betrayed him. These stories are frontal views of the incident seen from the perspective of each party. The plot is the same as [Akutagawa's] original novella [*Yabu no Naka* (In the Bush)] up to this point. In the film version, however, Kurosawa added another story, told by a woodcutter (the historian) who witnessed the incident from behind a bush (a side view). At first, it appears that Kurosawa was attempting to frame the multiple frontal views by this one side view. But in the end, the film reveals that the woodcutter took the knife from the crime scene, making him a party to the incident as well.

After this summary of the plot of *Rashōmon*, Hama comments that 'this is not an absurd story. It is an allegory for the interpretative conflicts that we are actually experiencing about war displays in historical museums, about the "forced transportation" of "comfort women", and about the Nanjing massacre' (Hama 2000: 195–6).

Certainly, in modern societies, all 'histories' appear to sit side by side with equal veracity. In terms of the discussion in this paper, it appears that multiple 'facts' are sitting side by side with equal veracity.

Yet what we are looking at here could be multiple 'non-histories' rather than multiple 'histories'. That is, perhaps they are not multiple 'facts' but multiple 'non-facts'.

Typically, some set of 'non-facts' competes for dominance, with each claiming that *it* is 'the true fact' until eventually a single 'fact' is selected and accepted. Questions must be asked: what happens in that process, and what is the context in which it happens? In order for a 'non-fact' to stand up as a 'fact', it requires an element of 'belief' because, after all, it is not a fact. It needs a procedure or a device to create an element of 'belief' that transforms a non-fact into the only 'fact'. However, what *Rashōmon* depicts is a situation in which multiple 'non-facts' are each presented as 'facts' with equal merit, or believability.

In *Rashōmon*, each of the four parties tells his or her own version of the incident. And each of these versions claims to be a 'fact' with the same level of believability. Although a woodcutter (a historian) enters the scene, who would otherwise be entitled to claim the only 'fact', he is found to also be a party to the incident; i.e. his is not a privileged account, hence he loses this entitlement. Hama comments that 'if the past is constructed by human recollections, history cannot be singular. History constructed by historical science is also merely one of multiple histories' (2000: 195). This suggests that historical science has already lost its claim to a privileged perspective from which to produce the 'only fact'.

This may appear to discredit the discipline of historical science, but it does not mean that there is no position from which to create a genuine 'fact'—the film also expresses the director's perspective which is the 'fact' that 'multiple facts exist'. This is precisely the perspective of 'sociology of history', which remains unquestioned. From this perspective, sociology of history promotes the 'belief' that the existence of multiple facts is the only fact.

In that case, we need to ask: what are the conditions that enable sociology of history to recognize multiple non-facts as multiple facts and present such a situation as the only fact?

Here it is worth briefly considering another narrative device that is commonly used to establish believability. The dead man's story is told through the mouth of a medium. In a society where this type of spiritual narration is commonly practiced, a story reported in this manner is accepted as a special 'fact', or 'history'. In a society where a medium's narration is accepted as a fact, the fact exists on the premise of 'faith' and there is no perspective from which one casts doubt on whether or not it is the fact. In this case, it is reasonable to call 'faith' a 'myth'. However, when a myth gives way to a history, historical science takes over as the basis for creating belief. At that point, a medium's narration is downgraded from a fact to a non-fact. The 'faith-based fact' is not an acceptable fact by current standards, and would never pass as evidence in a criminal investigation. It is clearly a non-fact in that sense.

In contemporary society, however, even historical science has exceeded its capacity to monopolize the creation of believable 'facts'. Neither a myth (the medium) nor historical science (the woodcutter) can create believable 'facts' any longer. They can only produce non-facts.

However, because this approach of treating the non-factual 'faith-based fact' and 'historical science-based fact' as 'facts' was discovered from the viewpoint of sociology of history, it is obvious that insufficient attention is paid to a difference found between a faith-based fact and a historical science-based fact when the former emerges as the subject of scholarly inquiry during its transformation from a myth to a history. In other words, given that even a historical science-based fact cannot claim to be the only fact, it seems that a faith-based fact is not important for the sociology of history.

This suggests that sociology of history has played a decisive role in dissolving the difference between faith-based facts and historical science-based facts rather than in relativizing a historical science-based fact. In other words, the sociology of history perspective from which it appears that the fact that 'multiple facts exist' is the 'only fact' is only possible by giving faith-based facts, which were clearly non-facts in the era dominated by historical science, the same degree of credibility as others.

However, if the definition of death is indispensable for the foundations of the social order,[1] it would mean that treating a faith-based fact, which is directly connected to the question of the state of a spirit after death, as one of multiple facts at the same level would consequently conceal the point that it is a fact belonging to a dimension that cannot be substituted by other facts. Now, let us consider this issue from another perspective.

Between a foreign culture and one's own culture

Anthropologists, whose work is to understand different cultures, have adopted an important principle, called 'cultural relativism'. Cultural relativism holds, 'that people's experiences and perceptions are defined by their culture (society)' and 'that people who belong to different cultures live in different worlds', which means 'that people who belong to different cultures see the world differently or organize their experiences differently' or 'that different cultures have different conceptual systems', etc (Hamamoto 1985: 246).

It is however, impossible to conduct anthropological research based on this principle alone. We would come to the conclusion, as Needham, a British anthropologist, did, that 'The solitary comprehensible fact about human experience is that it is incomprehensible' (Needham 1972: 246). Nevertheless, myriad ethnographies have been written by as many anthropologists. It is therefore not very useful to ask the theoretical question of whether or not it is possible to understand different cultures. For example, Evans-Pritchard describes the Azande's belief in witchcraft as follows.

> One can only obtain the full range of a Zande's ideas about causation by allowing him to fill in the gaps himself, otherwise one will be led astray by linguistic conventions. He tells you 'So-and-so was bewitched and killed himself' or even simply that 'So-and-so was killed by witchcraft'. But he is telling you the ultimate cause of his death and

> not the secondary causes. You can ask him 'How did he kill himself?' and he will tell you that he committed suicide by hanging himself from the branch of a tree. You can also ask 'Why did he kill himself?' and he will tell you that it was because he was angry with his brothers. The cause of his death was hanging from a tree, and the cause of his hanging from a tree was his anger with his brothers. If you then ask a Zande why he should say that the man was bewitched if he committed suicide on account of his anger with his brothers, he will tell you that only crazy people commit suicide, and that if every one who was angry with his brothers committed suicide there would soon be no people left in the world, and that if this man had not been bewitched he would not have done what he did do. If you persevere and ask why witchcraft caused the man to kill himself the Zande will reply that he supposes some one hated him, and if you ask him why some one hated him your informant will tell you that such is the nature of men. (Evans-Pritchard 1937: 71)

Evans-Pritchard examines the Azande's concept of causality, using their belief in witchcraft. Since his discussion is based on the modern European concept of causality and conducted by way of comparison, any explanation using witchcraft is interpreted as a 'cause', especially as an 'ultimate cause', as different to an 'usual cause'.[2]

What is notable for our purposes is that he has identified two different levels of causation, i.e. two concepts of 'fact'.

Interestingly, according to Evans-Pritchard, the Azande are well aware of the difference between these two concepts of 'fact': 'Witchcraft explains why events are harmful to man and not how they happen. The Azande perceives how they happen just as we do' (Evans-Pritchard 1937: 72). Anthropologists and their subjects thus appear to share a common awareness that there are two different concepts of 'fact' belonging to different dimensions, but they have different attitudes toward these two 'fact' concepts. The commonality is never actively picked up by anthropologists because they perceive an unbridgeable abyss between people who live in a world of faith-based facts and the anthropologists who attempt to explain these faith-based facts in a rational way. This 'unbridgeable abyss' is the 'cultural difference'. Hence, it is typical for anthropologists, as evidenced by Evans-Pritchard, to treat incomprehensible faith-based facts as a 'foreign culture' issue.

In other words, the gap between 'faith' and 'knowledge' is incorporated into a dualistic framework that polarizes the foreign (non-Western) culture and the anthropologist's own (modern Western) culture. In attempting to resolve the issues of 'fact' perception that arise between 'faith' and 'knowledge' as if the difference were that between a foreign culture and their own culture, they almost inevitably reach, it seems, a rigid cultural relativist conclusion.[3]

It is apparent that historical relativism, which arose by treating faith-based facts as equal to historical science-based facts, has become cultural relativism which generally treats faith-based facts and foreign cultures on a par.

However, in any society with an established intelligentsia, not only modern Western societies, similar issues arise between 'faith' and 'knowledge'—and indeed, this issue has been the subject of extensive debate.

Between faith and knowledge

> Pascal said that Descartes had actually wanted to do without God if possible. It seemed to him that Descartes' reasoning itself ran counter to the idea of faith. But this was simply a misunderstanding. Nevertheless, there is room for criticism of Pascal, too. It is unclear whether his main purpose was to clarify what the human condition was or to preach the need for faith using the human condition as a pretext; Pascal would merely be an apologist if the latter were the case.
>
> A similar problem exists with Norinaga Motoori. One critic, for example, commented that 'in my mind, although you feel deep in your heart that gods do not exist, you talk as if there are gods in order to justify ancient records of the country'. Of course Norinaga defended himself against such accusations, but I am very curious why the critic saw it this way.
>
> Certainly to the eyes of Shintoists, Norinaga's historical, philological (linguistic) pursuit of 'the Way' appeared to be proof of his lack of deep faith. (Karatani 1975/1987: 64–5)[4]

The passage above is from the introduction to a short essay titled *Yanagita Kunio no Kami* (Kunio Yanagita's Gods) by Kōjin Karatani. He first refers to Pascal's criticism of Descartes for a mismatch between 'reasoning' and 'faith', then comments that a similar problem is evident in Norinaga's work. In the latter case, the mismatch is between Norinaga's 'philological' work and 'faith'. What is common to both cases is the awkwardness that arises when 'faith' is explained by academic methods such as 'reasoning' and 'philology': a bizarre approach in the eyes of critics. In other words, the issue here is the state of the relationship between 'faith' and 'knowledge', the peculiarity of their connection. Generally, knowledge has been a threat to the survival of faith, and knowledge has increased its own importance by undermining and expelling faith. The state of 'knowledge' represented by 'science' clearly demonstrates this.

In Japan, it was only after the introduction of Neo-Confucianism in the early Edo period that the logical examination of 'faith' was established on the premise of this gap between 'faith' and 'knowledge'. Norinaga's classical divine word theory was also formed against the backdrop of Confucian intellectual discourse on the subject of faith in modern East Asian societies. This discourse is called the 'demon-god debate' (Koyasu 1992).

In order to examine the existence or nature of demon-gods—subjects of faith and religious rites rooted in the manners and customs of traditional societies—it is necessary to establish a standpoint that provides a certain cognitive distance from the beliefs in question. It requires, as a prerequisite, establishing a privileged intellectual position. The demon-god debate was conducted by Confucian scholars as the occupants of such a privileged position in pre-modern East Asian societies.

In their examination of faith, Confucian scholars as the bearers of rational knowledge cannot acknowledge it as a simple 'fact'. At the same time, however, they cannot totally deny faith either, as they support religious rites of the state and emphasize the importance of ancestor worship. Hence, they proffered various inarticulate arguments in their attempts to explain it in terms of natural philosophical concepts (such as *yin/yang*) or in advocating the use of faith in ruling the public. In that sense, the demon-god debate has been a perennial and compelling issue for Confucian and modern East Asian scholars.

Confucianism was adopted as the state religion sometime after the Early Han era (c. 200 BCE) in China. Over the centuries the ritualistic side of its canonical doctrine was gradually emphasized and expanded by bureaucrats and Confucian scholars as the establishment ideology, while its religious dimensions were separated from the ritualistic to remain at a more personal level of customs and faith, eventually losing all doctrinal weight (Kaji 1990: 145–7). This schism has led to the dissociation of 'faith' and 'knowledge', creating an opening for the demon-god debate as a theoretical discourse about faith from the knowledge point of view.

Interestingly, Nobukuni Koyasu draws a parallel between the Confucian schism that enabled the demon-god debate and the process of psychiatric discourse described in Foucault's history of madness.

> Similar to Foucault's discussions of the interrelationship between insanity and reason, as demon-gods on one hand retreated into the religion of the familial society, or sank to the bottom of the society as gods of a malicious heresy, demon-gods on the other hand emerged as the main subject of a discourse among Confucian intellectuals. That is the birth of the demon-god debate. The separation between faith and knowledge has created the demon-god debate as a monologue of Confucian intellectuals. (Koyasu 2002: 45–6)

It is certainly thought-provoking to consider similarities in the structural change of psychiatric discourse and the demon-god debate. But we must be careful to recognize that the abyss between 'faith' and 'knowledge' is not as unbridgeable as the one between 'insanity' and 'reason', where the separation is irreversible. If it was otherwise, no 'fact' whatsoever could be admitted on the side of faith just as no 'fact' could be admitted on the side of insanity.

Instead, if we are to follow Foucault's suggestion, as the psychiatric position was being formed, some part of 'faith' was re-categorized as 'insanity'. In which case, the question becomes, how should 'knowledge' treat the remaining 'faith' that has not been excluded as 'insanity'?

Unlike 'reason' that confronts 'insanity' with a totally detached attitude, 'knowledge' actively attempts to find some basis for 'faith' even though there is in principle an impassable chasm between them. This was exactly what Norinaga was attempting. However, the division between 'faith' and 'knowledge' which such attempts are trying to overcome, and (sometimes) trying to conceal, is always open to the criticism that Pascal leveled at Descartes. Therefore, the attempt to find a basis for 'faith' using 'knowledge' would require a logic that can preempt such criticism by negating the very position that grounds it.

Faith and knowledge in own culture

Let us return to Karatani's account. One thing that bothers me is that it begins with the passage cited earlier about Norinaga's gods, although it is titled 'Kunio Yanagita's Gods'. This trend continues throughout the work; that is, he is trying to discuss Yanagita but continues to discuss Norinaga instead.

This tendency to discuss Norinaga when trying to discuss Yanagita is not limited to Karatani, either; in fact it occurs more often than not. Typically, in the 'essential' part of the discussion, any difference between Norinaga and Yanagita vanishes and the two are treated as if they were one and the same.

How can one discuss Yanagita by discussing Norinaga? Or rather, why does one have to refer to Norinaga when trying to discuss Yanagita? What is it about Yanagita that demands reference to Norinaga?

In the late eighteenth century Edo era, Norinaga was the first to begin a self-referential discourse about the modern nation state of Japan in a scholarly manner. Through his annotated work on the *Kojiki* (Records of Ancient Matters), which was written solely in Chinese characters, Norinaga extracted a pure form of the 'self' embodied in the Japanese language, the people who speak this language and the country in which they live, by objectifying the Chinese characters and the culture behind them as 'foreign', or the 'others'. Norinaga continues to be remembered, with words of praise, as a pioneer of modern philology in Japan because of the modern knowledge and scholarship found within Norinaga's academic discourse represented by concepts such as *shikishima no yamato no kuni* (Japan), *shikishima no yamato kotoba* (Japanese language) and *shikishima no yamato gokoro* (Japanese spirit) (Koyasu 1992).

But why must he be evoked in discussions about Yanagita? Because Yanagita was a brilliant leader in setting the frame for the self-referential discourse in modern Japan. Questions such as 'what is Japan?' and 'who are Japanese?' underlie Yanagita's attempt to logically debate the identity of Japan and its people. Thus when Yanagita is discussed, Norinaga is remembered as a pioneer who shared and tried to answer the same questions.

The majority of scholarly comments on Japan and the Japanese that followed Norinaga's pioneering efforts merely refashioned his arguments. Multitudes of these rehashed versions have come and gone. While Yanagita's folklore is one of these self (Japan)-referential discourses, it does not seem to fully answer the question of why Norinaga is so often mentioned in association with Yanagita.

For example, since the 1990s, there has been much debate and criticism about the nationalism inherent in Yanagita's folklore and the relationship to colonialism (see Murai 1992; Koyasu 1993; Kawamura 1996 and others). At the same time, much research has been done to interpret the positive potential of 'Yanagita's method' (see Satō 1987; Uchida 1989, 1995).

These two approaches oppose one-another, in that one is an extremely negative critique and the other seeks the positive potential. Yet, one thing that they have in common is that both approach

Yanagita's discourse from outside of its own boundaries. Interestingly, another thing that they have in common is that both discuss Yanagita without actively referring to Norinaga.

Discussing Yanagita from outside his self-defined boundaries, even when searching for a positive interpretation, is itself already tinged with a critical tone. Although Norinaga is almost invariably referred to in discussions about Yanagita that approach the issue from within Yanagita's discursive frame, it is perhaps unsurprising that no active reference to Norinaga is found in the discussions about Yanagita from external perspectives. Still, we need to ensure that we clearly understand which aspects of Yanagita's arguments these external interlocutions refer to. It is obvious that they relate to a discourse that debates the identity of Japan and Japanese. Although they highlight key aspects of Yanagita's discourse quite well, they also seem to obscure other aspects that almost overlap it. In other words, there is something of a blind spot that cannot be seen from the external perspective, and this appears to explain the lack of reference to Norinaga.

In reference to the previously cited passage, Karatani observes that 'I ended up just talking about Norinaga while intending to write about Yanagita' because 'I felt increasingly strongly that the heart of the issue in Yanagita relates to that of Norinaga at the deepest level'. He states that 'the most important is not the interrelationship of these two nor a scholarly comparison' of Yanagita's new Japanese classics with Norinaga's earlier works. 'What we need to look for is not the similarity or commonality of their language. Rather, it is a shared underlying theme that is spoken in the languages which may seem totally different or even opposite' (Karatani 1987: 68).

According to Karatani:

> Yanagita tried to find 'faith' in the very 'fact' that people existed, rather than in the image of the world that was intellectually rearranged in some way… In trying to see 'human facts' clearly, it can be said that [Yanagita and Norinaga] shared a question of human existence, or what makes people live. (Karatani 1987: 68–9)

According to Karatani, 'faith' is a real 'human fact' for both Norinaga and Yanagita, which can therefore never be denied or expelled by knowledge. That is, 'faith' is an undeniable fact.

It thus becomes clear that reference to Norinaga tends to arise in discussions about Yanagita's specific concept of 'facts'—a concept shared by both—a distinctive view on faith-related phenomena that is normally not deemed to be 'factual'. Karatani looks to a universal dimension of human being for the basis of this concept of 'fact', as evidenced by his claim that 'faith' is a 'human fact'.

What we find here is a universalist discourse based on some concept of what is essentially 'human'. However, this universalism remains, as Karatani notes, an 'underlying theme' shared by Norinaga and Yanagita, truly lurking under the surface. That is, it remains implicit in both authors' work. This 'faith' becomes 'fact' only within the particular culture of Japan and the Japanese. Norinaga was the first in Japan to begin discussing this cultural identity in a scholarly style. The discourse that explains faith by knowledge and regards it as a fact and the self-referential (self-identifying) discourse of Japan and the Japanese are two sides of the same coin from Norinaga's perspective.

In his *Kojiki Den* (Tales from 'Kojiki'), which depicts the world of gods and the dead, Norinaga refers to the *Kojiki* as a 'sacred text', thus demanding acceptance without question; he accuses any doubters of being 'admirers of Chinese culture'.[5] In other words, he attempts to overcome the fundamentally impassable chasm between faith and knowledge by rejecting the critics' viewpoint as 'foreign (Chinese) culture' worship and demanding 'belief' in Japan's own culture.

Benedict Anderson observed that 'The reason is that neither Marxism nor Liberalism are much concerned with death and immortality. If the nationalist imagining is so concerned, this suggests a strong affinity with religious imaginings' (1991: 32). From this perspective, the formation of Norinaga's classical discourse that enabled 'faith-based facts'—such as questions about the state of a spirit after death—to be accepted as 'facts', using a self-defensive logic that turns cultural relativism to his advantage, can be regarded as a 'creation myth' of nationalism.

Soteriological universalism and facts

Proponents who try to retrieve Yanagita's positive potential, however, encounter this concept of 'facts' only with reference to Norinaga. Even though the concept is inextricably linked to the self-referential discourse about Japan, they hardly touch on this particular subject, instead attempting to extract a universal characteristic of human being.[6] This implies an assumption that Yanagita's concept of 'facts' can be retrieved and confirmed only if it is found in Norinaga's discourse, which in turn indicates how tightly their thinking is bound by the myth of Norinaga as the father of modern philology in Japan. Given that, in Norinaga, this specific concept of 'facts' is inextricably linked with the self-referential discourse on the inherent characteristics of Japan and the Japanese, it is unreasonable to try to extract the universal 'human' characteristic from it alone.

In an attempt to resolve this dilemma, Hiroyuki Torigoe comments on Norinaga's treatment of the concept of *Michi* (the Way) in *Naobi no Mitama*, then argues: 'In order to form a link with a political discourse of total affirmation of the emperor leading to the divine way, Motoori emphasizes Japan's inherent characteristics and explains that the philosophies of Lao zi and Zhuang zi in China are similar but different. I consider that they have the same roots. For example, even in Beijing today, the capital of a socialist regime, Taoism, embodying the philosophy of Lao zi who advocated abandoning artifice and being oneself, is very much alive among ordinary people. The same human way of life can be observed there'. He then adds 'I do not consider this to be inherent only to Japan' (Torigoe 2002b: 4).

From this perspective, in order to extract the essential 'human' concept from Norinaga, we must first release it from the framework of 'Japan'. Then, we can confidently say that 'In his early days, Yanagita was eager to understand human beings' and his original studies of folklore were interested in 'human nature' and the 'human way of life itself' (Torigoe 2002b: 5).

However, this line of argument, drawing comparisons to China in an attempt to extract a universal 'human fact' from 'faith-based facts' that are inherent characteristics of Japan, was not derived from Norinaga. On the contrary, it threatens Norinaga's self-referential classical discourse. Notably, this argument follows the same logic as Atsutane Hirata in *Shin Kishin Ron* (New Demon-Gods Theory) when he tried to prove faith-based facts by referring to Chinese classical books. Yet, Atsutane is never mentioned in this line of argument. What follows instead is typically speculation that Norinaga must have originally been interested in an overall or universal 'human way of life'.

This might be because Yanagita's advocates have been influenced by his contrasting assessments of Norinaga and Atsutane. For example, Yanagita quotes Norinaga:

> Many examples of exquisiteness from ancient times still remain not only in the language but in a myriad of things in the countryside… It is very regrettable that old things are disappearing everywhere… I would like to visit every village on the coast and in the mountains throughout the country to collect these examples and place them on record.

Yanagita lauds Norinaga's perspective as 'quite remarkable' but expresses puzzlement about Norinaga's lifelong dedication for the study of the classics, lamenting that he 'couldn't help but feel how powerfully the tide of the times governed and led scholars'. Still, he obviously respects Norinaga as the father of folklore. It is also clear from the way he addresses Norinaga as 'Motoori Norinaga Ou' and 'Motoori Sensei'. In contrast to his courteous treatment of Norinaga, he expresses a markedly different attitude toward Atsutane. For example, he says: 'The likes of Atsutane Hirata also took pleasure in listening to the country people and in particular had the virtue of not taking even uneducated views too lightly in his experimentation about the spirit world. But he was just preaching pre-existing theories and what he did was just select supportive evidence; therefore his approach is incompatible with the inductive approach we employ' (Yanagita 1935/1998: 237–8).

However, Shinobu Orikuchi notes that 'it is also true that my teacher (Yanagita) walked down the same path as the venerable Mr Hirata' and points out extraordinary similarities between Atsutane's interest in the spirit world and Yanagita's interest in ancestral spirits (Orikuchi 1955: 515–16). These influences from Atsutane's work are very well known in some quarters and have been examined in detail by, for example, Tokutaro Sakurai (Sakurai 1989). Yet those who try to ground Yanagita's contribution by reference to Norinaga would never recognize its essential significance, and never actively acknowledge the connection between Yanagita and Atsutane.

Atsutane explains that the purpose of his study is to strengthen the 'Japanese spirit' and, in order to achieve that, the first priority is to eliminate uncertainties about the afterlife to attain religious peace of mind by clearly explaining the 'peaceful destination of the spirits' (Hirata 1813/1998: 12). It is in agreement with Yanagita's purpose, which he describes as 'the way our contemporaries mostly and commonly imagine or feel about the afterlife is a fact we ought to know, which, indeed, guides this great advancement in the fortunes of the country' (Yanagita 1946/1969: 116). Yet, there is a difference between Atsutane and Yanagita. While Atsutane considered it a natural (universal) human feeling to seek spiritual peace in the afterlife, Yanagita's consideration was limited to spiritual peace in the afterlife of the 'Japanese people'.

In short, although Atsutane and Yanagita share a soteriological interest, Yanagita limits his focus to his own culture—Japan—while Atsutane perceives the issue at a more universal 'human' level. In this sense, Atsutane's classical discourse can be called soteriological universalism. This is exactly the argument made by those who try to find the argument that 'faith' is a 'human fact' in Yanagita. No one, to my knowledge, has discussed the 'soteriological universalism' found in Yanagita in relation to Atsutane.

This might be due to political consideration. Atsutane consistently assumes the supremacy of his own country, and hence, his soteriological universalism can be interpreted as supportive of a colonialist discourse that justifies the invasion of Asia under the pretext of 'salvation', as exemplified by his student, Nobuhiro Satō.[7]

It might be argued that Norinaga's classical Japanese discourse entails a self-defensive framework constructed to the 'exclusion' of 'foreign countries' whereas Atsutane's classical Japanese discourse is an expansionist framework enabled by 'subsumption' of 'foreign countries'. In this sense, although Atsutane's soteriological universalism takes a different form of expression from Norinaga's, it is nevertheless a limited universalism with the same cultural constraints.

This raises the question of how to break the vicious circle in which elicitation of soteriological universalism generates either colonialist discourse or, inversely, its containment 'inside' the 'own culture' and the resultant nationalist discourse. It requires a methodological position that allows a modern revival, using Atsutane's position as a guide, to regard 'faith' as a 'fact' on the basis of the universal 'human' concept formed against the question 'where is the soul after death?'

Conclusion: A folklore of happiness and unhappiness?

Atsutane's soteriological universalism is conducive to colonialism because it is an ethnocentric perspective. Yet, Norinaga mounts his criticism of Chinese culture worship from the same point-of-view. In this sense, these two logics comprise two sides of the same coin; the nationalist discourse to establish and substantiate Japanese identity. As long as the argument is grounded in such an ethnocentric perspective, the 'salvation' argument based on universally 'human' characteristics will continue to affirm the superiority of one's 'own culture'.

We should instead adopt a standpoint about the 'fact' of 'faith' that could not be resolved from within these existing paradigms—the 'fact' of 'faith' that could never be defined by 'knowledge', and which was already accorded before 'knowledge'. In short, we must assume the viewpoint of the 'dead'.

Ensuring the viewpoint of the dead means assuming a critical perspective from outside of the frame of reference of the 'living', who tend to treat multiple facts with equal merit. When a 'state' or 'national' paradigm is inextricable from the perspective of a living person, it is necessary to secure a point of view of the 'dead' that cannot be resolved within this paradigm. In this way, it is possible to secure the viewpoint of the dead which was previously hidden by political dynamics between nations and almost erased from our minds. It means not only reviving the viewpoint of long-lost victims but also securing the viewpoint of the dead who are not yet born. Otherwise, violent force brought on by the lopsided dualistic thought that divides one's 'own culture' and 'foreign culture', 'knowledge' and 'faith', 'reason' and 'insanity', and the 'living' and the 'dead' prompts the former (in each pair) to deny and expel the latter, possibly resulting in suppression of 'facts' for the dead.[8]

A folklore of happiness and unhappiness is only possible if we constantly remind modern academia, which is established upon the suppression of the viewpoint of the dead, of the existence of the dead, urge them to rethink their paradigm and appeal for the necessity of seeing things from the viewpoint of the dead.

In that case, what becomes important is an approach to folklore that tries to identify specific 'facts' in the realm where the worlds of the dead and the living overlap; the unsettling area where the boundary between the dead and the living is dissolved. Yanagita, however, substantiated such specific 'facts' by limiting them to something that can only be understood by 'fellow countrymen' and then absorbed the 'dead' as 'ancestral spirit' of the 'Japanese'. Consequently, what is needed here is to deconstruct folklore established on the existing paradigm of the 'self'. For this purpose, these specific 'facts' must be reconstructed into a non-static methodological frame of reference, just like the dead who unexpectedly appear in *Tōno Monogatari* (The Tales of Tōno).

In this sense, folklore of happiness and unhappiness will always be folklore for the 'dead'—which means that the possibility of a folklore of happiness and unhappiness only exists in its impossibility. However, thinking through this impossibility is perhaps an unavoidable challenge for modern societies, which must contend with many legacies of the twentieth century, including war, colonialism and environmental destruction.

7
Conditions for 'Well-being' in Surveillance Society: The Dubious Happiness of Being Watched

Kiyoshi Abe

Introduction

It has been one year since the COE program for the Study of Social Research for the Enhancement of Human Well-being was launched. I have been involved in this vast project mainly through the activities of the research team working on the subject 'Effects of Surveillance Technology on "Well-being" in Civil Life'. At this opportunity to contribute to the inaugural issue of the Advance Social Research, I would like to reflect on various struggles in my own research work over the year and pose some questions about how to critically examine 'conditions for well-being' in a surveillance society.

Paradox of well-being

The original concerns that set our research team in motion can be summarized as follows. Modern society increasingly appears to be a 'surveillance society'. This trend cannot be treated simply as a technological issue but needs to be understood in the context of the economic and political dynamics of modern society. Is the increasing level of surveillance beginning to encroach on people's freedom and privacy?

Is this why people do not have a sense of 'well-being' in a surveillance society?

We proceeded with our research based on these questions and concerns. After almost a year of work, I feel that our intuitive insights were not far off the mark except on one of these questions. Our society is certainly moving toward increased surveillance and we can see economic/political motives under the guise of 'security assurance' in this trend. And there is no doubt that the basic rights of civil society are being eroded through increased surveillance. I can proudly say that our research has shed some light on surveillance society. However, I cannot help but feel that our last question—about people not having a sense of 'well-being'—was grossly mistaken. Or, less bluntly, we overlooked another possibility. Specifically, we suspect that people are actually feeling a sense of well-being in surveillance society. This suspicion became a common perception among the group as our research progressed.

It is not necessarily a bad thing to encounter a new 'question' in the course of research. Rather, it is perhaps an essential prerequisite for a new discovery. However, being faced with the seemingly intractable question of how 'well-being' is perceived/felt by people in the first place was a rather disturbing situation.

Needless to say, 'surveillance' means keeping watch on someone or something. At the same time, it can also mean keeping watch 'for' someone. The same social act of 'surveillance' can be done with either suspicious eyes or kind heart depending on the context. The 'two faces of surveillance' (Lyon 2001) can be clearly seen in Japanese society today, too. With such an ambivalent state of surveillance, the ways that people perceive and feel 'well-being' present complexities that defy a simple explanation. Through discussions at our research meetings and interviews with participants, we gradually got a clearer picture of the 'conditions for well-being' in a surveillance society.

First, I would like to explain schematically the 'difficulty' we faced in regard to 'well-being in a surveillance society'. We began our research with a focus on the 'unfreedom' of 'being under surveillance = under suspicion'. I can still say with conviction that the starting point itself was correct. However, we underestimated how appealing it was for people to be able to feel a sense of security and comfort when they were 'under surveillance = under protection'. In considering the relationship between surveillance and well-being, we were not sufficiently aware of, or sensitive to, the fact that 'well-being under surveillance', a paradoxical state from our viewpoint, is perceived as a 'reality' in contemporary society.

Thus, I seem to have finally reached the front gate to the main subject of the COE program, 'human happiness', after one year of research. What we should do from now on is to address the issue of how we are going to look at the paradoxical situation of 'well-being under surveillance' with critical eyes. I would like to lay out my own ideas below, though fairly roughly, about how to deal with future challenges of researching surveillance society.

Truth/goodness/beauty in modernity

Let us give a name 'critical studies', for the time being, to discourses that seek an alternative future condition by pointing out problems in society rather than accepting it as it is. Our research team's attempt is, in this sense, a 'critical study of surveillance society'. The theorists of the Frankfurt School, who call themselves Critical Theorists, aims for a realization of truth, goodness and beauty in society under the ideal of liberation. Streams of critical theory have dreamed of the coexistence of truth, justice and beauty in a liberated society to come—to aspire for. According to Jürgen Habermas, a leading thinker of the second generation Frankfurt School, the condition for a liberated society is the satisfaction through rational communications of three validity claims: truth in sciences that deal with the objective natural world, rightness in moral-politics that deal with the social world of inter-personal relationships, and sincerity in the arts that deal with the subjective internal world (Habermas 1981b).

The idea of explaining the paradigms of society in relation to these three values (truth, rightness and sincerity) belongs to a noble path of Western philosophy and is more specifically based on Kant's critical philosophy (critiques of pure reason/practical reason/judgment). In developing his own theory of modernity, Habermas emphasizes the fact that truth, goodness and beauty have each become autonomous value domains in recent times. Compared with the concept of 'intellect' in which truth, goodness and beauty are not clearly distinguished by the religious and metaphysical knowledge of a pre-modern society, he sees a momentum for progress/liberation lurking in the modern era in the intellectual framework in which they are separated into independent values and developed under distinct logics.

I have presented this very simple outline of Habermas' 'concept of modern intellect' because analysis of its merits and shortcomings offer some clues for our critical discussion of the paradoxical situation of 'well-being under surveillance'. Faced with a situation in which people yearning for happiness in peace and quiet equate surveillance with the 'well-being of being watched over', on what grounds can we develop a critical discourse? I would like to attempt below to find some intellectual pointers to theoretical and practical issues of critical studies, drawing on Habermas' argument.

Habermas uses a mobile as a metaphor to describe a mission for critical philosophy of the modern age to fulfill in relation to the three value domains.

> ... how to open up the cultural spheres of science, morality, and art, organized as self-contained expert cultures and structured as cognitive complexes around specialized validity claims; and how to connect them to the impoverished traditions of the lifeworld, without violating the fragile autonomous meaning of each sphere, in such a way that would be reunited in everyday communicative practice. The interpretive role of philosophy in relation to the lifeworld should, as I now see it, consist in reactivating the interplay of the cognitive-instrumental, the moral-practical, and aesthetic-expressive elements–thus, as it were, enabling a blocked mobile to function again. (Habermas [1981a] 1984: 14)

A mobile is a decorative object with mutually independent parts that swing in sympathetic movements with each other. Habermas' argument that the relationship between science, morality and art mediated by 'philosophy' ought to resemble a mobile can be seen as pretty much commonsense. Nor is it a novel approach to argue that the three value domains should be inter-related, not divided, in the Western philosophical tradition.

However, what I would like to focus on is not the orderliness of Habermas' theory of modernity, but rather its 'vacillations'. In other words, I consider that the strength of Habermas' explication of modern society lies not at the end-point of Habermas' critical theory but in the uncertainties and aporias that appear in the 'process' of getting there. I will explore this vacillation with the help of Habermas' discussion of Benjamin.

Consciousness-raising and redemptive critiques

Detailing Habermas' discussion on Benjamin—often seen as a 'maverick' of the first generation Frankfurt School, clearly influenced by messianism—is not my purpose here. What is needed for the purpose of this paper is to find out what Habermas, who was trying to re-interpret modernity based on communicative rationality, saw in Benjamin's discourse. What uncertainties and aporias in Habermas' own thinking can this reveal?

Habermas refers to two types of critique in his discussion of Benjamin: a 'consciousness-raising critique' and a 'redemptive critique'. The former is a critical attempt to, for example, expose a structure of domination that is hidden to everyday consciousness through the light of reason. In this respect, it is a typical ideological critique. The latter, however, is a method of critique that sends a message of hope for a 'good life'; where the good life is equated with redemption at an emotional level that tends to be suppressed in society, as opposed to rational conscious awareness. Putting it fairly schematically, Habermas' critical social theory would fall under the former category and Benjamin's messianistic critique of culture the latter. Yet, I cannot help but think that Habermas' discourse—which tries to critically absorb the ideas of the Frankfurt School pioneers in its effort to establish the validity of its own communicative action theory—is ultimately proposing to merge 'redemptive critique' into 'consciousness-raising critique'.

Vacillations are clearly evident in the argument that Habermas develops through the dichotomy of consciousness-raising critique and redemptive critique. More specifically, in the context of Benjamin's messianistic materialism (mimetic theory of language), Habermas appears to express a fundamental doubt about the type of society sought by his own critical theoretical communicative rationality. This can be seen in the following:

> Here we are talking only about the doubt that Benjamin's semantic materialism suggests: can we preclude the possibility of a meaningless emancipation? In complex societies, emancipation means the participatory transformation of administrative decision structures. Is it possible that one day an emancipated human race could encounter itself within an expanded space of discursive formation of will and yet be robbed of light in which it is capable of interpreting its life as something good? The revenge of a culture exploited over millennia for the legitimation of domination would then take this form: Right at the moment of overcoming age-old repressions, it would harbor no violence but it would have no content either. Without the influx of those semantic energies with which Benjamin's rescuing criticism was concerned, the structures of practical discourse—finally well established—would necessarily become desolate. (Habermas 1983: 160)

It is notable that, in discussing the details of Benjamin's messianistic redemptive critique, Habermas admits that the communicative liberation of society will unavoidably become a 'meaningless liberation' unless the 'semantic energy' to achieve a 'good life' exists in every individual. In other words, Habermas himself clearly admits that realizing a 'just society' in the absence of a 'good life' is futile. Interestingly, the subsequent development of Habermas' theory somewhat stoically avoids any discussion of the 'good life', as observed by many Habermas scholars. Ironically, the claim that 'Habermas' communicative action theory is formalistic and lacking substance', which was heatedly debated in the 1980s seems to have already been expressed by Habermas himself in the 1970s.

Grotesque reality of 'meaningless liberation'

We have come to see, via Habermas' presentation of Benjamin, that a 'just society where personal happiness is not achieved' is an image of a coming dystopia. As a methodology to avoid the dystopia of 'meaningless liberation', Benjamin attempts a 'redemptive critique' from the position of his unique linguistic/cultural theory. Habermas pursues 'consciousness-raising critique' toward the completion of 'unfinished modernity'. Although there are differences between them—messianism aiming for the realization of personal, internal 'happiness' or a social theory focusing on the realization of social consensus-building—both suggest the necessity of intermediation between the internal world and the social world for the realization of a 'liberated society'. Conversely, a society lacking such intermediation is in fact merely a dystopia of 'meaningless liberation', even if it appears to have realized justice on the surface.

So, at the beginning of the twenty-first century, what is this 'meaningless liberation' that Habermas was concerned about in the early 1970s? In short, it may already have become reality in everyday life, in a grotesque form. Moreover, in an utterly 'unliberated' form…

The grotesque situation I refer to is the seemingly endless trend towards increasing surveillance in the name of 'security', driven by political leaders loudly proclaiming a continuing War on Terror. They maintain that a surveillance society must 'watch over' society and individuals in order to achieve a state of 'objective security' that allows individuals to live with a sense of 'subjective security'. And this surveillance trend appears to be welcomed by the very people who are being 'watched/watched over' as a protective gaze. In this situation, the policies and systems to arbitrarily check/control the society go unchallenged on the promise that individual 'security = happiness'. Yet the rush towards the assurance of security is exactly the opposite of the 'liberated society' sought by critical theory. A surveillance society works relentlessly to exclude 'others' under notions of an almost religiously dogmatized, self-righteous 'justice' rather than aspiring to form social relationships open to many people through rational discussion. And yet the majority of modern populations appear to accept this state of affairs, to ensure their own safety and security for a 'peaceful society'. They appear to not care about other people's suffering or injustice as long as they can secure their own 'happiness'...

Examining the present state of surveillance society leads to an undeniable sense that the separation of a personal world and a social world that Habermas feared would follow the 'meaningless liberation' of a culture that does not provide any semantic energy has been spectacularly realized in our time. Needless to say, a surveillance society cannot even be called a pseudo 'liberated society' because of its preparedness to restrict 'freedom' in the name of 'security'. Does this mean that, in today's society, we are simply engaged in empty pursuit of the realization of 'happiness' for individuals under self-righteous 'justice' that rejects communication with others, without even achieving 'meaningless liberation'? To borrow Habermas' words quoted earlier, we would have to conclude that 'culture would have all forms of violence but it would have no content' in such a society.

It is widely known that the word 'security' comes from a Latin word 'securus' comprising *se* (free from) and *cure* (care). Which means, 'security' aims for freedom from concerns and considerations, or the state in which one is not bothered by anything. In this sense, perhaps we should not be surprised by the ability of individuals to feign almost apathetic indifference toward a society in which they and others live for the sake of a little happiness called 'peace of mind' in a surveillance society that pursues 'security' unconditionally. I suppose the state of assured security obsessively sought after by the inhabitants of a surveillance society is a 'peaceful society' in which they do not have to care about others. In such a society, people must be forced to live in a completely transparent culture which 'has no content' and at the same time 'permits all forms of violence' without having consideration or concerns for society, others and even themselves.

Maybe we have already started on that road in our pursuit of the 'happiness of being watched over'. The future looming at the end of the road is none other than the ugly society that does not even recognize the importance of 'semantic energy' that Benjamin resisted all his life.

Toward politicization of peace

Now is the time for us to try to shine a critical light on the ominous symptoms hidden behind a 'peaceful society'. As mentioned at the outset, in our critique of surveillance society, we must patiently continue to examine problems implicit in the 'well-being' of 'peace of mind' apparently promised by 'protective' surveillance as well as the 'unfreedom' brought about by 'suspicious' surveillance. To do that, we must develop our imagination through sensitivity to the violence caused by 'meaningless security' rather than 'meaningless liberation'. Otherwise, critical discourses would be lost for words in the face of the happiness in peace of mind endlessly pursued/accepted by individuals in a world filled with social injustice and disparities.

Benjamin courageously spoke out against the Nazi's 'aestheticization of politics' and for 'politicization of art'. Benjamin devoted himself to a 'redemptive critique' aimed to release/liberate 'semantic energy'. To borrow from Benjamin, what is required of the critical intellect today—where 'politics of security' is accelerating in the name of peace of mind/safety with little debate—would be to advance a thorough 'politicization of peace' that exposes the grotesque ugliness hidden in the sense of the 'happiness of being watched over', which is, in fact, merely one aspect of the violence of surveillance.

8
Happiness and Unhappiness: A Clinical Sociological Approach

Eishō Ōmura

Introduction

The total number of suicides in Japan exceeded 34,400 in 2003. Some commentators have attempted to downplay the magnitude of this social phenomenon by observing that 'As many as 330,000 to 340,000 suicides are reported every year in (mainland) China'. Nevertheless, the Japanese figure is unprecedentedly high considering the population difference between the two countries. Either way, a situation in which almost one hundred people kill themselves each day (not counting failed attempts) is clearly abnormal. This situation seems to indicate that, to borrow Emile Durkheim's expression, the 'average level of unhappiness' has risen significantly in recent years, at least among middle-aged and elderly males, who account for nearly two-thirds of the total number of suicides in Japan.

Another 'unprecedented' figure has recently become a topic of frequent debate: the total fertility rate of Japanese women, which has reportedly fallen to 1.29. When this rate hit 1.34 in 2000, it was reported as a 'shock'. At that time, some demographers estimated that, at that rate, Japan's population would fall to about 130,000 in five hundred years and 130 in one thousand years. Understandably, then, when the figure dipped below the 1.30 mark in such a short period of time it was an even bigger shock to the people concerned. In 2000, some commentators observed that with the global population crisis as it is perhaps this declining birth rate was not such a bad thing. But this more recent figure of 1.29 seems to have silenced those voices.

There must be a multitude of factors contributing to the declining birth rate. It would therefore be overly simplistic to call it a sign that the 'average level of unhappiness' among women of child-bearing age is rising. However, it is perhaps safe enough to attribute this trend to some of the more general conflicts or strains in Japanese society taking a toll on a certain demographic, as we can with the high suicide rate. If so, then borrowing from Durkheim once again, we might say that there is an underlying '*collective conscience*' that discourages childbearing on one hand and stimulates suicide on the other hand—with the people of certain demographics a little more easily swept up in the trend than others. In any case, it is safe to say that the current *collective conscience* in Japan does not seem to be making the people happy.

Of course, one may well ask, 'What exactly is "average unhappiness"?'—thereby forcing recognition that such a question cannot be adequately addressed by positivist science such as Durkheim's, which demands reliance on statistical data and excludes the participants' subjective assessments. Even if we could exhaustively detail the contents of the *collective conscience*, we would nevertheless need to employ something along the lines of Max Weber's method of 'understanding motives' or C. Wright Mills' extension of this to interpreting the 'vocabulary of motives' of the affected subjects in order to ascertain why certain people are more affected than others. Either way, the origins of the underlying *collective conscience* can only be discovered via structural analysis based on economics and cultural anthropology.

However, perusing the theories espoused by economists—both within and outside Japan—seems to confirm my suspicion that most of them are still grounding their arguments in the Utilitarian maxim of 'the greatest happiness of the greatest number' or similar. The misguided-ness of this maxim seems all too obvious in the current situation, which seems to epitomize Durkheim's conception of 'anomic suicide'. Although, on the surface it may seem paradoxical that the suicide rate is higher (i.e. the 'average unhappiness' greater) in wealthier countries and states than in poorer regions, it is not really so surprising once we reflect upon the situation for a moment. We don't need to look as far as Nepal or Bhutan. It will suffice to look back just a few decades to remember Japan during the first several years after WWII. Most people were 'on the edge of starvation' (and certainly there were more murders than today because of that) but the suicide rate was low. Moreover, people seemed to be more vital, then, with more zest for life. I can still remember the joy on my parents' faces when I triumphantly brought home a slab of chocolate dropped in my school yard by the Allied Occupation soldiers (Van Houten if I recall correctly).

How was such 'happiness' possible then? I think it was because most people were poor. Rousseau expressed a similar view in *Emile* when he said that 'the surest way to make children *unhappy* is to give them everything they want when they want'. Don't you agree that these are words of wisdom? And don't you think that 'the greatest happiness of the greatest number' is rather self-contradictory logically? When everyone becomes wealthier, the amount of happiness for *everyone* should increase accordingly? Unfortunately, I must say it is far from the reality facing us.

This is not to question the good intentions of those who hope to rid the world of poverty and inequality. But we know quite well that well-meaning stupidity—called *kyomou funbetsuchi* (fallacious reasoning) in Japanese Buddhism—is extremely difficult to deal with. It would be even worse if it was forced upon us (by some 'imperialists') in the name of justice and equity. Therefore, I think we should take this opportunity to make it clear that poverty and inequality are matters belonging to different dimensions than the 'happiness—unhappiness' of people.

This is the very reason that this paper is titled 'clinical studies' instead of 'scientific studies'. To make this clear I begin by explaining how remote traditional (social) science discourses are from the real feelings/experience/everyday life of ordinary people.

Asymmetry of happiness and unhappiness

To begin with, let us look at the asymmetry of the words happiness and unhappiness in their everyday use. In a real sense, this asymmetry only arises when the two concepts are placed on a single scale, such that one increases as the other decreases. That is, the problem becomes obvious when 'happiness-unhappiness' are treated as measurable quanta. In contrast, I would argue that in the everyday conversations of Japanese today, happiness and unhappiness are not used as a simple dichotomous pair.

First, this is clear if you consider their relationship to a genuine dichotomous pair, for example, density and sparsity. In the Japanese language, *usui* (sparse) is used to describe lack of happiness, as in *sachi usuki hito* (a person with little happiness) and *hakkō no reijin* (a beautiful but unhappy lady) for example, but its opposite *koi* (dense) is never used to describe abundance of happiness. As you may argue, we say *kōfuku no zecchō* (climax of happiness) and how does it contrast with *fukō no donzoko* (nadir of unhappiness)? The word 'climax' clearly has the connotation of 'transitoriness' and sounds precarious. To paraphrase the density-sparsity contrast, people obviously consider that happiness, by nature, is not supposed to last, as opposed to a more enduring nature of unhappiness.

Happiness is seen as an ephemeral thing that slips out of your hand as soon as you try to grasp it, just like a dream. This nuanced understanding of happiness is shared by Japanese as well as many others around the world. I will return to the latter later. Of course we must acknowledge the particular religious sensitivity cultivated by Japanese Buddhism here, but I have written about that elsewhere and do not have the space to revisit it here.[1] Instead, let us concentrate on the point that, by shifting registers once again, unhappiness is tinged with inevitability whereas happiness has a hint of accidentalness. I have no time to examine the complete etymology here, but *Kōjien* dictionary explains that the original spelling of one of the Japanese words for happiness, *shiawase*, means a stroke of fate or luck. Importantly, prior to the Meiji era, the same word could mean bad luck as well as good luck.

On the other hand, scholars of Buddhism agree that another Japanese word for happiness *kōfuku* is not found in any of the Buddhist scriptures that were written in Chinese characters (Kawai and Nakazawa, 2003).[2] Which means that *kōfuku* was created as a translation for imported words such as 'happy' and 'bonheur'. The two characters that were combined to create *kōfuku* originally meant things like 'products of the sea and land' and 'the god of wealth'. They must have had more specific meanings at various times throughout Japanese history. Although they similarly describe abundance of specific things, *kō* implies something one has attained whereas *fuku* suggests something one has been given (by Heaven). After the newly created *kōfuku* became widely used the character *kō* was applied to *shiawase*. Eventually, the meaning of *shiawase* assumed the characteristics of '*kō*' and its connotation of accidentalness gradually diminished.

But this sense of the term has not been completely lost, as can be seen in novels and movies which skillfully reveal connotations of a word that have been hidden in day-to-day usage to arouse a sense of a word buried deep in memory. For convenience, I will comment only on Munesuke Mita's critique of Keita Genji's serialized story *Teinen taishoku* (Age-limit retirement), which was published in *Asahi Shimbun* over a period of almost a year in 1962. Mita, who was not preoccupied with the etymology of *shiawase*, followed the convention of using *kōfuku* for happiness (Mita 1965b). Despite terminological differences, though, in the quotation below he describes happiness as an accidental event caused by Heaven's providence, thus articulating an interpretation that coincides with the meaning I am trying to bring out from the etymological connotations of *shiawase*.

> With the sound of steady footsteps, unhappiness ... closes in on the central character with the inevitability of turning pages of a calendar. In contrast, happiness accidentally turns up. This inevitable sure-footedness of unhappiness in the primary theme of 'age-limit retirement' and the casual nature of happiness in various compensatory themes are described in vivid contrast.
>
> However, like the darkness of the sky in the background of fireworks on a summer night that goes unnoticed by the spectators, just a sprinkling of accidental happiness warms the heart of the readers and people tend to find enrichment of their lives *as if* it were an everyday occurrence. (In the world of popular literature, people's lives exist in the background and their dreams are painted in the foreground.) (emphasis added)

This passage demonstrates Mita's sharp insights into the 'asymmetry' of happiness and unhappiness. But my reason for quoting it is to highlight Mita's representation of the artifice of 'popular literature', which he argues, generally acts to divert the public's attention from the reality of their alienation. More bluntly, Mita considers the general 'happiness' of ordinary people to derive, after all, from a 'false consciousness', a deception to alleviate the unhappiness of reality. In fact, the passage continues:

> ...in the end, various problems relating to fundamental human conditions of today ... remain totally unresolved ... What each of us needs to face squarely now as a modern man is the problem of pettiness felt by modern people *that comes to the surface triggered by* this issue, and the things that created this sense of pettiness—the social structure that allows us to treat ourselves and others as a tool, a commodity, a resource or an object. (emphasis original)

With the benefit of hindsight, it is clear that Mita's *Gendai nihon no seishin kōzō* (Mentality of modern Japan)[3]—touted as a masterpiece at the time of publication—undoubtedly raised important questions about the 'alienation' and 'false consciousness' theories—we can collectively call them pulpit Marxist and Freudian modernism—that long dominated all fields of social science (Mita 1965a). It is safe to say that Marxist orthodoxy has been rather faltering, to say the least, both here and overseas since about this time.

But perhaps all fields of social science are faltering...[4] That is why I have been appealing for the need for clinical sociology and clinical studies of religion for the past several years. As can be seen see in the quotation above, 'happiness', when truly felt by people, has typically been treated by the social sciences as something that *shouldn't* be. Rather, according to most social science, people should be unhappy in this world. And the happiness promised in the afterworld (heavenly bliss) by various religions is regarded as the ultimate unscientific superstition (and opiate). Frankly, we cannot defend against the accusation that traditionally, the social sciences have never taken happiness seriously. Those who occupy the pulpits of academia have, however, never stopped seeking their own happiness, of course.

If those at the other end of the political spectrum (neoclassicists and competitive market mechanism theorists seem to be the dominant forces these days) propose 'the greatest happiness of the greatest number' as the only viable alternative, as I mentioned in the introduction, this is in fact the clearest evidence that they have not been thinking about it seriously. In short, all those theories about happiness devised by social science based on some kind of simulation have little to do with people's actual experience of 'happiness' in real life. Why? The truth is, social science is not so different from the 'popular literature' evoked by Munesuke Mita: it creates a form of fiction—a framed reality to be exact—but is perhaps insufficiently self-reflexive on that point.

The asymmetry between the accidentalness of happiness and the inevitability of unhappiness does not stem from one being fictional and the other real. Based on the reality of the feelings invested in the word in the everyday life-world, both feelings should be treated equally within the same frame. In other words, if one is fictional, the other should also be understood to be a product of fiction. However, as we have seen Mita does not agree, nor it seems, do most conventional social scientists, alienationists (including the Frankfurt

School) in particular. They maintain that only unhappiness is a reality (problem) and happiness is 'false consciousness'.

In contrast, clinical sociology places special importance on the common vocabulary in the ordinary life-world, as demonstrated above, considering this to be the data that best and most accurately represents reality. Especially, we think that what Miyahara calls deeply ingrained *karada kotoba* (personal words)[5] such as *shiawase* are more important data for understanding reality than translated words such as *kōfuku* (Miyahara 1998). From this perspective, the language of popular literature and popular songs better reflects the true life in the 'background' than does the language used in social science and philosophy books. Of course, translated words adopted into common parlance can also contribute to this understanding. *Kōfuku* is one of the better words in this sense, compared, for example, with *shūkyō* (religion), a translated word that cannot fully represent the true religious 'background' of Japan.

Certainly, *shūkyō* is widely used in academic and philosophy books. However, its use in the life-world is far removed from its use in academic books—so much so that we don't feel anything is particularly wrong when we hear of a 'religionless' or 'non-religious' memorial service. Before I had realized this, I was once quite befuddled by an interviewee who replied that he had no particular religion, or rather, he disliked religion, but then, after further questioning told me that he attended a certain shrine twice a week without fail (Shūkyō Shakaigaku no Kai 1985).[6] The late religious scholar Keiichi Yanagawa was correct in saying that the predominant religious sentiment of the Japanese is *shinkō naki shūkyō* (religion without faith), but when I asked 'Does that make sense when translated into English?' he could only reply, 'You are giving me a hard time'. That is, although it is understandable intellectually, in essence, the word *shūkyō* still infers something other than our religious feelings. Similarly, some people express regret that *kami* (a deity) has become the preferred translation of 'God', instead of *tenshu* (the Lord of Heaven) which was used for a while. In contrast with *shūkyō*, though, the regret here seems to arise from the fact that *kami* is capable of expressing and redefining the *traditional* religious feelings of Japan too well.[7]

In any case, clinical sociology takes the view that the world that is created in a real living language, even if it is a fictional world, resembles real life more closely than the academic world created with translated words. Let us now return to the connotations of *shiawase*.

We find a very clear articulation of its meaning in Takao's (1977) *Kōfuku no rinrigaku* (Ethics of happiness), which deserves to be called a real clinical study of religion.[8] His brilliant commentary on word connotations backed by his linguistic sophistication is most appropriate in this context.

> It certainly seems that the *feelings* of happiness we experience are very accidental and fragmentary and dependent on accidental good fortune we experience on occasions. Many of the words meaning 'happiness' also point to it. Happiness in English means 'happening to be', *glück* (German) means 'good fortune', and *bonheur* (French) means 'good timing'. It seems happiness does not lie in our own hands. In fact, the Greek word *eudaimon* means 'having a good protector god' and the Chinese script for happiness consists of two parts—one meaning 'divine' and the other meaning 'a plump-shaped full vessel'—and means 'abundance provided by gods'. *Shiawase* in Japanese seems to mean that things coincide well and *saiwai* derived from *sakihahi* which means to come across good prey by chance. They all seem to represent a similar feeling.

The accidentalness of happiness is apparent in all of these understandings. But we must also note another important dimension, pointed to by the saying 'happiness dwells on the other side of the mountain'. This theme is well explored in the story of *L'oiseau bleu*, by the Nobel Prize winning author Maurice Maeterlinck (1908). Rather unexpectedly for a story written for young children, observes Itsuki (2004), this story 'has a very sad ending in which, the moment they realize that the blue bird of happiness has always been in front of them, the bird flies away'. Itsuki continues:

> The ending of *L'oiseau bleu* has an indescribably bitter taste. Why did he have to tell young children who were about to embark on a journey to the future that real happiness was something that, as soon as you grab it, would slip through your fingers and disappear. I am yet unable to resolve this question… The word 'happiness' conveys good, cheerful feelings, but at the same time it hides some kind of sorrow. A saying in Europe asks, 'Why do people love things that are bound to be lost?' People do not love things that will remain in our hand forever with certainty. People desperately try to love things they anticipate will be lost or get away from them some day. (Itsuki 2004)

The potential of clinical sociology: Art and science

Basically clinical sociologists are engaged in the same business as fiction writers in that we rely on 'live' feelings of word but we have unfortunately chosen to work as professional scholars. We respect 'common sense' and 'subtleties of human nature' but nevertheless need to attain some 'special knowledge' in a different frame or level—that is, larger, interpretable, clinical knowledge. The reality created by academic literature is largely a world made of 'impersonal' words. This is how it can maintain a certain degree of universality that is easily translatable into foreign languages, unlike a world of 'personal words' that can absorb the very particular everyday feelings of the moment. For example, I freely use 'personal words' when I give a live lecture as a 'monk', but if I try to say the same thing to religious scholars, I feel a need to translate (transform) the message into 'impersonal words'. Putting the message into writing demands that it be translated into an even more specialized written language (jargon).

Of course, our problem is not just a matter of language. If accidentalness is an essential characteristic of happiness, science, which aims to find some kind of inevitability, be it a causal relationship or a structural association, quite logically leans toward a 'sociology of unhappiness' rather than a 'sociology of happiness'. However, as argued, the apparent inevitability also has an element of artificiality, constructed by certain frames. If one stands on the Marxist and Freudian frames mentioned earlier, there is no way of escaping this inevitability of unhappiness unless we make a *fundamental* revision. Worse still, from this perspective, unlike the *Theodizee des Leidens*, even death cannot change this helplessness.

In all of the pervasive, traditional religions, Western and Eastern, the inevitability of unhappiness in this world is explained more convincingly than in any social science. However, especially in those religions based on an absolute, single god, there is always a chance for a dramatic reversal after death. It can be said that inevitability of unhappiness transforms into inevitability of happiness (in the next world) when it crosses the boundary of death. Even for a religion like Buddhism, though, that does not evoke the *Theodizee des Leidens* as such, the apparent unhappiness in this world is nothing compared to 'eternal happiness'. Both perspectives offer an insightful view, no doubt based on a good understanding of the accidentalness of happiness and the inevitability of unhappiness in this world. But this paper is not about my own religious experience…

Once we understand the inevitability of unhappiness and the accidentalness of happiness, we should construct a universally framed reality that can be understood by the ordinary people who live in today's more secularized societies. We can take a clue from the field of medicine, where 'science' and 'art' have come to fairly well-established—competing but complementary—frames for constructing reality. From this perspective, the conventional evidence-based science can be contrasted to the framed reality constructed on art that I have in mind when I speak of clinical sociology. Figure 8.1, drawn by Yamanaka in *Rinshō bunka no yukue* (The future of clinical culture) (2005) is a good illustration of these different frames.[9]

The idea that students of medicine can only be transformed into physicians through contacts with 'live' patients—i.e. clinical experience—has not changed much even as the field is increasingly flooded with more and more advanced medical technologies. In fact, doctors of internal medicine do not prepare drugs, perform surgery, nor correct bones sitting astride a patient like an osteopath. They only see patients, think, diagnose and prescribe medication. This is the emergence of new medicine in the later half of the nineteenth century described by Michel Foucault in *The Birth of the Clinic*

Figure 8.1: Components of 'clinical culture' in medicine

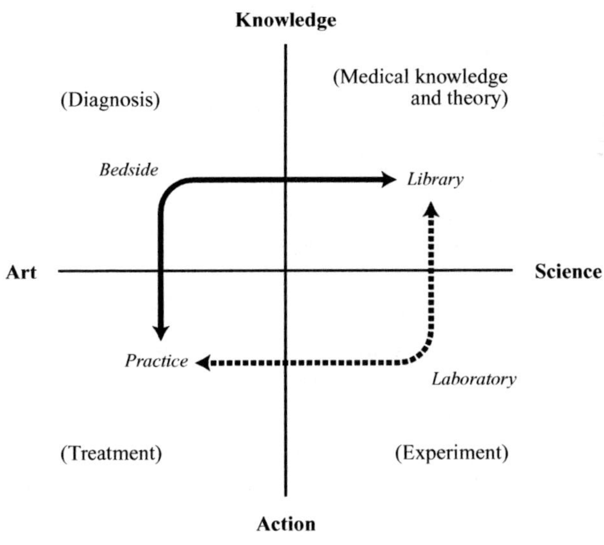

Source: Yamanaka (ed.), 2005.

(1963). Yamanaka observes that Foucault's approach is somewhat biased toward the activities of internal medicine physicians. 'Around the same time,' he says, 'surgical medicine made rapid progress and a move toward laboratory medicine wielding microscopes and chemical analysis started shortly thereafter, but Foucault focused on a medical reform movement by internal medicine physicians for some reason' (Yamanka 2005). He goes on to explain that the reason was that Foucault wanted to emphasize the groundbreaking significance of the invention of the stethoscope. What I want to stress is that the type of 'clinical knowledge' in question—an acquired art (skill) as depicted in the upper left corner of Figure 8.1—was already the very essence of a traditional 'diagnostician'.

Now, what problem has emerged in the field of medicine in recent years? Around May 1999, a report titled 'Chōshinki ga tsukaenai—Hensachi sedai no igakusei, kihon no ketsuraku (Cannot use a stethoscope: Medical students of the deviation value generation, lack of basics)' was broadcast by NHK's *Kurōzuappu Gendai* (Close-up today) program. Doctors interviewed for the program contend that medical diagnosis is still an art, not simply a science. That they have to point this out suggests that in some respects medicine has forgotten its essential spirit of care and has been focusing instead on organ (parts) treatment. In my experience, particularly at university hospitals, I have never had the pleasure of being examined with a stethoscope, not to mention palpation. One physician who I visited stared at his computer screen throughout his consultation and called out, "Next person, please...", without glancing at me even once. 'They see organs (parts) but not persons.' The type of modern medicine that has created this situation is depicted by the broken-line arrow running across the bottom and right side of Figure 8.1: 'science'. At the same time, what was traditionally considered the true value of an internal medicine clinician—the areas covered by the black arrow—has now become the nurses' task, as the role of 'care' has been virtually forgotten in pursuit of 'cure' (Noguchi and Ōmura 2000).

There is a growing momentum in Japan and elsewhere for a comprehensive review of the medical world as a whole. In the US, strong demand for holistic medicine is shifting Oriental medicine from the status of 'alternative medicine' to a more widely accepted mainstream position (somewhat surprisingly, this trend is apparently much stronger in the US than in Japan). In Japan, people have begun to express dissatisfaction with the scientific cure-oriented medical practices as they reassess the importance of terminal care. One influential factor in this reassessment is the rise in so-called 'lifestyle diseases' that cannot be cured by even the most radical treatment or wonder drugs, and thus leave both practitioners and patients alike with little option but to focus on improving methods and standards of care, rather than cure alone.[10]

And what is happening in this regard in the world of social science, which since its inception has supposedly been trying to resolve, in a sense, a much more troublesome social problem than lifestyle diseases—the inevitability of unhappiness? Isn't it faced with a need to change its priorities too?

In my view, social science originated from the liberal arts, then became increasingly segmented and specialized in its efforts to become more scientific. It is now roughly divisible into two groups—one which looks towards science, represented by modern economics and experimental psychology, and the other which doesn't go so far as to revert to its origins but tries to recognize and reassess the value of clinical knowledge as liberal art. Just as modern medicine has come under attack for having become 'dehumanized', the once-popular 'social engineering' project is recoiling from similar criticism. This has created a situation in which the relationship depicted in Figure 8.1 between the broken-line two-headed arrow (cure) and the black two-headed arrow (care) is being thoroughly and critically reassessed in the social sciences (exemplified perhaps by the flourishing of clinical psychology). To be sure, I am not in any way suggesting that the frame depicted by the right (science) side of Figure 8.1 is unnecessary or could be discarded. Far from it. I am simply stressing that we cannot be satisfied with social science knowledge constructed in the science frame alone—it must be counter-balanced with knowledge derived from the different frames on the art side. In fact, the failure of the 'social engineering' proponents lies in their misperception that the specialized theoretical knowledge of the upper right area could be translated unchanged to the upper left area as valid as 'clinical knowledge'.

We can apply this model more specifically to social science to clarify the position of clinical sociology. This model is depicted in Figure 8.2, again adopted from Hiroshi Yamanaka.

The caption in each quadrant indicates a 'ground', so to speak. 'Actual contact' is on the knowledge side rather than the action side, because it refers to the ground in which clinical knowledge is cultivated. The same applies to 'theoretical knowledge' on the right side. In the old days, pure theorists were called armchair sociologists

Figure 8.2: Components of clinical sociology

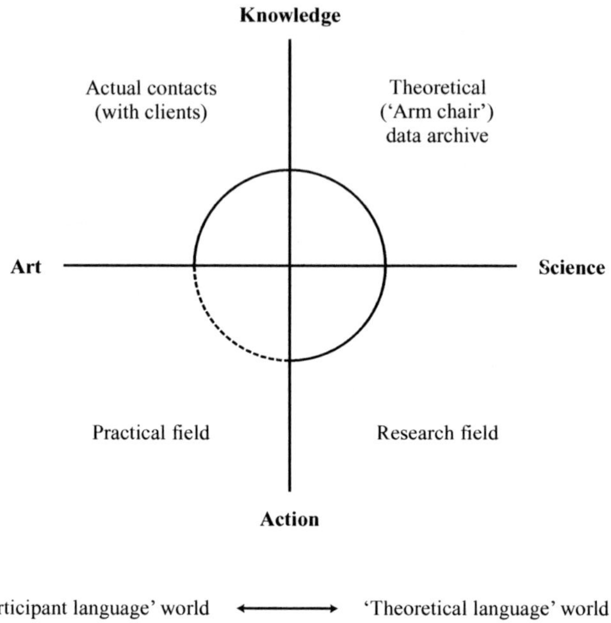

but these days not even theorists are allowed to simply sit back and think. It means that modern sociology theories are worked out by scholars secluded in a library, or rather, 'immersed in a data archive'. And of course they must work in the research field as well.

Is it possible to be a theorist based solely on the two fields of art, on the left side? No. While a pure theorist might work only with knowledge and action on the science side, someone who relied only on the two areas on the art side might be a practitioner, but could not be a theorist. 'Clinical knowledge' referred to here is not merely common sense or wisdom for life. Although like common sense, it is grounded in a 'participant language', it is very different from common sense in that 'clinical knowledge' as we define it is also specialized knowledge. Again, we saw this with the black-arrowed 'care' in Figure 8.1, which covers three quadrants, including specialized medical knowledge. We can see this best, perhaps, among those practitioners called, 'expert nurses' by the leading nursing theorist, Patricia Benner, who also place great importance on learning from medical theories. Likewise, the clinical sociology theorist must be a true expert who encompasses the three areas marked by a solid line in Figure 8.2—all except the lower left (art-action) area. In other words, clinical sociology is not simply a matter of shifting the ground from science to art.

We can look to Erving Goffman as one of the great precursors of clinical sociology theorists, a true expert. His methodology, known as the dramaturgical perspective, was much closer to art (skill) than science (not that he said so himself). Interestingly, he humbly claimed that his method was just crude empiricism, perhaps in anticipation of a critique of his methodology from the defenders of the science perspective. But his use of the word 'crude' is rather tricky.[11]

First, the word is full of Goffman's characteristic sarcasm about conventional sociology. More particularly, it seemed to him that conventional sociologists formed arbitrary theories—almost prejudices in his eyes—even before observing the various facts of the real life-world, then misguidedly believed their constructed realities (frames) to be social facts. Goffman advocated accurately observing and describing the surface facts as they are to start with. He once called his own method a 'snapshot view', suggesting a camera taking several still images of actual, visible, social interactions. If done properly, some invisible order, some feeling or rules that govern the interactions should manifest themselves in the resulting description. This is the methodology that he deliberately describes as 'crude'.

At the same time, Goffman certainly did not ignore conventional sociological theories. In particular, it would be no exaggeration to say that he respected Durkheim's sociological theory more so than anyone previously had in the American sociology community. And yet he dramatically reframed this Durkheimian legacy. While Durkheim literally relied on science—that is, completely excluding the subjectivity of participants—and argued that 'social facts' should be observed as if they were objects, Goffman maintained that social facts could only be extracted with good artistic skill and by not bracketing-out the subjectivity of the participant. This perspective and methodology is exemplified in the way that Goffman was able to extract invisible 'social facts' in the earliest stages of his field research in the Shetland Islands, for example, a finding that cannot be seen as anything other than true art.

To understand the strength of this methodology, it is useful to compare Goffman's dramaturgical perspective to the role played by the stethoscope for the clinical doctor of internal medicine. Determining the right distance from a client or a subject is a perpetually difficult question for clinical knowledge—hence its position on the art side. Citing Foucault's observation that a stethoscope represents a fixed distance to a clinical physician, Yamanaka states that 'Two desires of clinical medicine—a desire to get as close to the patient's body as possible and a desire to keep as much distance from the patient's influence as possible—can be satisfied simultaneously'.

In contrast to the science that requires everything to be treated dispassionately and with detachment, clinical knowledge is not possible without some level of empathy. The twin desires above must pose a difficulty for sociologists too. Something like a 'neutral attitude' might suffice for simple 'common sense' but it does not provide an adequate ground for specialized knowledge. Goffman therefore proposed to observe every life situation as a performance on a stage—linking the performer to the audience, like a stethoscope, not the type of approach that clearly separates the subject and the observer.

As he refined the approach he seems to have become increasingly adept at viewing his own action as that of a performer on a stage. He developed the ability to move freely between the science and art frames while remaining fully aware of both. Even a researcher does not live in isolation from the real world. He must have acquired common sense and 'cunning' as an ordinary person, as do psychiatric patients. The practiced ability at switching between front stage and backstage, might have enabled him to deal with patients more skillfully than other researchers or psychiatric hospital staff. Using the stethoscope analogy, we might say that Goffman was often listening to his own breath, or using a theater analogy, he was playing the roles of both performer and audience, often *at the same time*. We can call this the 'double life' of Goffman, which is also definitive of the methodological perspective that he established (Ōmura 1985).

Action and expression: Role and character

A major advantage of viewing every life-world situation as a performance on a stage lies in its capacity to unveil the invisible script or story that manifests through visible performance. It is perhaps common knowledge by now that the front stage performance and the backstage performance are played out according to completely different scripts, as is the fact that 'what one says and what one really means' can be quite different. Strangely, although conventional sociological theories aptly use 'roles' as a drama metaphor, they immediately eliminate the visible components such as behaviors and movements to 'extract' the invisible actions that are supposedly the 'true functions' of the performance. For example, the specified role may be 'father' but all that that these theorists read in the script are the functions that he performs in the family. Goffman outlined the dilemma of action versus expression to draw our attention to this omission prevalent among role theories in general and *literal functionalism* in particular (read this 'ism' as 'addiction').

In my own critique of functionalist theories that are content with simply extracting invisible 'functions', I described them as 'invisible man models'. That is, they depict only the functions, with no expression. For example, if we locate the 'father' role in Figure 8.2, on the science side we find only abstract general meanings and functions of a typical father in a generalized family but cannot discuss the role that is *actually* being performed by any particular person in any given family. At the same time, many advocates do not seem to recognize that the 'family' defined on the science side alone is a framed reality.[12] This is not to deny the important contribution that functionalists have made to understanding social life. For example, there can be no denying the significance of the way Talcott Parsons described 'seeing a doctor' as 'assuming the sick role' for clearly highlighting the obligations and rights that attach to this role. But if we focus solely on the (latent) functions or outcomes of a role—such as any associated rights and obligations—we occlude the processes by which particular people assume such a role in the first place (including when/how they might be forced to assume such roles). Such an approach would also preclude an analysis of social action from the researchers' toolkit, thus closing off any opportunity for understanding the particular ways in which actors perform some of their functions. From our standpoint on the art side we might consider the 'character' to be played rather than the 'role'.[13]

For example, within a stage set in which the doctor sits comfortably in a large armchair and the patient shrinks on top of an unstable (for some reason) swivel chair, the client may have some feelings of resistance at first but as s/he realizes that there is *no* other role available to play, s/he learns that s/he will be rewarded most (i.e., particularly on the emotional level) when s/he plays the sick role in accordance with expectations. It is very clear that a stethoscope has an important theatrical value here in that the patient has to stop talking when the stethoscope is placed on his/her body. The strong normality of this response is highlighted by a caricature of the counter-example, the patient who chats away while the doctor is trying to listen through the stethoscope. Clearly, the appropriate actions for the sick—whether classified as essence or identity—are prompted one at a time through a very 'obvious', superficial (scripted) process of interactions between the doctor and the patient. Assuming the sick role with its associated rights and obligations as described by Parsons is only one of the outcomes of this 'obvious' process. More importantly, (operating at the unconscious emotional level) the latent functions of the hierarchical structures built into this process are not fully explicable by Parsons' role theory.

Goffman's study *Asylums* (1961) provides a good point of comparison. It might be asking too much for the powers of observation that could fully comprehend the backstage formed by patients, to extend understanding far beyond the front stage interactions of institutional staff and inpatients, and extract from their actions the true 'under life'. But much research has been done recently from various perspectives on the (latent) functions of the script concealed behind the front stage. So much, in fact, that I do not need to define constructionism. Yet one example, the so-called *netakiri-rōjin* (bedridden elderly people) issue raised by Yukiko Ōkuma (2000) will serve to illustrate our methodology.

Ōkuma argues that the people typically referred to as 'bedridden elderly people' in Japan are actually the *nekasekiri-rōjin* (the elderly confined to bed). This disparity came to her attention when she visited aged-care facilities in the Nordic countries. She was surprised to learn that wherever she went the people did not understand the term 'bedridden elderly people'. Inspecting their facilities, she found no elderly person who fitted that description. After a detailed analysis to discern how they were different from Japanese facilities, she sharply criticized the Japanese practice as self-interested kindness. Although it appeared to be attentive care, the facility staffs' convenience was the highest priority, and the easiest way to manage elderly residents was to confine them to their beds with restraining devices. We must not ignore the importance of Ōkuma's realization coming from her observation of expression rather than action—her observations of different actions were directed/focused by her observations of expressive differences. She further noted that while it is common in Japanese aged-care facilities to see elderly residents with cropped hair and dressed in identical grayish pajamas, in stark contrast, the residents of the Nordic facilities dressed with abundant individuality. What she revealed was that the common social role 'bedridden elderly' was really a socially constructed character that people were forced to play.

Perhaps even worse for such patients than the aged-care 'uniform' is being addressed as ...-*chan* (a suffix of endearment) in a wheedling voice by young nursing staff. When the elderly are addressed in this patronizing way repeatedly over time, most of them become easy-to-handle grandpas and grandmas who willingly wear diapers to satisfy the staff's expectations. This situation was identified by Goffman in reference to some patients in an asylum: 'Sympathetic patients in mental wards will sometimes feign bizarre symptoms so that student nurses will not be subjected to a disappointingly sane performance.'

Of course, there are degrees of conformance to this script. The patients who go furthest—who are most complicit—are treated in a subtly different way by other patients as well as by the staff. In *Stigma*, Goffman pays close attention to these people who become 'mascots' of a sort, calling them 'in-group deviants' (Goffman 1963). Considering that this type of in-group deviant exists in every classroom at every school, a 'shorty' or a 'fatty' for example, understanding the process by which these figures are created would seem an urgent issue in today's bullying problem. In some respects, the current pet boom (apparently even bigger in the US than in Japan) may be understood as an overt manifestation of the middle-class family's urge to create in-group deviants—it is a group mechanism.

To be fair, we should acknowledge strong counterarguments from the proponents of specialized medical knowledge against these arguments from clinical knowledge. Ōkuma's conclusions, for example, were harshly criticized by specialist doctors who had visited the same Nordic countries. They claimed that those countries do not provide medical services as actively as Japan does to the aged on the brink of becoming bedridden. The extreme argument was that most elderly people die in those countries before they become bedridden. Much of the criticism against Ōkuma from specialist doctors was along the line of 'that's the only reason, no more and no less'. Non-doctors like Ōkuma and us cannot argue about actions of a medical nature. So, to quickly return to our main topic: the scenario of a drama concealed in the hierarchical structure will manifest itself if one observes the 'obvious' interactive situation in detail.

In this context, it is worth turning to Michel Foucault again, for he placed the 'watch-watched' relationship at the center of his analysis of power although, unlike Goffman, he never outlined a dramaturgical perspective (Foucault 1975). 'Spectacular' power which was once displayed for the purpose of demonstrating its strength has now hidden itself inside institutions and structures. Foucault invokes Bentham's Panopticon as the epitome of this new power. The Panopticon was designed such that the observers (guards) were concealed from the observed subjects (prisoners) but the subjects could not conceal themselves from the observers. Foucault's point was that under these circumstances the subjects would learn to observe—and discipline—themselves. In such a place, a search light will unilaterally shine on us (albeit softly) for the purpose of corporeal discipline, just like the stethoscope placed on our bodies. Children, sick people and mentally ill people are examined more closely than adults, healthy people and mentally stable people and subjects are sharply 'individualized' according to minute differences. Foucault argues that 'The individual is no doubt the fictitious atom of an "ideological" representation of society; but he is also a reality fabricated by this specific technology of power that I have called "discipline".' That is, the individual in any 'idealistic theory' is a role, a framework, but in reality one has to become a complex character.

By focusing on visible, superficial facts rather than invisible actions Foucault exposed the disciplinary power concealed in the hierarchical structure. By adopting a methodology that, like Goffman and the stethoscope, moves simultaneously back-and-forth between the observer and observed, while focusing on action and expression rather than function, Foucault revealed that 'power aiming for corporeal discipline', although appearing to be a superficial form of control, can actually act on the depths of people's unconscious better than a juridical form of control. It is even capable of controlling their emotions.

Miyahara's contrast between impersonal and personal languages discussed earlier was formulated with due consideration for Foucault's theory on power. While impersonal language is only understood intellectually, personal language can pick up emotions from the unconscious depths. However, Foucault did not stop at the different languages in use, tracing the modern mind:body split back to the duality of power in general.

> The real, corporal disciplines constituted the foundation of the formal, juridical liberties. The contract may have been regarded as the ideal foundation of law and political power; panopticism constituted the technique, universally widespread, of coercion. It continued to work in depth on the juridical structures of society, in order to make the effective mechanisms of power function in opposition to the formal framework that it had acquired. The 'Enlightenment', which discovered the liberties, also invented the disciplines. (Foucault 1975)

In this passage Foucault contrasts the 'real' and 'effective' disciplinary control extending to the emotions to the 'formal' and 'ideal' effects of juridical control that is no more than intellectually perceptible, and is thus superficial control. Connecting this directly to our discussion, Foucault is warning that action-centric (and functionalist) theories have ignored expression (corporeality), which may help to understand 'formal' and 'ideal' contractual relationships, but the real control system that we're actually experiencing will be left unexamined and thus continue to work behind-the-scenes. The classificatory techniques of modern society are so intricate that they even control emotions at unconscious depths, thus controlling expressions rather than actions. The orthodox social sciences, represented by sociology and economics, are unfortunately not keeping up with the evolution of this 'effective' control system. The inability of the social sciences to explain the control system which is actually in operation lies in its desire to justify the social order, especially its legitimacy, on the basis of 'action' functions (i.e., contribution-reward relationship). (I will return to this in more detail in a later section.)

This 'action' centrism is a common bias that has long been entrenched in Western ideas in general, not only sociology and economics. Yamazaki noted that, at the extremes this manifests as a conviction that actions are real and expressions fake, and hence the spirit of dramatic performance itself had long been discounted in Western modernist thought (Yamazaki 1975). Paralleling Goffman's observations about the dilemma of action versus expression, Yamazaki noted that 'Paying attention to how we eat food (expression), rather than just eating food (action), is a human trait that other animals do not have. It is no exaggeration to say that this is the precise distinction that underlies all human cultures.' This is perhaps why there is no sense or culture of 'shame'—a concern with expression—comparable to the sense or culture of 'guilt' in Western thought.

Whether approached through Sigmund Freud's psychoanalysis or Ruth Benedict's comparative study of cultures, the sense of guilt is considered to be mature and sophisticated while a sense of shame is considered to be immature and unsophisticated. Similar to functionalistic theories of action confusing the movements of 'invisible men' for real actions, these analysts appear to have mistaken a sense of 'guilt' generated at a shallow (ideal) level of consciousness by certain ideologies for something much deeper, and therefore failed to see the sense of 'shame' that actually wells up at the corporeal emotional level and manifests as expression rather than action.

To skip from this theoretical shortcoming to a clinical sociological conclusion, actors are gripped by a sense of guilt only when they fail to perform their roles (action) but *secretly* feel ashamed when they have behaved in a way that is inappropriate for themselves (character) in *all* of their more common situations. And when shame arises, it is unmistakably an emotion that wells up from the deepest parts of one's being. Because it is a universal emotional mode of human-beings irrespective of ideologies, 'it is no exaggeration to say this is the very attitude that underlies all human cultures' as Yamazaki argued.

It is perhaps no accident, then, that the subjects of concern to Foucault and Goffman were those who appeared to be more sensitive to a sense of shame than to a sense of guilt. These are the (post-modern) inhabitants of the Secular City, supposedly liberated from particular religion (ideology). But they haven't necessarily managed to become independent-minded individuals. There are obvious parallels between Foucault's warning of 'descending individualization', and Goffman's discovery of a small space to escape to in the 'under life' of the backstage—and the corresponding realization that he could only manage to catch a glimpse of independent individuals in their acting skill as expressed through the role distance of the front stage. But this incapacity to capture more than a glance at the 'independent individual' suggests that perhaps it is merely one of the roles (it is really a character mistaken as a role…) created by various theories of action-ism—from Christianity to modernist philosophy, *in toto*. From this perspective it appears that both Foucault and Goffman were looking at the projected illusion of the 'independent individual' against the reality of the life-world in the right way.

Semiotics of behaviors

From one perspective, the theory I have been outlining here may appear to be merely a variant of alienation theory. From the dominant Western perspective—where, for example, only a reality framed by science (a role, for example) is considered to be 'real' while that skillfully created by art (a character, for example) is necessarily 'fake', or a form of alienation—my argument certainly appears to be following in the footsteps of conventional sociology (ideology). However, once the bias against expressive feelings (shame, for example) is overcome, it becomes clear that the 'independent individual' and its 'identity' are usually not "scientifically" 'real' in themselves, but are merely characters performed on a stage. This realization is almost synonymous with understanding the accidentalness of happiness.

In other words, one of the conditions for happiness is freedom from 'action' or 'function' (reality)-centric ideology. Scientifically framed reality is the very contrivance which leads us to believe that the scenes of our lives are unavoidably scenes of alienation. Although acting on stage often gives rise to a sense of shame, Yamazaki observes that people have never given up the joy of dramatized acting throughout the ages. Someone who 'feigns bizarre symptoms' for a student nurse, is surely somewhat overacting. However, he is playing the patient in an asylum because he finds some kind of joy in it. Of course, I am not trying to criticize your 'normal' senses (ideology, rather) which regard this as an unfortunate joy... One thing which is certain, based on Goffman's awareness of the problem, is that the asylum staff shared the 'normal' ideology with everyone else.

To make this clear we need a more vigorous examination of what acting means in our theory. It is useful to begin with an examination of general behaviors modeled on semiotics. Contemporary mass consumption has been described as 'semiotic consumption'. There is a sense in which this trend represents a blackout on the stage, so to speak, which sets the scene for modern actors. This 'blackout' is evidenced by the changing usage of the word 'produce', which once meant to make 'things' but now often means to create 'characters'.

This reinterpretation has ramifications for not only our understanding of contemporary society but for the longer view of human history as well. For example, the origins of the customs of clothing was previously naively explained in terms of the need to adapt to temperature changes—a classic example of functionalist reasoning. If you start from the end result and follow its development backwards through history, it certainly appears as if the need for clothing came first and its supply was an outcome of civilization. However, from the perspective of semiotics, that explanation of 'social history' has gotten its facts upside down. The earliest production of clothing was ignited by a desire for creative expression—to display one's status, skill or similar. Once the practice habitualized or instituted, the human animal gradually lost its corporeal capacity to cope with its climatic conditions and became the people of today who could not live without clothing. In short, the supply of clothing came first, and the demand-cum-need for clothing was merely a product of a *subsequent* course of events.

Nevertheless, the wrong-headed delusional view about demand and supply is more pervasive—grounded in the dominant action-centric (functionalist) ideology. The gravity of this situation must be explained from a broader perspective. I will return to this later. For the moment, I would like to outline the perspective that emerges if we regard behavior as semiosis. Please bear with me as this is rudimentary semiotics.

Let's say we have two sentences here. One says, 'The apple is red' and the other says, 'Apple has five letters'. The same letter sign 'apple' means a fruit in the first sentence but not in the second. According to linguistics (pragmatics in particular), 'apple' is used transparently in the former but is a reflexive or a 'mention' in the latter. In fact, not only letter arrangements but also phonetic or any other sign has these two parts inextricably linked—one used transparently at the object level and the other (physical/corporeal level) reflects the sign itself at the meta-level.

Yet, if one wants to secure unambiguous meaning (at the object level), the corporeality hiding at the meta-level is a hindrance. It is therefore in many respects preferable for the sign to stay as transparent as possible, or remain in hiding. There is little doubt that increasing the purity of a sign means diluting its corporeality for this purpose. We can see this process of 'transparentizing' clearly in the history of money. According to cultural anthropologists, many ages ago hominids expanded their area of interactions by using their 'females' as exchange goods. In a sense, the establishment of exogamy by imposing a taboo on the 'internal consumption of kinswomen' was the first step in the evolution of a flock into 'society'. But the 'female' was a rather ambiguous medium of exchange. They signified many meanings because their own corporeality (literally) could not be occluded or covered over.

Gradually, however, other goods began to be used as media for exchange. From shells and beads, to gold, numbers printed on pieces of paper, and eventually ones and zeros in virtual space, money gradually shed the corporeality of its signs. Yet, numerous studies have indicated that young children from poor families tend to prefer the physically larger low denomination coins to the physically smaller larger denomination coins. Similarly, as signs become increasingly transparent, even adults continue to be bedazzled by their physicality (manifesting as 'expression', of course). For the Japanese people, for example, who have command of multiple sets of hieroglyphic symbols, including *kanji* characters, appreciation of the beauty of the symbols themselves, independently of their linguistic meanings, is enshrined in the culture in numerous ways. Likewise, certain phonetic signs can be enchanting in their sounds alone. This may suggest that the 'visible' physical part on the surface has more appeal at the deep (unconscious) emotional level.

Interestingly, *hiragana* and *katakana*, both of which are reportedly simplifications of *kanji*, had distinctly different uses. The former was used for soft evocative writing as in songs and the latter for rigid or authoritative writing such as religious teachings. In pre-modern days, however, students were not taught to read this type of text quietly, alone, but rather to appreciate the 'pre-meaning' of their sounds (at an emotional level) by reading them aloud with others. It is no exaggeration to say that one effect of 'action' (or 'function')-centric modernism lies in the loss of the enjoyment associated with enacting such rituals.

But quite independently of modernism, signs tend to evolve in such a way that the transparent part is gradually separated from the physical. This also applies to the history of languages in general. In the days when there was only phonetic language, 'big' was probably signaled by a louder voice or a larger gesture than 'small', but with the introduction of numerals and the standardization of written texts, larger numbers mean 'big' no matter how small they are written. The ever widening use of computerized word processors and the corresponding decline in handwriting may also be leading to a further shedding of corporeality. This serves to isolate the emotional level 'pre-meaning', enabling the equivalence of meaning to be secured more reliably. But there cannot be a totally transparent sign. No matter how close it gets to transparency, it cannot totally occlude or disguise its physicality (expression), whether it is a sound wave, an ink blot or an electrical stimulation. The 'density of signs' cannot be wiped out—and is perhaps the very thing that guarantees that the potential for meaning in our world remains rich at the emotional level. Contrast this to the emptiness of 'speed reading' techniques which aim only to extract the content.

This becomes clearer if we compare a word-processed letter with a handwritten one. To convey meaning transparently, a word-processed letter is certainly better than a more-or-less illegible handwritten letter. The more independent (liberated) from corporeality the medium, the more conducive to the creation of unambiguous meaning. Yet many continue to cherish handwritten letters, precisely because they communicate such things (at the meta-level) as genuineness or sincerity of the conveyed message through the physicality of the signs. It also has a better capacity to convey a double meaning—not semantically but pragmatically—where the content of the message (action) presented as sincere *feels* insincere at the meta-level (expression, for example). This has been pointed out by Gregory

Bateson in the Double Bind theory, as well as others. I would like to illustrate it through a personal experience in which I was able to successfully exploit this subtlety of human psychology.

My students still have to handwrite most of their examination papers. Like most teachers, I suppose, I am tired of trying to read their bad writing. But I have noticed a curious tendency: that part of the answer with which the student is confident is written very clearly while the part s/he is not confident about is written more faintly. Because the latter part typically determines whether the paper passes or fails, I am in the habit of using a magnifying glass to assist my aged eyes to read it. One day I casually remarked to a class that I would know whether the answer was correct without reading, based on whether it was written clearly and legibly or not. That group of students wrote clearly and legibly even when the answer was total nonsense (and I chuckled to myself, 'I fooled you!').

Joking aside, it is perhaps safe to say that signs tend to evolve towards transparency, and the more transparently they convey the message, the less ambiguous is the meaning-world they create. At the same time, this meaning-world invariably tends towards logical consistency. It is difficult to maintain two logically inconsistent cognitive elements within the same meaning frame. This was of course Leon Festinger's point in *A Theory of Cognitive Dissonance* (1957) and *When Prophecy Fails* (1956), where he and his colleagues demonstrated how efforts to avoid 'cognitive dissonance' can push some people to extreme fanaticism. In less extreme cases, we regularly encounter people who stubbornly reject facts or data that do not fit into their pre-formed (prejudiced) views.

In short, more transparent signs are useful for reducing ambiguity in the meaning-world, but the meaning-world thus created is more likely to become 'false/untrue' (*kokefujitsu* in Japanese Buddhism)—i.e., further removed from the reality of multiple meaning layers. Of course, we cannot reduce all of our behaviors to signs. But at the same time, behavior always has a signitive or communicative dimension (as in 'body language') since it is always conduct accompanied by some sort of expression. And because emotions at unconscious depths are expressed physically more so than verbally, it is necessary to pay close attention to semiosis on the surface. Yet, the rich signification of such (particularly human) behaviors is almost completely ignored by the 'invisible man models' of 'action'-centric or functionalist theory. The latter approach literally strips the physicality from behavior, abstracting it such that only its transparent (instrumental) dimensions are apparent. With this approach, it has created unambiguous meaning-worlds that are logically consistent, but void of real feelings.

Of course, criticisms of this model of explanation are as old and as varied as sociology itself. The 'theory of play' for example, points out that such an approach only recognizes the instrumentality of behavior and ignores or dismisses its expressive or autotelic aspects. I did not introduce the semiotic model simply to explain something of this sort. Rather, my purpose was to raise the question of whether the 'unambiguous meaning-world' thus created might attribute some kind of necessity to the interrelationships among various factors which are only arbitrary or accidental by nature. In other words, I aim for an answer to a broader question—which includes the prevalence of the 'wrong-headed delusional view' about demand and supply discussed earlier.

Firstly, the extremely arbitrary nature of the link between a sign and what it signifies is at the very basis of semiotics and probably requires no further explanation. However, those of us who live in the world of Chinese-derived languages tend to be somewhat shocked at comments such as 'play with the arbitrary' because our understanding of the history of *kanji* formation is firmly grounded in 'reflection theory'. Therefore, it is perhaps better to discuss this at the pre-writing, phonetic level. To take but one simple example, what we call '*inu*' in Japan is called 'dog' in the English-speaking world. The total absence of (phonetic level) commonality here is more than sufficient to establish how arbitrary the link is between an animal and its name.

If you were asked why the animal was called '*inu*', you would probably have no better answer than to say that this is what the animal is called by everyone in the Japanese-speaking world. And in fact, there is no other basis for everyone to use this name than the fact that everyone uses this name. I would like to call this tautological relationship—this obvious arbitrariness of semiosis—'ungrounded systematicity'. That is: 'no ground exists for its currency other than the fact that it is actually in currency'. 'Semiotic consumption' is a typical example here, but many other things and events are based in this 'ungrounded systematicity' than is allowed for by the dominant explanatory paradigms of our information society.[14]

What economists call 'network externalities' provide a useful illustration of 'ungrounded systematicity'. Toshihiko Hayashi (Hayashi and Ōmura 1994) provides a simple definition of 'network externalities': 'Network consumption is the type of consumption for which the utility value of a product or service is determined based on how much the product or service is being used'. 'For example, the value of a telephone for many people is crucially dependent on how many people you can talk with on the phone if you join the network—much more than on the telephone functions or the line quality'. This mechanism through which 'the more subscribers it has, the higher its value becomes for individuals' is among what economists call 'network externalities'.

In other words, no matter how good its quality, a telephone not connected to anywhere is useless except as a child's toy. From this perspective, then, consider the wide range of phenomena in modern societies for which the value is determined by the number of people belonging to *the relevant category* rather than by the quality of the object itself. While popular fads may provide the most obvious cases of such 'semiotic consumption', a more dramatic form can be seen in the so-called 'standards wars' between manufacturing corporations. Again, let me cite Hayashi's discussion of the battle that erupted at the end of 1970s between Panasonic (VHS format) and Sony (Beta format) to establish the standards for video recording and playing.

> A standard or a norm means a network for both manufacturers and consumers. If there are two standards, X and Y, a manufacturer must produce a machine which meets one of them. The company knows its costs of production under each standard. But what is more important than the relative production cost for the company is to determine which standard is (will be) the mainstream in the marketplace. That is, which standard is in greater demand and will therefore be used to manufacture more machines. That one standard is attracting more users than the other means that more units are being manufactured according to it. Manufacturers would naturally follow the standard supported by the greater demand (number of buyers/users) unless the cost difference is too great. [...] Since the video war of the late seventies, we have seen various struggles over standards—in Japan, over language processors for the personal computer, and internationally over high-resolution television broadcasting and each new generation of telecommunications, etc.—all of which are typical examples of network competition.

It may be quite obvious, but is nevertheless worth stating that one of the problems with this type of network competition is that the (supposed) law of the survival of the fittest is not necessarily upheld—in fact, it is frequently invalidated. In the VHS-Beta war, for example, the fact that professionals continued to use the Beta format long after VHS had 'won the war' suggests the technical superiority of the former. Which brings us back to the inu/dog example: the only convincing answer any member of the general public can give when asked why they consumed the VHS format more than the alternative is that it is more widely circulated. In short, there is no grounds for the VHS format to dominate the marketplace (circulation system) outside of the system itself (i.e., its dominance is not attributable to any "objective" properties, such as machine performance, for example). This is what I have called 'ungrounded systematicity'.

In the 1960s, the Esperantists advanced a seemingly sound argument that the artificially created language, Esperanto, should be used for all international exchange so that no party would derive either advantage or disadvantage from the use of an existing language. But since then, the already dominant English language has become ever more pervasive, passing the point of no return not only in academic communities but far more widely. And this can not be attributed to English being superior to other languages. So, again, besides the fact that English is widely used throughout the world, there are no grounds for this widespread use of English. Like Sony in the video war, the Esperantists were unsuccessful in the international language struggle. Both were unable to expand their networks adequately—perhaps because they were overly confident about the superior performance of their product. In the next section, I would like to examine this 'ungrounded systematicity' from a wider angle with the fundamental suspicion that it may actually point to the essence of various social phenomena.

The world of 'ungrounded systematicity'

The cliché, 'might is right'—while perhaps highly problematic as an ethical principle—has strong explanatory resonance in relation to the network competition and externalities discussed in the previous section. In particular, it explains two situations very well: there is often no reason to explain a victory other than the fact that the victor won; but victors (and others) nevertheless tend to want to think that there was some objective ground for their victory. In particular, the subtleties of that uniquely human characteristics of 'wanting to think' (according to certain logics or standards) is a crucially important point. I would like to take an indirect approach to this subject, beginning with a brief discussion of a phenomenon called 'branding shrines for New Year's visits'.

The rankings of the ten most popular temples and shrines in Japan have not changed significantly for a very long time according to the numbers of New Year's visitors each year. Why do so many people visit these particular temples and shrines? Do they fulfill the worshippers' wishes a lot better than other temples and shrines do? Imagine commemorating New Year's at a temple that nobody else goes to. In fact, the more people who attend the same temple, the more they make each other think that the temple must be effective in fulfilling their wishes. Other than the fact that these temples and shrines attract larger crowds, there is virtually no reason for them to attract so many people. Another characteristic of what Hayashi identifies as network consumption is useful here. He notes: 'Even if there are competitive conditions between the networks, the switch does not occur quickly because of the excessive inertial force working from the consumer side'. This at least gives a partial explanation for the long-term stability of the top ten rankings.

Recreational religious practices such as the New Year's visit are not a serious sociological problem. The fraudulent sales of spiritual goods and the rise of religious cults are a more serious problem. During the so-called new religion boom of the post-war reconstruction period, the growth in religious cults could be largely explained in terms of deprivation—poverty, sickness and conflict (inevitability of unhappiness)—but this is no longer the case. Interviewing people who attended a mass for aborted fetuses and those who had joined 'new' new religious sects (as defined by Shigeru Nishiyama), it soon became apparent that the number of people who appeared to have reflected deeply and seriously prior to attending/joining was smaller than one might have expected. The majority seemed to offer rather trivial reasons for their participation, such as 'my friend invited me to join…' or 'someone recommended it to me very enthusiastically'.

This example helps to tease out a hidden trick of conventional thinking which is related to the upside down view of demand and supply (discussed in the previous section). If we take a mass for aborted fetuses as an example, we see that initially, people went casually, thinking it would be better to go than not. But as they talked to other people there, they gradually became more anxious, and continued attending the mass regularly in a considerable number of cases. This indicates that the real need for attending the mass might have arisen for the first time after their casual attendance. In other words, our belief that the motive, or the need, for joining a religious organization is acquired outside of that religion (external to the religious meaning system) prior to joining it may be false. The reality may be different. I suspect that it is quite common for people to "learn" the motives for their initial interest in such organizations only after they have joined.

Of course, some reasons are not totally unfounded and thus too hard to swallow. They must at least give a suitable shape to a vague anxiety—a level of anxiety that everyone would have. Yet this does not change the fact that the need for a religious organization is actually created and supplied by the organization itself. These subtleties become more apparent if we focus on the fraudulent sales of spiritual goods. Interpreting the responses of my interviewees who had 'fallen' into the cult's trap, they did not typically purchase such goods because of any pre-existing need, but rather bought them 'casually' because the price was affordable, which in turn made them feel that they 'needed more', thus creating the need for more expensive goods of a similar nature. Just like the first "casual" attendance at the mass for aborted fetuses, the initial 'small' purchase conceals a surplus value in the form of stimulating an anxiety that creates a need or motive to purchase more expensive goods.

I am sure that there are many who think nothing of such spiritual goods, yet still visit temples and shrines to pray for protection against evil. And if asked why they do it, they cannot provide a satisfactory answer—because there is no reason for them to do it other than the fact that everyone does it in perilous times. The need or motive is no more than the common anxiety about protection from evil. It is really a tautological world which has no justification outside of itself. Ivan Illich detected a similar dimension in the medical and education systems, observing that the medical and education systems proliferate because they have created a need (or hunger) for themselves such that people cannot do without them (Illich 1976, 1971).

> School makes alienation preparatory to life, thus depriving education of reality and work of creativity. School prepares for the alienating institutionalization of life by teaching the need to be taught.

Undoubtedly, his is a one-sided view. Nevertheless, he accurately depicts the type of illusion we are susceptible to. We falsely come to believe that the reason why we cannot get out of it is the same reason why we needed it in the first place, as in the religiously-based examples discussed above. If 'hospital dependency' is real, then 'school dependency' and 'religious dependency' are also possible manifestations of the same condition. Summing up what we have seen so far, I buy product A only 'Because everyone else is buying it'. The demand for product A grows under this mechanism, for that reason alone. As Illich found in the automotive industry, it is via this mechanism that supply simultaneously creates demand. Attending the mass for aborted fetuses and purchasing spiritual goods are merely two examples of this phenomenon.

Notice the underlying (vicious) cycle, or 'principle of accumulation' between the various factors here. The structure of this vicious cycle was explained as the principle of accumulation by Gunnar Myrdal in *An American Dilemma* and as a 'self-fulfilling prophecy' by Robert K Merton. In Merton's analysis, the presumption by white union members that 'black workers are strikebreakers' lead to discrimination in the form of excluding black workers from the union, leaving the (unemployed) black workers with no motivation to not take positions as 'scab' labor during a strike, which consequently fulfills the 'strikebreaking' prophecy. Similarly, a prophecy that product B will not sell as much as product A may drive more people toward product A—the value of product B thereby decreases further and the prophecy is fulfilled. Moreover, with hindsight it appears that the prophecy had legitimate grounds to start with. This is clearly the same as the mechanism at work in the competitions between networks.

The same mechanism is described in labeling theory, which highlights how a presupposition (prophecy) that was initially groundless becomes 'self-fulfilling' and then appears to have had legitimate grounds (justified prejudice) from the beginning. For example, a white boy A and a black boy B have both been caught shoplifting (both for the first time) in a convenience store. The security guards who catch them release boy A after cautioning him, thinking 'he should be OK'. But, assuming that boy B is 'bad', they hand him over to the police... Several years later, boy A becomes an ordinary college student as predicted by the security guards, whereas boy B has become a full-fledged rogue. Again, the security guards' judgment looks as if it was correct from the beginning.

This is not criticism of racial prejudice in the US in particular. The current public worries about the future of juveniles in Japan are perhaps likewise self-fulfilling to the extent that the data showing 'a trend towards a lower age of juvenile delinquency' is actually caused by the 'early detection, early correction' policy of the police and their meticulous 'zero-tolerance' for even trivial misconduct.[15] Strangely, people tend to feel relieved when this type of data is announced and find their worry has turned out to be justified. Festinger called this the 'rumors to justify anxiety' (1957). It should be clear that the mass for aborted fetuses and the sale of spiritual goods are various forms of a rumor to justify people's anxiety (although not reducible to that).

Let us now look more closely at the notion of 'self-fulfilling prophecy'. The issue here is that an initial, seemingly trivial and perhaps accidental 'trigger' can lead to unexpectedly serious and irreversible outcomes. Take the earlier example of the boy who was caught shoplifting. Boy B eventually became a rogue and was incarcerated in prison on serious charges, but the process may well have been triggered by the rather trivial and seemingly random incident of being caught by those security guards. However, whether such a 'trigger' will lead to such serious results cannot be fully explained by the mechanism of self-fulfilling prophecy alone. On this point, the idea of Second Cybernetics, which was proposed somewhat flamboyantly by Magoroh Maruyama, has some merit and deserves attention (Maruyama 1963).

While the cybernetics systems first described by Wiener aim to prevent deviation and maintain system equilibrium by means such as thermostat and body temperature control (deviation counteracting system), that is, a negative feedback loop incorporating various factors, Maruyama's Second Cybernetics is a systems theory that refers to a positive feedback loop incorporating various factors, which is a deviation-amplifying mutual causal process. To illustrate, Maruyama explains how the precise spot in a once homogeneous plain on which a city begins to develop is initially defined by an accidental event such as an enthusiastic farmer happening to turn the soil for the first time on that particular spot. Although a valid example of the randomness of morphogenesis in general, this is a rather abstract discussion. I suggest that we ought to focus on something closer to everyday life, such as those points in the biographies of successful people in which they reminisce about those 'chance encounters' that 'started it all', for example. In this case, the approach is to look at someone's career pattern through a narrative life history or story (Kobayashi 2000).

Reflecting upon my own extremely ordinary life (as theater), I recall quite a few chance encounters that in one way or another triggered a change in the set (stage), and thus shaped the subsequent 'act'. Of course, like everyone else, the opening scene of the first act (birth) was dependent upon an encounter with my parents that was entirely accidental (no logical reason can be given for it). I would not be here were it not for this accidental encounter. Nevertheless, sociological theories (especially social stratification and mobility theory) argue that this first accidental encounter has little to do with defining the life course that follows in modern societies.

Some more recent sociological theories have begun to argue that weak ties, such as 'an acquaintance's acquaintance', are more likely than strong ties such as blood and work relations to provide the chance encounter that may change one's career path (Ueno and Dentsū Network Kenkyūkai 1988). Furthermore, career paths do not always tend upwards. In fact, there is solid evidence that an increasing number of people are intentionally seeking gentle downward mobility—or 'downshifting'. For those whose downward mobility is not intentional—those undergoing cancer treatment, for example—the self-help groups that they form may be more or less effective ways of alleviating the anxiety of downward mobility (Hase 2000; Ishikawa 1995). The more accidental and transitory an encounter is, the more precious the bond of fate is for the people involved. Unfortunately, all of these subtleties of human behavior are disregarded by functionalist role theory.

Yet 'happiness' cannot be adequately understood without examining these subtleties. Thus it is no surprise that sociology as science can endlessly discuss the inevitability of unhappiness but cannot shed much light on the accidentalness of happiness. To see this problematic more clearly, I believe, we need to experience a paradigm shift—particularly in relation to certain 'domain assumptions' in the dominant theories of our 'competitive society'. A discussion of these dimensions will perhaps clarify why I approached a discussion of behaviors through semiotics.

Ideology dressed as scientific theory

To my eyes, there are two major defects apparent with orthodox economics and sociology. Both are domain assumptions that are blindly postulated by a conventional orthodoxy. Conscious intellectual thinking alone will never identify their problems as long as it remains trapped within these domains (i.e., without realizing that it is just one way of framing realities). From outside of the domains, however, they are readily apparent.

First, assuming that the secular society we live in is a 'competitive society', a problem arises from the form of the competition itself—it is a knockout tournament. In this form of competition, everyone drops out sooner or later: we all die without exception; there are no winners (Takeuchi 1987). But there is no scientific discourse that squarely addresses this glaringly obvious fact of the life-world. In contrast, a casual survey of popular novels and films in recent years reveals that most of them deal with this inescapable reality in one way or another. Clearly, if the world created by 'theoretical language' is so far removed from the life-world created by 'participant language', it follows that a reality constructed as scientific theory is more fictitious than fiction. I present this merely as another piece of evidence that genuine 'happiness' has never been seriously thought about by the social sciences.

Here it is worth returning to Erving Goffman once again. In the early 1950s, Goffman wrote 'On Cooling the Mark Out', an interesting essay about how losers come to accept their own failures (Goffman 1952). He observes that if a victim of a confidence game is left alone, he may complain to the police or discuss his bad experience in public, which may be unfavorable for the future business of the conmen. So one of the conmen stays with the victim, consoling him with platitudes such as 'it was bad luck' or 'you'll lose face if you talk about it' in an effort to restrain his anger and let the matter drop. Goffman reports that the pacifier role was called a 'cooler' in the con industry. He thus named this process of consoling the mark 'cooling out' and explained that the process was typically successful because the victim was deeply hurt—not so much by the financial loss but by the fact that he had been deceived and was afraid of further humiliating himself.

From our perspective, Goffman's observation was progressive in two ways: his attention to repercussions for losers and dropouts; and his focus on intangible aspects of character, such as honor and saving-face rather than action (role) alone. He extends the first point to cover all areas of social life, observing how the cooling mechanism operates more generally at a macro-cultural level. To this end, he notes, for example, that the phrase 'participation is what counts' encourages failures to accept their lot. This observation offers support to my claim that religion is a 'mechanism of calming culture' and informs my further argument that a 'competitive society' needs both calming culture and agitating culture (Ōmura 1996b).

His corresponding focus on character should not require any further explanation. It will suffice to mention only one issue that intersects with the previous point. That is, although people tend to consider financial loss from bankruptcy or redundancy to be the central (or most common) motive for the recent increase in the suicide rate among middle-aged men, we must question whether it is that simple. For example, research indicates that those who lose their jobs find telling their family about the job loss to be the hardest part, suggesting that it is a sense of humiliation rather than the financial loss itself that most damages these (hardworking) middle-aged men. Similarly, the notes left by children who have committed suicide without confiding to their parents about the terrible bullying that they had suffered might suggest that a sense of humiliation attached to being '*weak enough to be bullied*' may be the real reason that drove them to suicide. In any case, we must remember that a loss of honor or face—a slight on one's 'character'—may be more capable of deeply hurting people than a failure to perform the functions of one's 'role'.[16]

But this is not typically recognized by the orthodox social sciences, blinded as they are by the previously mentioned domain assumptions, which fail to take into account the downward mobility (both social and physical) that invariably occupies at least half of our life course (unless we die "prematurely" of course). These disciplines can therefore offer no instruction on how to 'get off' a life—which is supposedly an urgent issue for all members of super-aging societies. Among the types of adaptation to anomic strain proposed by Robert K Merton, for example, 'ritualism' and 'retreatism' were hardly looked at by American sociologists. Insights such as Kazuko Tsurumi's, who interpreted these as two types of 'self-respecting defeat', are very rare exceptions (Tsurumi 1977).[17]

The second defect of the domain assumptions is a problem deeply connected to my suspicion that the causality of the demand-supply process is construed in reverse order. The 'contribution-reward' dimension of role performance is well-established in sociological theories and need not be outlined here. And it should be clear from what I have argued so far that this 'defect' results from an over-emphasis on the instrumentality of behavior at the expense of its expression. It follows from such a schema that any variation in the distribution of rewards in a competitive society is determined by an individual's contribution to the system functions. A typical example of such an approach can be seen in the Functional Theory of Stratification proposed by Davis and Moore, which states:

> If the rights and perquisites of different positions in a society must be unequal, then the society must be stratified, because that is what stratifications means. Social inequality is thus an unconsciously

> evolved device by which societies insure that the most important positions are conscientiously filled by the most qualified persons. Hence every society, no matter how simple or complex, must differentiate persons both in terms of prestige and esteem and must therefore possess a certain amount of institutionalized inequality. (Davis and Moore 1945)

Like Parsons' systems theory, the Functional Theory of Stratification has long been criticized for its conservatism that merely justifies the existing social order. However, most of this criticism was raised from the perspective of 'social change theory', with its illusion of fundamental social change, which happened to be highly popular at the time—that is, it was merely the discourse presented by certain 'academic characters'—a perspective that rapidly vanished into thin air as reformist forces declined worldwide. Yet, the premises implicitly assumed by economics and sociology today continue to advocate the principles of the Functional Theory of Stratification. In fact, some theories today appear to be even more degenerate for intentionally trying to ignore both the logical assumptions and the logical conclusions of the Functional Theory of Stratification.

The previously mentioned anecdotes found in biographies often contain certain elements that aim to explain various interludes between the acts on stage. These elements are of a completely different nature than the 'contribution-reward' relationship; they include chance meetings, of course, but also things such as 'luck' and personal 'connections'. Mita identified similar elements in 'popular literature', referring to them as the 'artifice' that distorts people's perceptions of reality. I believe, however, that these narrative elements are widely accepted in ordinary society because they closely reflect the actual feelings of ordinary people going about their everyday lives. Indeed, it is the effort- or merit-based ideology embedded in the 'contribution-reward' relationship that should be considered to be the 'artifice' that distorts reality and brings unhappiness to people. For example, someone who considers themselves to be 'allergic to mathematics' may attribute this 'allergy' to having done poorly in math at high school, when the true reason is that one particularly nasty mathematics teacher at high school uttered an unfounded prophecy: 'You have no aptitude for mathematics and science'. If this person were to sit down and seriously review a sociometrics textbook, he would probably discover that he could easily handle this level of mathematics. Such a 'discovery' is perhaps too late for someone like me, though, who is well past the halfway point in life—so it would be best for me to begin exploring the possibility of playing the role of a 'dandy' after my retirement. In other words, sad and feeble personalities like 'him' and 'me' were triggered by some causeless, accidental events—although the unfolding of the process seems to be somewhat inevitable once the subject is trapped in a vicious cycle. The very thing that stops one from escaping the cycle is belief in the artifice of merit- and effort-based ideologies.

This becomes clearer if we look at an experiment that skillfully exposed this artifice. This research was reported by Robert Rosenthal and Lenore Jacobson in *Pygmalion in the Classroom: Teacher Expectation and Pupils' Intellectual Development* (1968). The title invokes George Bernard Shaw's famous play *Pygmalion*—perhaps better known as *My Fair Lady*, from the musical based on the play. They quote the play:

> You see, really and truly, apart from the things anyone can pick up (the dressing and the proper way of speaking, and so on), the difference between a lady and a flower girl is not how she behaves, but how she's treated. I shall always be a flower girl to Professor Higgins, because he always treats me as a flower girl, and always will; but I know I can be a lady to you, because you always treat me as a lady, and always will.

Rosenthal and Jacobson had previously reported experimental data which indicated that even rats had a tendency to fulfill experimenters' expectations or prophecies. The experimenters were told of studies that had shown that maze-brightness and maze-dullness could be developed in strains of rats by successive inbreeding of the well- and the poorly performing maze-runners. Now they went further, and claimed that previous studies had demonstrated that the bloodline reproduction of 'wise' rats and 'dull' rats over generations can generate their artificial varieties. They presented this (false) explanation to experimental psychology students and then had them repeatedly conduct maze learning and more complex Skinner-box experiments with the rats.

Sixty untrained rats with no individual differences were randomly divided into two groups, labeled 'bright' and 'dull'. Furthermore, over the course of the research, these two groups were totally replaced with new rats (unbeknown to the students) and the experimenters were swapped back-and-forth between working with the 'bright rats' and the 'dull rats'. Nevertheless, the group labeled 'bright' consistently and performed significantly better than the 'dull' group. The post-experiment comments revealed that the experimenters tended to treat the 'bright rats' more favorably and encouragingly and paid more careful attention to them than the 'dull rats'.

The results of this experiment indicated that the rats that were expected to perform well actually performed well and the rats that were not expected to perform well performed as badly as anticipated. Rosenthal and Jacobson deduced from these results that it might be reasonable to expect that a school teacher's optimistic or pessimistic 'definition of a situation' concerning their students' learning potential could affect the students' academic performance. They set-up an experiment in a public elementary school (fictitiously) named Oak School to test the hypothesis that 'in any given classroom, the pupils for whom the teachers have higher expectations of intellectual growth actually experience accelerated intellectual growth'.

It would not be ethical to use the same 'wise' and 'dull' group distinction on humans as they had with the rats. So they devised an IQ test using the same principle. They called it the Harvard Test of Inflected Acquisition (a simple test not overly dependent on verbal skills). They then randomly selected a group of pupils and, supposedly on the basis of this test, labeled them as the 'top 20%'. This groups' performance was monitored and compared with a control group of the remaining 80% of the pupils. Most of the details of this experiment and the findings are beyond the scope of this discussion, but their findings largely confirmed their hypothesis that teachers' expectations could significantly affect pupils' academic performance. I can mention only one point which clearly shows Rosenthal's and Jacobson's observations about the Pygmalion Effect.

The minority Mexican pupils at Oak School who were allocated into the 'high expectation' group showed markedly higher academic growth than other pupils in the same group, and the tendency was more notable among pupils whose appearance was more distinctly Mexican. Teachers were perhaps bedazzled by the prestige of 'Harvard' and surprised by these experts' identification of these students' excellent 'intellectual growth potential'. Then, prompted by a sense of guilt about this evidence of their own prejudice against minority groups, they paid even closer attention to them to draw out any signs of such potential.

As with the university students in the rat experiment, the teachers at Oak School were in fact the subjects of this experiment. Naturally, conducting further tests of a similar nature becomes difficult once the fabrication has come to light (see below). Consequently, there are few available reports of such experiments except for the Crest School (also fictitious) experiment conducted at about the same time and which produced very similar results. In fact, as one would expect, *Pygmalion in the Classroom* attracted a hysterical response.

Such an experiment would never have been allowed in Japan in the first place. Japanese public schools are currently in the process of gradually doing away with IQ tests, for although they are supposed to measure natural talents unrelated to efforts, these claims are increasingly dubious. Although Americans are more tolerant of such measurements, the Pygmalion Effect theory was harshly criticized because it was taken to challenge the orthodoxy of their supposedly meritocratic culture.

Most people perhaps think that in general a person is treated the way that he is treated because of the way that he has acted in the past and is acting in the present. But I have argued that the causal chain goes round and round in circles and that certain intentional and/or accidental occurrences may induce the process in some cases to operate in the reverse direction. That someone is a 'rogue' or a reasonably 'competent person' today is perhaps because he was treated like one for no particular reason in the first place. In more general terms, the 'contribution→reward' causal process proposed by Functional Theory of Stratification and others should be the other way round. People can exercise their abilities appropriately only by being treated appropriately. In other words, the empirical fact must be the 'reward→contribution' causal process.

If so, then, it is clearly a tautological world that we live in. We are again looking at the familiar world we have been discussing, where a person fulfills the role of, say, a corporate manager simply because everyone treats her (or him) as one—there is no other ground whatsoever.

Substitute for a conclusion

This has been a long-winding argument, which may have given an impression that the 'accidentalness of happiness' has still not yet been addressed adequately, while the inevitability of unhappiness has been discussed once again. I have attempted to drop numerous hints and suggestions here and there, and regret that the front stage narrative has concentrated on unhappiness. I must confess that I had a feeling that if I tried to discuss 'happiness' in a positive light I would have to wear my other hat as a clinical Buddhism scholar. At the risk of being audacious, I have accumulated a rich variety of religious experience in the 'clinical field' and feel that I almost already know what the conditions for happiness are.[18] I also feel that such an approach might be inappropriate, considering the nature of this publication. I therefore have tried my best to take a stand at the edge of 'clinical sociology', but a 'thorough bias' might be heard occasionally on the front stage. I beg your pardon for the resultant 'negativity' of my argument with its disapproving comments.

To present my argument in a slightly more positive tone, Figure 8.3 depicts a version of Frame Analysis which might be regarded as the armor beneath the 'crude empiricist' dress that Goffman revealed in his final work (Goffman 1974). It also the *sacré-profane-jeu* (sacred-profane-game) trinomial that is commonly used in the field of cultural sociology (Inoue 1977). After discussing this framing process I will then conclude by summarizing the background of this paper.

1. The first thing to make clear about the *sacré-profane-jeu* division is that each field is firmly anchored to the world of things—what Goffman called 'resource continuity'—but in human experience all three fields are wholly constructed in language. Therefore none of the three fields can go against its 'semiotic fate' and each may take its own course towards 'unambiguousness', typically developing 'ungrounded systematicity'. In simple terms, this

Figure 8.3: Framed realities classified on the basis of different 'meaning' layers

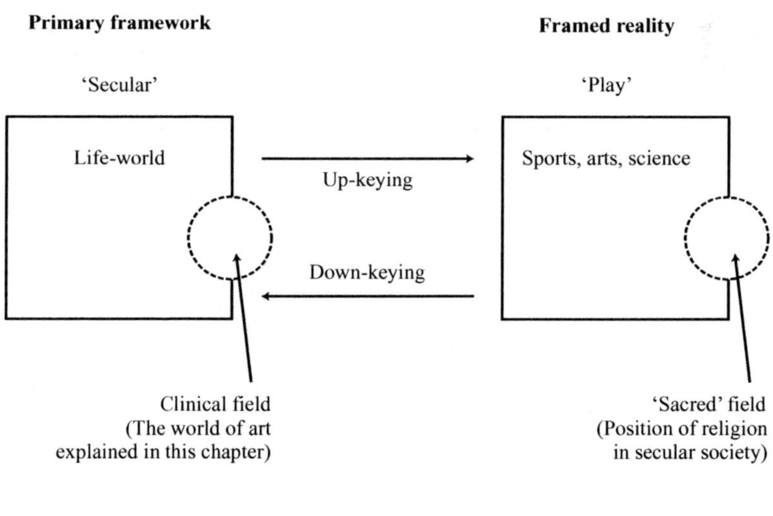

explains why we are such precarious beings; hanging on the webs of meaning that we have woven for ourselves. Many consider this to be the ultimate source of unhappiness, but I contend that it can also be the source of happiness, for it enables free movement between the fields through—as I will explain shortly—'up-keying and down-keying'.

2. Turning now to the two dotted-line circles, note that they both protrude from their respective fields of the 'secular' and 'play', unable to fit in completely, but their contents are entirely different. While the dotted circle named 'clinical field' on the left side of the diagram fits partially within the life-world, its frame is not dependent on mere 'common sense', but requires the art/skill of clinical knowledge as discussed earlier. It thus represents a constructed reality that draws on—or is supported by—'specialized knowledge'.

   In contrast, the corresponding circle on the right represents the position of religion in 'secularized' modern societies. With the exception of the US, the proportion of the population who are religious (who report having religious beliefs) is generally between 25–30% in the developed countries, including Japan. Those who have faith are clearly in the minority. In these same countries (and perhaps many others), the world of sports, which has its origins in the field of 'play', has in many respects become a functional substitute for the 'sacred'—as can be seen in feverish excitement of the soccer World Cup. The position of religion, overhanging the edge of the 'play' field, reflects this situation. But how is it that the sports world can generate higher levels of religious-type frenzy and excitement than the 'sacred' world? I would argue that the sufficient condition for happiness is in place here. For example, a sporting victory is unmistakably transitory. Discursively, many more pages of sports journalism are devoted to the 'nobility of failure' than to the glory of the victorious. From this perspective it is clear, as I have repeatedly argued elsewhere, that sport is a 'calming culture device' which can be a source of 'happiness' for those who inhabit that reality (Ōmura 2004).

3. Two of the fundamental points of frame analysis, as mentioned in (1) above, are that realities are created in languages even in the real life-world, and that these constructions rely on 'ungrounded systematicity' where 'a situation defined by someone as real becomes real as a consequence of being so defined', without other foundation. This occurs when the 'definition of a situation' is

shared by everyone. We can recognize a certain type of activity (define a situation) between two people as a 'fight', for example, because we share the same meaning system.

However, according to Goffman, this shared meaning system is not a singular system but a plural structure with multiple 'meaning layers'. Usually we can immediately distinguish different meaning layers, because there is normally some clue or device in place to enable differentiation. For example, watching otters comically frolicking, Bateson observed that two otters struggling with one another appeared to know when it was a fight and when it was play even though seemingly engaged in the same activity. It appears then that even animals can interpret a singular action through different (meaning) frames, as do humans. He identified the meaning layers as frame levels. Drawing on Bateson, here, Goffman developed a 'plural reality' theory of meaning. This is the theoretical frame that underpins Frame Analysis.[19]

Humans, however, can distinguish (differences in) more layers of meaning than other animals, and must therefore be able to move between the layers more freely as well. But of course, we occasionally select an incorrect/inaccurate frame (illusion) and can create devices that deliberately trigger incorrect selections. For example, a set of actions which is defined as a 'fight' or a 'brawl' in the ordinary life-world becomes the sport 'boxing' when transformed into the 'play' field. Goffman described this transformation using a musical metaphor of 'keying'. While the (shared) meaning framework that supports the reality of the life-world (a 'fight' in this case) is called the 'primary framework', the transformation process of adding another layer of meaning that supports the reality of a sport ('boxing' in this case) is called 'up-keying'—however, Goffman himself uses 'up-keying', as well as down-keying, only at the frame breaking phase and hence using 'up-' for other transformation processes is a deviation from Goffman's usage of the term. Conversely, this is a common occurrence among children but when a playful 'pushing and poking' eventually deteriorates into a real 'fight', this is certainly called 'down-keying' according to Goffman's usage because it involves a breaking down of the frame.

4. Where would we fit science into Figure 8.3? Our first impulse might be to regard it as a framed reality in the 'play' field with sports and art. But considering the extent to which science is 'worshipped' in modern societies, we should perhaps regard it as

a framed reality in the 'sacred' field. Thus it is probably best to see it as a reality such as the dotted circles that do not totally fit into either field, but perhaps overlaps both. Here we might learn from the reflections of Japan's leading astrophysicist, Professor Fumitaka Satō, who commented—with reference to my theory of 'calming culture mechanisms'—that scientists had made many mistakes as members of the 'agitator cultural mechanism' (Satō 1995). While he did not specifically place science in the 'play' field, he appears to be instructing us to be 'an artisan rather than a priest' if we are to be professional scholars. In this sense, we must know our limitations, as must professional sports people and artists.

In other words, he is calling our attention to the fact that scientific theory is a reality outside of the real world, if not always of the 'play' field, and typically 'down-keying' real world phenomena into theoretical terms. Mr. Satō was speaking as a physicist, primarily concerned with nuclear issues. But his call for greater awareness of the position of science is highly relevant today, and much more broadly, especially in view of the amazing advances of the life sciences in recent years which have steadily encroached ever further into the realm of God. The connection to our discussion is that delusions of scientific omnipotence in the life-world or clinical field are instances of down-keying or frame breaking. I have often said that I would like life science researchers to pause and ask themselves if they are truly thinking about the happiness of real people.

5. Stepping out-of one's own frame, Goffman thought, could be a technique for cheating. He called it 'fabricated keying'. What he meant was that there are cases in which one party secretly engages in down-keying with the intention of taking-advantage of others. Contrast this with the previously mentioned case of children unknowingly and unintentionally stepping out-of a play frame and into a real fight. Match fixing is a good example of fabricated keying. Spectators cheer for players, believing that they are watching a (pure) sports match, but the players have down-keyed to the life-world frame from the start and merely 'go through the motions' of the actions that they would have performed in the 'play' frame. But fabricated keying can also be used in the other direction: up-keying. In essence, then, 'fabricated keying' refers to secretly shifting to another frame—up or down—while leaving the others behind. In Rosenthal's and Jacobson's Oak School experiment, the researchers up-keyed to the scientific experiment

frame, leaving all of the students and teachers behind in the world of primary frameworks. Goffman decided cheating by up-keying was generally a lesser crime, because the object is typically not something vulgar, like money, as in the case of match fixing, but it's not so clear, for advantage and hence other forms of control can still be achieved…

Similarly, for sociologists, Satō's position can be interpreted as a warning that we should not attempt to directly apply conclusions reached within a frame of scientific theory to the needs arising from the life-world frame. He did not specifically say that down-keying in scientific work is necessarily fabricated keying. What his reflections highlight, however, is that if the general public blindly believes what scientists tell them because of some form of science worship, the public may not notice it if the scientists secretly shift-frames and thereby take advantage of their trust. Importantly, any attempts to apply theoretical conclusions from research findings to the clinical field are rife with possibilities for fabricated keying whereby researchers achieve advantage over lay people. Thus even though clinical sociology opens real possibilities for better understanding the social world, and therefore, for engaging in it, it also carries this enhanced capacity for manipulation and control, and to some extent precisely through its deeper immersion in the life world. The authoritarian attitude of pulpit academism which was alive until a decade ago manifested as academics talking seemingly endless nonsense to lay people, but it did not have this manipulative potential—in contrast to, say, match fixers—because the public was well aware that what the academics were telling them did not correspond to the needs of the life-world. It is obviously imperative for clinical sociologists to be inhabitants of the ordinary life-world before we start offering advice. But if we do, can we still talk about 'clinical sociology' as specialized knowledge and different to mere 'common sense'? The dotted circle on the left side of Figure 8.3 represents the position that I aspire to.

Finally, I would like to comment on the 'happiness' that we actually feel. In Goffman's schema, each of us is situated in different meaning frames at different times, and can shift back and forth between them. There is a 'me' that routinely produces in a 'secular' frame and another 'me' that non-routinely plays in the sports frame. Much of what is produced as the real 'me' never appears directly on the front stage; I may or may not take pleasure in 'bluffing' people in this manner.

Most importantly, whichever 'me' is performing, another 'me' is watching the performance as a member of the audience. Goffman presents a typology of audience members, based upon their mode of participation. He called those who remain in their seats all the time the 'theatergoers'—for example, those who continue eating their popcorn even when moved to tears by the play—in distinction from the 'onlookers', who laugh and cry by integrating themselves into the frame on stage. He further observed that of the two, the 'theatergoer' is the more expert audience. The theatergoer remains less engaged in the performance than other audience members, adopting a more-or-less critical perspective on the performance. If the theatergoer 'me' is a hyper-critical 'super-ego' of the type that Sigmund Freud hypothesized, unhappiness is perhaps inevitable. To experience happiness means that we must also be able to be absorbed in the audience as onlookers. Whichever frame one is in, one must also be an 'audience' who can feel and value the transience of a meeting or encounter, and who can connect with the fate of co-performers. Each of the many 'me's' I perform is created with its ultimate foundations in some chance encounter that happened with no necessity or particular reason whatsoever. I have come to learn to appreciate and cherish the 'me' being performed earnestly in the long-term, if I am to experience some moments in which I actually feel 'happiness'. Fortunately, my participation in the COE program afforded the opportunity to experience 'happiness' from watching 'me' performing so earnestly that I ended up showing all of my cards (only from stock in the sociology frame, though). I am thankful for that.

Notes

Introduction

1 An example of psychological studies on subjective well-being is Michael Argyle (1987). In the field of economics, see Bruno S. Frey and Alois Stutzer (2002). This book is not limited to economics but introduces and incorporates a large literature on the subject of happiness. Ruut Veenhoven (1984) creates a global base for collection of empirical data on happiness. All 'quality of life' studies have been dealing with the 'happiness issue' from some perspective or other. For the latest in this field, see Wolfgang Glatzer, Susanne von Below and Matthias Stoffregen (2004).

2 This classification of the view of happiness and the respective definition were first provided by Masahiro Ogino (the author of Chapter 3 in this volume).

Chapter 1

1 'Killing many innocent people' is a translation from '*Shikiri ni* (continually), *muko o* (the innocent people), *sasshō shi* (killing)' (Takeyama 1998: 143). The expression was used in the Japanese Imperial Rescript to report the defeat at the end of World War II. For the composition of the Imperial Rescript, see Takeyama (1998), Komori (2003), Chaen (1989). From those sources, one might surmise that the phrase 'killing many innocent people' replaced the passage in the draft of Rescript discussed at the first Court on 10 August: '...if we continue the battle a severe devastation and cruel carnage would eventually not only threaten the existence of our people...' The phrase was possibly inserted at the Cabinet meeting on 14 August. However, it is not certain on whose initiative the change was made.

According to Dower, the Imperial Rescript was an endeavour 'to turn the announcement of humiliating defeat into yet another affirmation of Japan's war conduct and of [the Emperor's] own transcendent morality', and 'the opening pronunciamento of an urgent campaign to maintain imperial control' (Dower 1999: 36, 38).

2 See Tomomi Endō (1989) for Western notions on 'well-being' prior to the nineteenth century. It was not until the eighteenth century that 'well-being' was considered as an obvious human 'right' and discussed, argued and celebrated as such.
3 Sen based his study on poor Indians. For present purposes, his principal contributions are: identifying 'why economic growth does not lead to happiness' (Kamiyama 2004) and introducing the concept of human capabilities. Strictly speaking, however, human capabilities have to be ordered on the 'capabilities' or a set of 'functions vector' available to individuals. It is a difficult task and Sen was unsuccessful in his attempt to do so (Roemer [1996] 2001: 219–23).
4 The expression and inspiration for 'missed opportunity' was taken from the dialogue between McNamara, the US Secretary of Defence during the Vietnam War, and Nguyen Co Thack, a high-ranking official and ex-Foreign Minister of the North Vietnam government. The dialogue was held over four days in 1997, and focused on the question 'was there truly no opportunity' to avoid the war or end it sooner? (Higashi 2000)
5 Incidentally, the Japanese translator of Collins' book translates the term 'non-obvious' differently according to context, using terms such as 'out-of-common sense', 'unusual', 'beyond common sense' and so on.

Chapter 2

1 Here the term 'state' always refers to 'social state'. Let us consider, for example, Mr A, who likes having a drink. Let us suppose that he is suffering from a hangover and is asked if he would like a glass of beer before going to work for an important business meeting. On this occasion, even Mr A with his fondness for a drink, would prefer not to drink. In this case Mr A compares the two states: 'being hung over and having a beer before going to work' (x) and 'being hung over and not having a beer before going to work' (y) and decides that y is better. He simply considers state y to be the one more conducive to well-being. This is a general definition of 'social state', one which takes full account of the individual's environment and of the actions of others.
2 The preference relation of individual i is expressed as R_i, with n number of people having a preference ($i = 1, 2, \ldots, n$). xR_iy means that 'for individual i social state x is at least as good as social state y'. The individual preference relation is assumed to satisfy the following three conditions.

1. Reflexive $\forall x \in X, xR_ix$. Social state x is at least as good as x itself.
2. Transitive $\forall x, y, z \in X, ((xR_iy) \vee (yR_iz)) \Rightarrow xR_iz$. The preference is transitive.
3. Complete $\forall x, y \in X, (x \neq y) \Rightarrow ((xR_iy) \vee (yR_ix))$. If x and y are not the same, then either xR_iy or yR_ix holds.

Preference relations satisfying all three of the above conditions are called 'order'. Also, in $xPy \Leftrightarrow [(xRy) \wedge \neg(yRx)]$ relation P is called a 'strict preference'. Different disciplines employ different terminologies and it should be noted that other disciplines refer to the term 'order' used here variously as 'partial (*han*) order', 'partial (*bubun*) order' or 'weak order' (Sen [1970] 2000: 14).

3 The Pareto principle is often criticised as being an inappropriate basis for welfare judgements as it is unethical.

4 When $x \in X$ satisfies $\forall y, y \in X \Rightarrow xRy$ (when x is as good an option as y), x is the best element of X in the binary relation R. The set of the best elements in X is called the choice set of X and is expressed as $C(X, R)$. A choice function $C(S, R)$ defined over X is a functional relation such that the choice set $C(S, R)$ is nonempty for every nonempty subset S of X.

In other words, the social decision function is a social preference by which the best elements of a social state can be determined (Sen 1970: 14).

5 The form of the function, the 'weighted sum total of the income gap' is not itself derived from the axiom. It is, however, successful in deriving a specific form of function regarding an inequality measurement—namely, the Theil Entropy Measure—from the general nature (Lorenz criterion, continuation and additive decomposability) assumed by Shorrocks (1980).

6 See Dagum (1997) regarding decomposition in cases where there is overlap. See Hamada (2004) regarding parametric analysis.

Chapter 3

1 This paper is part of the results of a 2003 Kwansei Gakuin University Individual Special Research project, 'Sociological research regarding negative historical heritage'.

2 Bourdieu would define fate as an 'objective survival condition'.

3 The proposition that the exchange of goods creates desire is not unique to Durkheim; it can be seen in nineteenth century Japanese philosophy, particularly in Mitogaku (Mito School) and Kokugaku (national studies) (Aizawa [1825/]1973: 74).

4 An example of the victims of an incident in which direct murder charges were not laid can be found in *Kukai jōdo* (Paradise in the sea of sorrow) by Michiko Ishimure (1972), which deals with Minamata Disease patients. These days there are literary works which focus on the victims of events, such as *Underground* by Haruki Murakami (1999). Murakami interviewed victims of the sarin gas subway incident in 1995, and published his account of these interviews. He wrote about the lives that the victims of the incident were leading rather than about the perpetrators of this random mass murder, followers of the Aum Shinrikyo Cult. In this case, however, the focus on the victims comes at the expense of the offenders, whose existence becomes vague. Unlike literature, sociology should follow a different path, focusing neither on the assailant nor victim, but on the encounter between them, and the space in which this encounter became possible.

5 Western social theory has the following characteristics.

   i. The exertion of violence is seen as an opportunity to organize the social order.
   ii. There is a tendency to seek the basis for this organization/violence in an uncivilized society.
   iii. (It reveals that) the use of violence which triggered the organization of a social order is concealed.

The secrets of modern society itself remain hidden by sociologists who continue to see opportunities for organizing the social order through the exercise of violence. The French Revolution is a prime example of how modern society was established by violently exterminating the opposing power. Few would now dispute that the French Revolution was a highly significant historical incident in that it created a society where freedom and equality were constitutive ideals. Perhaps fewer still ever mention the many, some say 2 million, violent deaths that occurred in the process. The circumstances which necessitated this extreme violence at the birth of modern society have been obscured, and instead projected onto 'uncivilized' societies, which, unlike modern society, were not necessarily born of violence. In this sense it is modern society, not uncivilized society, which created a society out of violence.

6 In an article titled 'Distorted reporting by the mass media—Truth of the Minamata Disease compensation issue' in the December 1971 edition of *Jitsugyō no Nihon*.

7 The interview was conducted in February 2004.

Chapter 4

1 In his last years, Bentham deleted the qualifier 'of the greatest number' from this motto, to focus upon 'the greatest happiness' alone, because society's 'total mass of happiness' cannot be maximized when a great deal of unhappiness is experienced even by a small number of people.

2 Nietzsche's 'last men' already had subconscious anxiety—they 'blink' each time they say 'We have discovered happiness'. But at the conscious level, they maintain a steady sense of relaxed happiness.

3 The *Painless Civilization Theory* is littered with similar passages whose persistent repetition eventually induces an almost nauseating unpleasantness. The end of the book is filled with sexual delusions not unlike a B grade animation film.

4 The 'young child' is a part of the 'übermensch' concept. The general image of the übermensch is a coercive and violent 'powerful man' who gives orders to the whole world. Owen called this the 'world-historical übermensch' and pointed out that there was a 'quiet übermensch' within Nietzsche (Owen 1994). The former is a 'man of legislature', represented by military or politically powerful men, while the latter is 'one who sets an example', represented by artists. The 'young child' enjoys the 'play of creativity' as an instinctive artist and is exactly the latter, the 'quiet übermensch' (Miyahara 1999).

5 Ryōkan (1758-1831) was a Buddhist monk in the late Edo period. In his pilgrimages throughout Japan, he enjoyed wine (sake) with local peasants and played ball with their children. Free of all kinds of greed and worry, he produced wonderful poems and calligraphy.

6 *Enjo kōsai* (literally: assistance dating)—when a middle-aged man gives money and/or gifts to a young girl in exchange for dates. Also translated as compensated dating, school girl prostitution, mutually helping prostitution, assisted dating, etc. (translator)

7 While writing this paper, a strange question occurred to me: *who* is writing it? The content and style would differ greatly depending on whether my inner 'slave', 'master' or the 'young child' writes. It thus seemed necessary

to appoint one of these three if I was to write a consistent 'paper'. I finally appointed the 'master' as the lead writer, with the 'slave' and 'young child' helping as assistants. If I had a chance to write another essay on the same topic, I would try to appoint a young child as a lead writer. Needless to say, a new essay would be quite different from the present essay in its tone and content.

Chapter 5

1 This research was conducted as part of the Kwansei Gakuin University's 21st Century COE Program 'The Study of Social Research for the Enhancement of Human Well-Being'. I would like to express my gratitude to my friends in many parts of Africa and the Deaf people around the world who gave me inspiration for the ideas I have explored in this paper by showing me the affluent world of their languages and cultures.
2 This heading is borrowed from the title of Yokozeki's presentation.
3 The Universal Declaration of Human Rights, Article 2: 'Everyone is entitled to all the rights and freedoms set forth in this Declaration without distinction of any kind, such as race, colour, sex, language, religion, political or other opinion, national or social origin, property, birth or other status' (United Nations 1948).
4 UNESCO supports the World Conference on Linguistic Rights (Universal Declaration of Linguistic Rights 2004).
5 This paper focuses on the language communities of the permanent residents of nation-states; hence the following issues are beyond its scope: multilingual education in response to globalism (English education in Japan, etc.); variations within a language (the power relationship of dialects and the standard language, etc.); languages used by temporary residents of a country (issues involving overseas students, migrant workers and refugees, etc.).
6 Among the ideas for establishing apartheid was a consideration for protecting traditional black cultures (Mine 1996). There are two types of discrimination, namely assimilation and segregation. It has been observed that anti-assimilationist ideas readily lend themselves to segregation, while anti-separationist ideas lean towards assimilation (Taguieff 1987). The South African apartheid policies, unfortunately, exemplified this observation.
7 Much research has been conducted into sign language and cultures of the Deaf, and a great number of books for the general public have been published on these subjects (see Padden and Humphries 1988, Sacks 1989, etc).
8 Although there are a total of 121 sign languages listed in *Ethnologue*, two of them no longer have any signers.
9 We need to be careful in emphasizing permanent residents as it may lead to neglecting issues concerning temporary residents. However, the state should be expected to at least affirm the permanent residents' pursuit of well-being.
10 There are deaf people who use a spoken language but not a sign language (the hard of hearing and deafened adults). Depending on the linguistic

environment, the age at which hearing was lost, the parents' views on education and individual values, language usage varies from one deaf person to another. In this paper, "the Deaf" is used to indicate members of a community who share a sign language and a culture, while "the deaf" means people with hearing loss in the medical view. However, Deaf signers universally agree that signing is the most natural language for them, regardless of when or where they live.

11 Although it is extremely difficult for the Deaf to assimilate into a speech community, they are strongly seeking to execute their right to the official language with regards to written language. Deaf people in Japan, for instance, are seeking opportunities to acquire not only signing competence in Japanese Sign Language but also reading and writing competence in Japanese.

12 The current linguistic surroundings of the Deaf can be compared to what spoken language users would find themselves in if they should live as a minority in a world of aliens who talk in a telepathic language (Akiyama and Kamei 2004). What kind of linguistic rights would the spoken language users seek in a situation where their lack of telepathic facilities denied them acquisition of the majority language?

13 It is not clear whether sign languages were being autonomously formed in all of these areas before Foster's school education. It is also worth noting that since it spread, ASL has gone through such regional pidgenizations that today some people are using a sign language unaware of its origin.

Chapter 6

1 On this point, see Masahiro Ogino (1998: 8–25).

2 The 'causal relationship' concept with regard to intercultural understanding has been examined in detail by Hamamoto (1989: 55–92). When this problem is cast in terms of intercultural understanding, it raises the need to reflect on the modern (Western) concept of the 'causal relationship'.

3 Clifford Geertz proposes 'anti anti-relativism' (1984/2002: 59–94), but this is effectively no different from relativism and anti-relativism, in that it remains an intercultural issue.

4 According to Norinaga, the concept of 'the Way' was fiercely debated in China because the country was in turmoil. There was no equivalent word in ancient Japan, not because the concept did not exist but because it was so indisputably established that it did not warrant discussion (Yoshikawa 1969: 288–9). This argument about 'the Way' in *Naobi no Mitama* is widely recognized as demonstrating Norinaga's typically rhetorical line of argument.

5 Norinaga's criticism of 'the worship of Chinese culture' is repeated consistently throughout his oeuvre. For example, he states in *Ui Yama Fumi* that those who aspire to study 'the Way' must first 'discard their admiration for Chinese and Confucian cultures and strengthen their Japanese spirit' (Yoshikawa 1969: 31).

6 Torigoe has written the best analysis tracing this specific concept of 'fact' to Norinaga's theory of poetry (2002a). My argument agrees with Torigoe's view in principle. Yet I am primarily interested in confronting the 'dark

area' underneath the concept of 'fact' shared by Yanagita and Norinaga and finding a way to overcome it.

7 Ogino (1998: 149–90) discussed the relationship between Atsutane Hirata's classical thought and Nobuhiro Satō's colonialist concept.

8 Refer to Yama (1996) for an epistemological discussion of using the perspective of the dead to open this dualist paradigm.

Chapter 8

1 See my book *Rinshō Bukkyōgaku no susume* (An invitation to clinical studies of Buddhism) (Ōmura 2003), and my paper 'Japanese Buddhism and happiness' presented at the symposium titled 'Rinshō shūkyōgaku no kanōsei—kōfuku to meifuku wa ryōritsusuruka (The Potential of clinical studies of religion: The dilemma of happiness in this or the other world)' at the 19th World Congress of the International Association for the History of Religions (IAHR Tokyo 2005) in March 2005.

2 Kawai and Nakazawa (2003) provide a very detailed discussion of the differences between the word '*kōfuku*' and the Buddhist concept.

3 Mita's *Gendai nihon no seishin kōzō* (Mental structures of modern Japan) includes the chapters 'Sukurappu no kōfuku to hisan: teinen taishoku to sararīman (Happiness and misery of being scrapped: Age-limit retirement and salarymen)', from which the above passages are quoted, and 'Gendai ni okeru fukō no shoruikei (Types of unhappiness in modern times)'.

4 The Public Philosophy at the Kyoto Forum held an international conference entitled 'Shihonshugi wa 21-seiki no jinrui no kōfuku ni kōkensurunoka? (Will capitalism contribute to human happiness in the 21st century?)' in October 2002. The general consensus view was that 'the current form' of capitalism was a system that made people unhappy, broadly paralleling John McMurtry's view about 'the loss of happiness in capitalism'. Shin Chiba's summary report on the conference in the journal *Kōkyōteki ryōshikijin* (Common sense people) (February 2003) asked what former Marxist economists were doing now. He complained, 'Now is the time we really want to hear criticism, proposals for revision and alternative suggestions from them on the rampancy of global capitalism and financial capitalism but they are nowhere to be seen' (Chiba 2003).

5 Just to be clear, Miyahara's 'personal language' has nothing to do with what has been called body language.

6 This is one of the few field surveys I have conducted. The interpretation of the mass for aborted fetuses and the fraudulent sale of spiritual goods presented here is based on my experience in this field survey.

7 See Miyahara (1998) for a detailed discussion on a series of studies into the 'culture of translation' by Akira Yanabu.

8 Toshikazu Takao, studied under the famous Professor Paul Tillich at Columbia University graduate school in his youth, went to Union Theological Seminary, returned to Japan with some unresolved theological questions and continued serious dialogues with some notable people, including Katsumi Takizawa. This book deserves much greater attention than I can give it here.

9 I contributed a chapter entitled 'Rinshō bunka no shakaigaku (Sociology of clinical culture)' to the same book (Yamanaka 2005).

10 The 44th conference of the Public Philosophy at Kyoto Forum (March 2003) was a symposium entitled 'Kenkō to iryō to fukushi niokeru kōkyōsei (The public nature of health, medicine and welfare)'. I presented a report entitled 'Kea no kōkyō tetsugaku—shūkyōshakaigaku no kanten kara (Public philosophy of care: From the viewpoint of a sociology of religion)'. I learned a lot about care and cure from the forum participants, who included leading experts on nursing theory and oriental medicine.

11 My comment here is mainly based on J. Lofland and R. Collins in Ditton (1980).

12 This is why I suggested the possibility of seeing a family as the 'smallest religious community' in my (1995) paper 'Kazoku o meguru sezokusei to datsu-sezokusei (Secularity and unsecularity concerning the family)'.

13 I have written many times about the distinction between 'role' and 'character', but the one that most closely touches on this discussion of Foucault is 'Kanjō seido to kenryoku (Emotions, system and power)' (in Ōmura 2002).

14 Regarding 'behavior as a semiotic phenomenon' in general, please see the bibliography in Hayashi and Ōmura (1994).

15 It is worth noting here that this 'self-fulfillment' may be merely statistical—that is, not reflecting real changes in society. The statistical evidence that juvenile delinquency is beginning at an earlier age may be merely indicating that the zero-tolerance policy is now reporting trivial misconduct that previously went unrecorded. It does not tell us whether there is actually any change in the amount of such misconduct.

16 Ōmura (2002) includes 'Gekijō hanzai no shutsugen: Glico Morinaga jiken ni miru tasō na riaritī (The emergence of theatrical crimes: Multilayered reality seen in the Glico and Morinaga incidents), analyzing the Glico and Morinaga incidents using the frame analysis which I will explain shortly. (First published in *Chuokoron*, April 1985)

17 I cannot help but feel that the maladaptive patterns exhibited by today's youth in the midst of agitating culture, *furītā* (part-time worker) and *hikikomori* (withdrawal), are respectively 'ritualism' and 'retreatism' according to Tsurumi's interpretation. I emphasize the need for 'calming motif' theory against 'achievement motif' theory and 'calmative level' theory against 'aspirational level' theory because, in essence, I believe that the 'agitating culture' dominant in modern society cannot make people 'happy' (Ōmura 1996b).

18 From the beginning of our current research project, I knew that the International Institute of Advanced Studies had conducted a joint research project on 'comparative studies of happiness' led by Mr. Hisayasu Nakagawa between April 1992 and March 1998. I had its final report at hand and consulted it several times. Especially, Yoshida's research paper 'Hikaku kōfukugaku no hitotsu no kenkyū no puroguramu (A research program of comparative studies of happiness)' contained exhaustive discussions on theoretical frameworks and proved to be a very valuable work for me (Yoshida 1999). Even more interesting for me is the supplementary essay entitled 'Kōfuku to kōfukukan: chichi ni gan o kokuchi shite (Happiness and

the perception of happiness: Having informed my father of his cancer)' that followed his thoroughly theoretical research paper. I knew his late father somewhat, and had attended his wake upon his passing, which deepened my understanding of what was expressed in that essay. Seeing a research paper advocating universal validity juxtaposed with an essay which was almost a confession of faith made me wonder whether perhaps even a great theorist must touch upon the mysterious bonds of fate if he is to think about people's happiness seriously. Or, maybe an 'incorrigible theorist' is compelled to 'break the frame' to express his honest feelings. In either case, I consider Yoshida's to be a valuable record of earnestness working on the edge of the frame.

19 It is curious to note that the Pygmalion Effect experiments mentioned earlier were prompted by the observation of rats and that frame analysis was inspired by otters.

Bibliography

Adorno, Theodore W. (1966), *Negative Dialektik*, Frankfurt am Main: Suhrkamp Verlag.

Aitchison, John and James A. C. Brown (1957), *The Lognormal Distribution with Special Reference to Its Uses in Economics*, London: Cambridge University Press.

Aizawa, Seishisai ([1825/]1973), 'Shinron (New theory)', *Nihon shisō taikei 53: Mitogaku* (Japanese philosophy series 53: Mito School), Tokyo: Iwanami Shoten.

Akasaka, Mari (2001), '"Shōgai" to "sōzetsu jinsei" bakari ga naze yomarerunoka (Why "disability" and "heroic life" books are so popular)', *Chuokoron*, June.

Akiyama, Nami and Nobutaka Kamei (2004), *Shuwa de ikou* (Shall We Sign?), Kyoto: Minerva Publishing.

Anderson, Benedict (1991), *Imagined Communities: Reflections on the Origin and Spread of Nationalism*, London: Verso.

Aoki, Masahiko (1979), *Bunpai riron, dainihan keizaigaku zenshū* (Distribution theory, economics series, second edition) 13, Tokyo: Chikuma Shobo Publishing.

Argyle, Michael (1987), *The Psychology of Happiness*, London: Methuen.

Aron, R. (1969), *Les désillusions du progrès*, Paris: Calmamn-Lévy.

Atkinson, Anthony B. (1970), 'On the Measurement of Inequality', *Journal of Economic Theory*, 2: 244–63.

Bauman, Zygmunt (1992), *Modernity and the Holocaust*, Cambridge: Polity Press.

Benjamin, W. (1974), 'Das Kunstwerk im Zeitalter seiner technischen Reproduzierbarkeit', *Gesammelte Schriften*, Bd. I, Ffm, Frankfurt am Main: Suhrkamp. Edited and translated by Kenjirō Asai and Tetsushi Kubo (1995), 'Fukusei gijutsu jidai no geijutsu sakuhin (Works of art in the age of reproduction technology), *Benjamin Collection I*, Tokyo: Chikuma Shobo Publishing.

Bentham, Jeremy ([1789] 1948), *A Fragment on Government and an Introduction to the Principles of Morals and Legislation*, Oxford: Blackwell.

Berlin, Isaiah (1954), *Historical Inevitability*, Oxford: Oxford University Press.

Bhattacharya, Nikhileah and Bimalendu Mahalanobis (1967), 'Regional Disparity in Household Consumption in India', *Journal of American Statistical Association*, 62: 143–61.

Bourdieu, Pierre (ed.) (1993), *La misère du monde*, Paris: Le Seuil.

Bourdieu, Pierre and Jean-Claude Passeron (1970), *La reproduction*, Paris: Edition de Minuit.

Canetti, Elias (1966), *Masse et puissance*, Paris: Gallimard.

Chaen, Yoshio (1989), *Misshitsu no shūsen mikotonori* (Imperial edict to end the war, written behind closed doors), Tokyo: Yushodo.

Chiba, Shin (2003), '"Shihonshugi wa 21-seiki no jinrui no kōfuku ni kōkensurunoka?" sōkatsu hōkokubun ("Will capitalism contribute to human happiness in the 21st century?" Summary report)', *Kōkyōteki ryōshikijin* (Common sense people), vol. 2, Kyoto: Kyoto Forum Jimukyoku.

The Chugoku Shimbun (ed.) (1980), *Zōho Hiroshima no kiroku: Hibaku 35 nen shashinshū* (Record of Hiroshima: Photographs of 35 years of atomic bomb victims, expanded edition), Hiroshima: The Chugoku Shimbun.

Cohen, Robin and Paul Kennedy (2000), *Global Sociology*, Great Britain: Palgrave Publishers Ltd.

Collins, Randall (1982), *Sociological Insight: An Introduction to Nonobvious Sociology*, Oxford: Oxford University Press.

Comte, August ([1822]/1895), *Plan des travaux scientifiques necessaries pour reorganizer la société*. In *Système de politique positive, IV, Société positiviste*. Paris: Appendice Général.

Comte, August ([1844] 1926), *Discours sur l'esprit positif*. Paris: Garnier Frère.

Comte-Sponville, André (2000), *Le bonheur deséspérement*, Nantes: Éditions Pleins Feux.

Dagum, Camilo (1997), 'A New Approach to the Decomposition of the Gini Income Inequality Ratio', *Empirical Economics*, 22: 515–31.

Dai, Le Cao (2000), 'Agent Orange in the Viet Nam War: History and Consequences', Vietnam Red Cross.

Davis, Kingsley and Wilbert E. Moore, 'Some Principles of Stratification', *American Sociological Review*, April 1945: 242–49.

Deuleuze, Gilles (1962), *Nietzsche et la philosophie*, Paris: P.U.F.

Dinh Xuan Lam (ed.) (2004), *Lich Su* 12, Hanoi: Nha Xuat Ban Giao Duc (Education Publishing House).

Ditton, Jason (ed.) (1980), *The View from Goffman*, New York: Macmillan Press Ltd.

Dower, John (1999), *Embracing Defeat: Japan in the Wake of World War II*, New York, London: W.W.Norton and Company/ The New Press.

Durkheim, Émile ([1897/]1981), *Le Suicide*, Paris: P.U.F.

Durkheim, Émile ([1893] 1960), *De la division du travail social: étude sur l'organisation des sociétés supérieures*. Paris: P.U.F. Translated by Otoyori Tahara (1971), *Shakai bungyōron*, Tokyo: Aoki Shoten.

Durkheim, Émile (2000), *De la division du travail social*, Paris: F. Alcan.

Easterlin, A. Richard (2004), 'Life satisfaction: Can we produce it?' in Wolfgang Glatzer, Susanne von Below and Matthias Stoffregen (eds), *Challenges for Quality of Life in the Contemporary World*, The Netherlands: Kluwer Academic Publishers, pp. 347–57.

Endō, Tomomi (1989), *Seiyō kindai ni okeru 'kōfuku' no gensetsu: Chishiki shakaigaku-teki kenkyū* (Notions of 'happiness' in the Western modern period: A study in the sociology of knowledge), MA thesis in Sociology A, University of Tokyo.

Ethnologue, http//www.ehtnologue.com/, visited on 1 January 2006.

Evans-Pritchard, Edward Evan (1937), *Witchcraft Oracles and Magic among the Azande*, Oxford: Clarendon Press.

Fararo, Thomas J. and Kenji Kosaka (2003), *Generating Images of Stratification: A Formal Theory*, The Netherlands: Kluwer Academic Publishers.

Festinger, Leon (1956), *When Prophecy Fails*, Minneapolis: University of Minnesota Press.

Festinger, Leon (1957), *A Theory of Cognitive Dissonance*, Stanford: Stanford University Press.

Foucault, Michel (1963), *Naissance de la clinique*, Paris: Presses universitaires de France.

Foucault, Michel (1975), *Surveiller et punir: naissance de la prison*, Paris: Gallimard.

Foucault, Michel (1984), *Histoire de la sexualité II: l'usage des plaisirs*, Paris: Gallimard.

Frey, Bruno S. and Alois Stutzer (2002), *Happiness and Economics*, Princeton University Press.

Fry, Dennis (1977), *Homo Loquens: Man as a Talking Animal*, Cambridge: Cambridge University Press.

Fukuchi, Toshio (1999), 'Gengoken-ni kansuru ronriteki-kōsatsu (Theoretical issues on linguistic rights)', Master's thesis, Tokyo: Graduate School of Language and Society, Hitotsubashi University Graduate School.

Furukawa, Akira (2004), *Mura no seikatsu kankyōshi* (A history of environmental conditions in villages), Kyoto: Sekaishisosha.

Geertz, Clifford (1984), 'Anti Anti-Relativism', *American Anthropologist*, Vol. 86(2): 263–78.

Gengoken Kenkyūkai (ed.) (1999), *Kotoba e no kenri: Gengoken to wa naki ka* (Rights toward languages), Tokyo: Sangensha.

Giddens, Anthony (1984), *The Constitution of Society: Outline of the Theory of Structuration*, California: University of California Press.

Girard, René (1961), *Mensonge romantique et verite romanesque*, Paris: Editions Bernard Grasset.

Glatzer, Wolfgang, Susanne von Below and Matthias Stoffregen (eds) (2004), *Challenges for Quality of Life in the Contemporary World*, Netherland: Kluwer Academic Publishers.

Goffman, Erving (1952), 'On cooling the mark out, some aspects of adaptation to failure', *Psychiatry*, 15(4)(November): 451–63.

Goffman, Erving (1961), *Asylums: Essays on the Social Situation of Mental Patients and Other Inmates*, Garden City, NY: Anchor Books.

Goffman, Erving (1963), *Stigma: Notes on the Management of Spoiled Identity*, Englewood Cliffs, NJ: Prentice-Hall.

Goffman, Erving (1974), *Frame Analysis: An Essay on the Organization of Experience*, New York: Harper and Row.

Habermas, Jürgen (1981a), *Philosophisch-politische Profile*, Frankfurt: Suhrkamp. Translated by Osamu Komaki and Takao Murakami (1984), *Tetsugakuteki seijiteki purofīru* (Philosophical-political profile) vol. I and (1986) vol. II, Tokyo: Mirai-sha Publishers.

Habermas, Jürgen (1981b), *Die Moderne: Ein unvollendetes Projekt*, Kleinere politische Schriften (I-IV), Frankfurt am Main: Suhrkamp. Edited and translated by Kenichi Mishima (2000), *Kindai: Mikan no purojekuto* (Modernity: Unfinished project), Tokyo: Iwanami Shoten.

Habermas, Jürgen (1983), *Philosophical-Political Profiles*. Translated by Frederick G. Lawrence, Cambridge, MA.: The MIT Press.

Hama, Hideo (2000), 'Rekishi no shakaigaku (Sociology of history)', *Jōkyō* (State of affairs), August supplement issue: 185–200.

Hamada Hiroshi (2004), 'Parametric Decomposition of the Gini Coefficient', mimeographed.

Hamada, Hiroshi and Atsushi Ishida (2003), 'Fubyōdō shakai to kikai no kintō (Social inequality and equal opportunity)', *Shakaigaku hyōron* (Essays on sociology), 54 (3): 232–49.

Hamamoto, Mitsuru (1985), 'Bunka sōtaishugi no daika (Price of cultural relativism)', *Risō* (Ideal), 8: 105–21.

Hamamoto, Mitsuru (1989), 'Fukō no dekigoto: Fukō no katari ni okeru "gen'in" to "hi gen'in" (Unhappy events: 'cause' and 'non-cause' in talks of unhappiness)', in Teigo Yoshida (ed.), *Ibunka no kaidoku* (Decoding of foreign cultures), Tokyo: Hirakawa Shuppansha.

Haq, Mahbub (1995), *Reflections on Human Development*, Oxford: Oxford University Press.

Hara, Junsuke and Kazuo Seiyama (2005), *Inequality and Affluence: Social Stratification in Japan*, Melbourne: Trans Pacific Press.

Hase, Masato (2000), 'Serufu herupu gurūpu no chōsa jisshū kara (From survey practice on self-help groups)', in Eishō Ōmura (ed.), *Rinshō shakaigaku o manabu hito no tameni* (For the students of clinical sociology), Kyoto: Sekaishisosha, pp. 24–46.

Hayashi, Toshihiko and Eishō Ōmura (1994), *Bunmei toshiteno nettowāku* (Network as a civilization), Tokyo: NTT Publishing.

Higashi, Daisaku (2000), *Wareware wa naze sensō o shitanoka: Beikoku, Betonamu: teki tono taiwa* (Why did we fight the war? America and Vietnam: Dialogue with the enemy), Tokyo: Iwanami Shoten.

Hirata, Atsutane (1813), *Tama no mihashira* (Central pillar of spirits), annotated version by Nobukuni Koyasu (1998), Tokyo: Iwanami Shoten.

Honda, Katsuichi (1981), *Senjō no mura* (Vietnam: A voice from the villages), Tokyo: The Asahi Shimbun Company.

Hyslop, Jonathan (1999), *The Classroom Struggle*, Scottsville: University of Natal.

Ichii, Saburō (1971), *Rekishi no shinpo towa nanika* (What is the progress of history?), Tokyo: Iwanami Shoten.

Illich, Ivan (1971), *Deschooling Society*, New York: Harper and Row.

Illich, Ivan (1976), *Limits to Medicine: Medical Nemesis; The Expropriation of Health*, London: Marion Boyars.

Inglehart, Ronald (1990), *Cultural Shift in Advanced Industrial Society*, Princeton: Princeton University Press.

Inoue, Mariko and Eishō Ōmura (eds) (1995), *Famirizumu no saihakken* (Rediscovery of familism), Kyoto: Sekaishisosha.

Inoue, Shun (1977), *Asobi no shakaigaku* (Sociology of play), Kyoto: Sekaishisosha. Re-released in 1999.

Ishikawa, Jun (1995), 'Shōgaisha no oya to atarashii "shinsei" no tanjō (Parents of the handicapped and the birth of new "parenthood")', in Mariko Inoue and Eishō Ōmura (eds), *Famirizumu no saihakken* (Rediscovery of familism), Kyoto: Sekaishisosha, pp. 25–59.

Ishimure, Michiko (1972), *Kukai jōdo* (Paradise in the sea of sorrow), Tokyo: Kodansha.

Ishimure, Michiko (ed.) (1974), *Ten no yamu* (Ailing heaven), Fukuoka: Ashisyobo.

Itsuki, Hiroyuki (2004), *Ima o ikiru chikara* (Strength to seize the day), (NHK Kyōiku Terebi 'Ningen kōza' textbook [NHK Educational Television humanities lecture series text book]), Tokyo: NHK Japan Broadcast Publishing.

Japanese Deaf News (2004), 'Shuwa no teigi no mondai de Takada Zennichirōren riji ga shuchō (Mr. Takada, executive board member of the Japanese Federation of the Deaf, discusses the definitional issues of Sign Languages), *Japanese Deaf News*, 1 July.

Kaji, Nobuyuki (1990), *Jukyō towa nanika* (What is Confucianism?), Tokyo: Chuokoron-Shinsha.

Kamei, Nobutaka (2002–2006), 'Africa no Rōsha (The Deaf in Africa) (1)–(12)', *Shuwa komyunikēshon kenkyū* (Sign language communication studies), Nos. 46–59.

Kamei, Nobutaka (2003a), 'Africa rō-kyōiku no chichi Foster (Foster, the Father of Deaf Education in Africa)', *Africa Report*, 36(2003.3): 36–9.

Kamei, Nobutaka (2003b), 'Africa-shokoku no Rōsha ni yoru Rō-kyōiku jigyō (Education by the Deaf for the Deaf in African countries)', *World Trend of the Institute of Developing Economies*, 96(2003.9): 35–8.

Kamei, Nobutaka (2004), 'Africa no shuwa-gengo (Sign languages of Africa)', *Africa Kenkyū* (Journal of African Studies), 64(2004.3): 43–64.

Kamiyama, Hidenori (2004), 'Naze keizai ga hattatsu shitemo shiawase ni narenainoka (Why can't we be happy despite economic progress?)', in Gaku Doba, Jun Kobayashi, Yoshimichi Satō, Naoki Sudo, Kazuto Misumi and Tsutomu Watanabe (eds), *Shakai o moderu de miru: sūri shakaigaku eno shōtai* (Looking at society in 'models': An invitation to mathematical sociology), Tokyo: Keisoshobo, pp. 154–7.

Karatani, Kōjin (1975), 'Yanagita Kunio no kami (Kunio Yanagita's gods)', in Sōichirō Gotō (1987) (ed.), *Yanagita Kunio kenkyū shiryō shūsei* (Kunio Yanagita research materials collection) 18, Tokyo: Nihon Tosho Center, pp. 64–71.

Kawai, Hayao and Shin'ichi Nakazawa (2003), *Bukkyō ga suki!* (I love Buddhism!), Tokyo: The Asahi Shimbun Company.

Kawamura, Minato (1996), *'Daitōa minzokugaku' no kyojitsu* (Truth and falsehood of 'Great East Asian folklore'), Tokyo: Kodansha.

Kobayashi, Tazuko (2000), 'Jinsei no katari to naratibu apurōchi (Narratives of life and the narrative approach)', in Eishō Ōmura (ed.), *Rinshō shakaigaku o manabu hito no tameni* (For the students of clinical sociology), Kyoto: Sekaishisosha, pp. 71–91.

Komori, Yōichi (2003), *Tennō no gyokuon hōsō* (Emperor's broadcast to end Japan's war), Tokyo, Gogatsu Shobo.

Konishi Hideki (2002), 'Shotoku kakusa to Gini Keisū (The income gap and the Gini Coefficient)', in Hiroshi Miyajima and Rengō Sōgō Seikatsu Kaihatsu Kenkyūjo (ed.), *Nihon no shotokubunpai to kakusa* (Income distribution and income disparity in Japan), Tokyo: Toyo Keizai.

Koyasu, Nobukuni (1992), *Motoori Norinaga*, Tokyo: Iwanami Shoten.

Koyasu, Nobukuni (1993), *Kindaichi no arukeorojī* (Archeology of modern knowledge), Tokyo: Iwanami Shoten.

Koyasu, Nobukuni (2002), *(Shinban) Kishin ron* (On demon-gods, new edition), Tokyo: Hakutakusha.

Kukathas, Chandran and Philip Pettit (1990), *Rawls: A Theory of Justice and Its Critics*, Cambridge: Polity Press.

Kyōdai Nihonshi jiten Hensankai (ed.) (1990), *Shinpen Nihonshi Jiten* (Encyclopedia of Japanese History), Tokyo: Sogensha.

Lane, Robert E. (2000), *The Loss of Happiness in Market Democracies*, New Haven: Yale University Press.

Lanzmann, Claude (1995), 'Deau made ni 10 nen no saigetsu o yōshita, Nihon no dokusha ni (To readers of Japan, that took me ten years to meet)', in Lanzmann, Claude, *Shoā* (Shoah), translated by Taketomo Takahashi, Tokyo: Sakuhinsha, pp. 1–10.

Lévi-Strauss, Claude (1943), 'Guerre et commerce chez les Indiens de l'Amérique du Sud', *Renaissance*, 1.

Linguistic Society of America (1996), 'Statement on Language Rights'. *http://www.lsadc.org/info/lsa-res-rights.cfm* (Accessed on 1 January 2006)

Lyon, David (2001), *The Surveillance Society: Monitoring Everyday Life*, Buckingham and Philadelphia: Open University Press. Translated by Ichirō Kawamura (2002), *Kanshi shakai*, Tokyo: Seidosha.

Lyon, David (2003), *Surveillance after September 11*, Blackwell: Polity. Edited by Yasuhiko Tajima and translated by Tomoko Shimizu (2004), *9-11 ikō no kanshi*, Tokyo: Akashi Shoten.

Maeterlinck, Maurice (1908), *L'oiseau bleu*. Translated by Daigaku Horiguchi (1960), *Aoi tori* (Blue bird), Tokyo: Shinchosha.

Mannheim, Karl (1940), *Man and Society in an Age of Reconstruction: Studies in Modern Social Structure*, New York: Harcourt, Brace and Company.

Maruyama, Magoroh (1963), 'The second cybernetics, deviation-amplifying mutual causal system', *American Scientist,* 51.

Maruyama, Masao (1961), *Nihon no shisō* (Japanese philosophies), Tokyo: Iwanami Shoten.

Masuda, Sumio (ed.) (1978), *Gengo-sensō* (Language wars), Tokyo: Taishukan Publishing.

Mine, Yōichi (1996), *Minami-Africa: 'Niji no kuni' e no ayumi* (South Africa: Steps towards the rainbow nation), Tokyo: Iwanami Shoten.

Mita, Munesuke (1965a), 'Gendai ni okeru fukō no shoruikei (Types of unhappiness in modern times)', in *Gendai nihon no seishin kōzō* (Mental structures of modern Japan), Tokyo: Koubundou Publishers. (Originally published in Ryūkichi Kitagawa (ed.) (1963), *Sogai no shakaigaku* (Sociology of alienation), Gendai shakaigaku kōza 6, Tokyo: Yuhikaku Publishing.)

Mita, Munesuke (1965b), 'Sukurappu no kōfuku to hisan: teinen taishoku to sararīman (Happiness and misery of being scrapped: Age-limit retirement and salarymen)', in *Gendai nihon no seishin kōzō* (Mental structures of modern Japan), Tokyo: Koubundou Publishers. (Originally published in *Bungei shunjū*, October 1964.)

Mita, Munesuke (1979), 'Manazashi no jigoku (Hell in his eyes)', *Gendai shakai no shakai ishiki* (Social awareness in modern society), Tokyo: Koubundou Publishers.

Miura, Nobutaka (1997), *Ta-gengo-shugi to wa nani-ka* (What is multilingualism?), Tokyo: Fujiwara Shoten.

Miyadai, Shinji (1998), *Owari naki nichijō o ikiro* (Live the endless daily life), Tokyo: Chikuma Shobo Publishing.

Miyahara, Kojiro (1992), *Kijinron: shisō no genzai aruiwa Genji Monogatari* (On the noble persons: Current thoughts on *Genji Monogatari*), Tokyo: Sin-yo-sha.

Miyahara, Kojiro (1998), *Kotoba no rinshō shakaigaku* (Clinical sociology of speech acts), Kyoto: Nakanishiya Shuppan.

Miyahara, Kojiro (1999), 'Shizukana chōjin ni tsuite (On the quiet übermensch)', *Sōbun*, 407: 1–4.

Miyahara, Kojiro (2004), '"Nagaiki shakai" to iu kanten (From the perspective of the "mass longevity society")', in Kazuhisa Nishihara and Kyōko Utsunomiya (eds), *Kuritīku to shiteno shakaigaku* (Sociology as a critique), Tokyo: Toshindo Publishing.

Miyamoto, Masaoki (1998), 'Multilingualism to Africa: Ningen to shakai no kaihatsu no shiten kara (Multilingualism and Africa: From the perspective of the development of human beings and societies)', *Gekkan gengo* (Monthly language), 27–8(1998.8): 47–54.

Miyazawa, Nobuo (1997), *Minamatabyō jiken yonjūnen* (Forty years of the Minamata Disease), Fukuoka: Ashisyobo.

Mori, Takemaro (1993), 'Ajia/ Taiheiyō-sensō (Asia/ The Pacific War)', in *Nihon no rekishi* (History of Japan), vol. 20, Tokyo: Shueisha.

Morioka, Masahiro (2003), *Mutsū bunmeiron* (Painless civilization theory), Tokyo: Transview.

Morris, Ivan (1975), *The Nobility of Failure: Tragic Heroes in the History of Japan*, London: Secker and Warburg.

Murai, Osamu (2004), *Shinban Nantō ideorogī no hassei* (The origin of the south island ideology, new edition, originally published in 1992), Tokyo: Iwanami Shoten.

Murakami, Haruki (1999), *Andāguraundo* (Underground), Tokyo: Kodansha.

Myrdal, Gunnar (1944), *An American Dilemma: The Negro Problem and American Democracy*, New York: Harper and Brothers (3rd edition, 1996, New Brunswick, NJ: Transaction).

Nakagawa, Yutaka (1996), 'Shōsū-gengo to gengo no hoji (Minority languages and language maintenance)', in Osahito Miyaoka (ed.), *Gengo-jinruigaku o manabu hito no tame ni* (Introduction to linguistic anthropology), Kyoto: Sekaishisosha, pp. 263–80.

Nakaoka, Tetsurō (1979), *Gijutsu o kangaeru 13 shō* (Thirteen chapters on technology), Tokyo: Nippon Hyoronsha.

Namita, Katsunosuke (1998), 'Tagengo-shugi no kosuto: Canada o rei ni (Cost of multilingualism: The case of Canada)', *Gekkan gengo* (Monthly language), 27–8(1998.8): 62–8.

Naono, Akiko (2004), *'Genbaku no e' to deau: Komerareta omoi ni mimi o sumashite* (Encountering the 'A-bomb paintings': Listening to the voices of the images), Iwanami booklet No. 627, Tokyo: Iwanami Shoten.

Needham, Rodney (1972), *Belief, Language and Experience*, Chicago: The University of Chicago Press.

Nietzsche, Friedrich (1883–85), *Also sprach Zarathustra* (Thus spoke Zarathustra). Translated by Thomas Common and edited by Paul Douglas, *http://www.luminary.us/nz/zarathustra.html.*

Nietzsche, Friedrich (1885–86), *Jenseits von Gut und Böse* (Beyond good and evil). Translated by Helen Zimmern, *http://www.gutenberg.org/etext/4363*

Nietzsche, Friedrich (1887), *Zur Genealogie der Moral* (On the Genealogy of Morals). Translated by Ian Johnston, *http://www.mala.bc.ca/~johnstoi/Nietzsche/genealogytofc.htm*

Nietzsche, Friedrich (1888), *Der Antichrist* (The Antichrist). Translated by H.L. Mencken, *http://www.primitivism.com/antichrist.htm*

Nishio, Kanji (1999), *Kokumin no rekishi* (History of the Japanese people), Tokyo: The Sankei Shimbun.

Noguchi, Yūji and Eishō Ōmura (2000), *Rinshō shakaigaku no susume* (An invitation to clinical sociology), Tokyo: Yuhikaku Publishing.

Nussbaum, Martha C. (1993), 'Non-Relative virtues: An Aristotelian approach', in Martha C. Nussbaum and Amartya Sen (eds), *The Quality of Life: A study prepared for the World Institute for Developing Economics Research (WIDER) of the United Nations University*, Oxford: Clarendon Press, pp. 242–69.

Nussbaum, Martha C. (2000), *Women and Human Development: The Capabilities Approach*, Cambridge: Cambridge University Press.

Obara, Hideo (1995), *Petto-ka suru gendaijin* (Modern humans becoming pets), Tokyo: NHK Japan Broadcast Publishing.

OECD (1974), *Subjective Elements of Well-Being*, Paris: The Organization for Economic Co-operation and Development.

Ogburn, William F. (1922), *Social Change: With Respect to Culture and Original Nature*, New York: Viking Press.

Ogino, Masahiro (1998), *Shihonshugi to tasha* (Capitalism and others), Nishinomiya: Kwansei Gakuin University Press.

Ogino, Masahiro (2001), 'Burudyū to gendai shakaigaku (Bourdieu and modern sociology)', in Joukyou-Shuppan Henshū-bu (ed.), *Shakaigaku riron no 'kanōsei' o yomu* (Reading the 'potential' in sociology theories), Tokyo: Joukyou-Shuppan, pp. 261–69.

Ogino, Masahiro (ed.) (2002), *Bunka isan no shakaigaku: Rūburu Bijutsukan kara Genbaku Dōmu made* (A sociology of cultural heritage: From the Louvre Museum to the Atomic Bomb Dome). Tokyo: Sin-yo-sha.

Oguma, Eiji (2002), *'Minshu' to 'aikoku': Sengo Nihon no nashonarizumu to kōkyōsei* ('Democracy' and 'patriotism': Nationalism and communality in postwar Japan), Tokyo: Sin-yo-sha.

Ōkuma, Yukiko (2000), 'Fukushi to iryō to jōhō to (Welfare, medicine and information)', in Yōichirō Murakami (ed.), *21-seiki no "i"ryō wa dokoni mukau* (Where is the 21st century "medical" service headed?), Tokyo: NTT Publishing.

Ōmachi, Tokuzō (1937), 'Ie no seisui (Rise and fall of *ie*)', in Kunio Yanagita (ed.), *Sanson seikatsu no kenkyū* (Research on mountain village life), Tokyo: Iwanami Shoten.

Ōmura, Eishō (1985), 'Goffman ni okeru daburu raifu no tēma (The theme of double life in Goffman)', *Gendai shakaigaku* (Contemporary sociology) 19, Kyoto: Akademia Shuppankai, pp. 4–29.

Ōmura, Eishō (1994), 'Kūtensuru sekai—shisutemugai mukonkyosei to iukoto (The spinning world: About ungrounded systematicity)', in Toshihiko Hayashi and Eishō Ōmura, *Bunmei toshiteno nettowāku* (Network as a civilization), Tokyo: NTT Publishing, pp. 101–44.

Ōmura, Eishō (1995), 'Kazoku o meguru sezokusei to datsu-sezokusei (Secularity and unsecularity concerning the family)', in Mariko Inoue and Eishō Ōmura (eds), *Famirizumu no saihakken* (Rediscovery of familism), Kyoto: Sekaishisosha.

Ōmura, Eishō (1996a), *Gendai shakai to shūkyō: Shūkyō ishiki no hen'yō* (Modern society and religion: Transformation of religious consciousness), Tokyo: Iwanami Shoten.

Ōmura, Eishō (1996b), *Nihonjin no kokoro no shūkan: Shizume no bunka ron* (Spiritual habits of the Japanese: A theory of calming culture), Tokyo: NHK Japan Broadcast Publishing.

Ōmura, Eishō (2002), *Hikō no riaritī: Futsū no danshi no ikizurasa* (Reality of delinquency: Hardships of life for ordinary boys), Kyoto: Sekaishisosha.

Ōmura, Eishō (2003), *Rinshō bukkyōgaku no susume* (An invitation to clinical studies of Buddhism), Kyoto: Sekaishisosha.

Ōmura, Eishō (2004), '"Shizume no bunka" toshite no supōtsu (Sports as a calming culture)', *Supōtsu shakaigaku kenkyū* (Research in sports sociology), 12: 1–14.

Ōmura, Eishō (2005), 'Rinshō bunka no shakaigaku: rosu no itami to shizume no bunka sōchi (Sociology of clinical culture: Pain of loss and calming culture apparatus)', in Kōji Yamanaka (ed.), *Rinshō bunka no shakaigaku: Shokugyō, gijutsu, hyōjunka* (Sociology of clinical culture: Vocations, skills and standardization), Kyoto: Showado.

Orikuchi, Shinobu (1955), 'Sensei no gakumon (My teacher's science)', *Orikuchi Shinobu zenshū* (Complete work of Shinobu Orikuchi) 16, Tokyo: Chuokoron-Shinsha.

Ormel, Johan, Siegwart Lindenberg, Nardi Steverink and Lois M. Verbrugge (1999), 'Subjective Well-being and Social Production Functions', *Social Indicators Research*, 46: 61–90.

Owen, David (1994), *Maturity and Modernity: Nietzsche, Weber, Foucault, and the Ambivalence of Reason*, London: Routledge.

Padden, Carol and Tom Humphries (1988), *Deaf in America: Voices from a Culture*, Cambridge, MA.: Harvard University Press.

Parsons, Talcott (1937), *The Structure of Social Action*, New York: McGraw-Hill Company, Inc.

Phillipson, Robert and Tove Skutnabb-Kangas (1995), 'Linguistic Rights and Wrongs', *Applied Linguistics*, 16:4.

Pinker, Steven (1995), *The Language Instinct: The New Science of Language and Mind*, London: Penguin.

Ragin, Charles (1987), *Comparative Method: Moving beyond Qualitative and Quantitative Strategies*, Berkley, CA.: University of California Press.

Rawls, John (1971), *A Theory of Justice*, Cambridge, MA.: The Belknap Press of Harvard University Press.

Rawls, John (1982), 'Social Unity and Primary Goods', in Amartya Sen and Bernard Williams (eds), *Utilitarianism and Beyond*, Cambridge: Cambridge University Press.

Roemer, John E. (1996), *Theories of Distributive Justice*, Cambridge: Harvard University Press. Translated by Shinobu Kitani and Takashi Kawamoto, *Bunpaiteki seigi no riron: Keizaigaku to rinri no taiwa*, Tokyo: Bokutakusha.

Rosenthal, Robert and Lenore Jacobson (1968), *Pygmalion in the Classroom*, New York: Rinehart and Winston.

Ruiz, Richard (1984), 'Orientations in Language Planning', *National Association for Bilingual Education Journal*, 8: 15–34.

Sacks, Oliver (1989), *Seeing Voices: A Journey into the World of the Deaf*, Berkeley-Los Angeles: University of California Press.

Sakurai, Tokutaro (1989), *Reikonkan no keifu* (The images of spirits: a genealogy), Tokyo: Kodansha.

Satō, Fumitaka (1995), *Kagaku to kōfuku: 21-seiki mondaigun bukkusu* (Science and happiness: The 21st century issues books) 7, Tokyo: Iwanami Shoten.

Satō, Kenji (1987), *Dokusho kūkan no kindai: Hōhō toshiteno Yanagita Kunio* (Modern age of literary space: Kunio Yanagita as a method), Tokyo: Koubundou Publishers.

Satō, Kenji (2002), 'Kyōdo (Native land)', in Kazuhiko Komatsu and Kazutoshi Seki (eds), *Atarashii minzokugaku e: No no gakumon no tameno ressun* (Toward new folklore: Lessons for field study) 26, Tokyo: Serica Shobo.

Schmaling, Constanze (2001), 'ASL in Northern Nigeria: Will Hausa Sign Language Survive?', in Valerie Dively, Melanie Metzger, Sarah Taub and Ann Marie Baer (eds), *Signed Languages*, Washington DC: Gallaudet University Press, pp. 180–93.

Schmaling, Constanze (2003), 'A for Apple: The Impact of Western Education and ASL on the Deaf Community in Kano State, Northern Nigeria', in Leila Monahan, Constanze Schmaling, Karen Nakamura and Graham Turner (eds), *Many Ways to be Deaf*, Washington DC: Gallaudet University Press, pp. 302–10.

Schütz, Alfred (1967), *Collected Papers I: The Problem of Social Reality*, The Hague: Martinus Nijhoff.

Sekiya, Shigeru and Yoshie Sakamoto (1998), *Tonari ni dassōhei ga ita jidai* (The times when a deserter lived next door), Tokyo: Shisō no Kagakusha.

Sen, Amartya K. (1970), *Collective Choice and Social Welfare*, San Francisco: Holden-Day. Translated by Kiyoshi Shida (2000), *Shūgōteki sentaku to shakaiteki kōsei*, Tokyo: Chikuma Shobo Publishing.

Sen, Amartya K. (1976), 'Poverty: An Ordinal Approach to Measurement', *Econometrica*, 44: 219–31.

Sen, Amartya K. (1985), *Commodities and Capabilities*, New York: Elsevier Science Publishers B. V. Translated by Kōtarō Suzumura (1988), *Fukushi no Keizaigaku*, Tokyo: Iwanami Shoten.

Sen, Amartya K. (1992) *Inequality Reexamined*, Oxford: Oxford University Press. Translated by Yukio Ikemoto, Hiroo Nogami and Hitoshi Satō (1999), *Fubyōdō no saikentō*, Tokyo: Iwanami Shoten.

Sen, Amartya K. (1997), *On Economic Inequality,* expanded edition with a substantial annex by James E. Foster and Amartya Sen, Oxford: Clarendon Press. Translated by Kōtarō Suzumura and Kōichi Suga (2000), *Fubyōdō no Keizaigaku*, Tokyo: Toyo Keizai.

Shorrocks, Anthony F. (1980), 'The Class of Additively Decomposable Inequality Measures', *Econometrica*, 48: 613–25.

Shūkyō Shakaigaku no Kai (Association for Sociology of Religion) (Representative: Tsutomu Shiobara) (ed.) (1985), *Ikoma no kamigami: Gendai toshi no minzoku shūkyō* (Gods of Ikoma: A folk religion in a modern city), Osaka: Sogensha.

Shuzui, Hajime (1936), 'Ie no seisui nitsuite (About the rise and fall of *ie*)', in Kunio Yanagita, Tokuzō Omachi, Shunchō Higa and Hajime Shuzui (eds) (1984), *Sanson kaison minzoku no kenkyū* (Research on folk customs of mountain and coastal villages), Tokyo: Meicho Shuppan.

Skutnabb-Kangas, Tove (2003), 'Linguistic Genocide and the Deaf', World Congress of the World Federation of the Deaf, Montreal, Canada.

Smith, Adam (1776), *An Inquiry into the Nature and Causes of the Wealth of Nations*, London: Strahan and Cadell. Translated by Kazuo Ōkōchi (1978), *Kokufu-ron I*, Tokyo: Chūkō Bunko.

Spencer, Herbert (1851), *Social Statics or the Conditions Essential to Human Happiness Specified and the First of Them Developed*, London: John Chapman.

Strack, Fritz, Michael Argyle and Norbert Schwarz (eds) (1991), *Subjective Well-Being: An Interdisciplinary Perspective*, Oxford: Pergamon Press.

Suzuki, Seiji and Minoru Nakamichi (1997), *Kōdo seichō no shakaigaku* (Sociology of high economic growth), Kyoto: Sekaishisosha.

Tachibanaki, Toshiaki (2004), *Fūin sareru fubyōdō* (Sealed inequality), Tokyo: Toyo Keizai.

Taguieff, Pierre-André (1987), *La force du préjugé: essai sur le racisme et ses doubles*, Paris: Gallimard.

Takada, Eiichi (2004), 'Rōsha no negai: Shuwa o hōtei-gengo ni mitomete (Desire of the Deaf: Please recognize sign language as an official language)', *Yomiuri Shimbun*, 25 August.

Takao, Toshikazu (1977), *Ningenteki ikikata eno shuppatsu* (The beginning of a humanistic life), Tokyo: Dentō to Gendaisha.

Takayama, Noriyuki (1979), 'Poverty, Income Inequality and Their Measures: Professor Sen's Axiomatic Approach Reconsidered', *Econometrica*, 47(3): 747–59.

Takeuchi, Hiroshi (1988), *Senbatsu shakai: Shiken, shōshin o meguru 'kanetsu' to 'reikyaku'* (Selective society: 'Overheating' and 'cooling' surrounding tests and promotion), Tokyo: Recruit.

Takeuchi, Shōsuke (1999), *Mon no higeki: Abakareta 'Kennedy no sensō' no tsumi* (The Hmong tragedy: The crime of 'Kennedy's war' exposed), Tokyo: The Mainichi Newspapers.

Takeyama, Akiko (1998), *Gyokuon hōsō* (The Imperial announcement of the end of the war), Tokyo: Banseisha.

Torigoe, Hiroyuki (2002a), *Yanagita minzokugaku no firosofī* (Philosophy of Yanagita's folklore), Tokyo: University of Tokyo Press.

Torigoe, Hiroyuki (2002b), 'Motoori Norinaga to Yanagita minzokugaku (Norinaga Motoori and Yanagita's folklore)', *UP*, 360: 1–5.

Tsuchiya, Keiichirō (1993), *Bensamu to iu otoko* (A man called Bentham), Tokyo: Seidosha.

Tsurumi, Kazuko (1977), *Hyōhaku to teijū to: Yanagita Kunio no shakai hendō ron* (Wandering and settling: Kunio Yanagita's theory of social changes), Tokyo: Chikuma Shobo Publishing.

Uchida, Ryūzō (1989), *Shakai ki jo* (Social record: Introduction), Tokyo: Koubundou Publishers.

Uchida, Ryūzō (1995), *Yanagita Kunio to jiken no kiroku* (Kunio Yanagita and records of incidents), Tokyo: Kodansha.

Ueno, Chizuko and Dentsū Network Kenkyūkai (1988), *Joen ga yononaka o kaeru* (Women's connections will change the world), Tokyo: Nihon Keizai Shimbun.

Ui, Jun (ed.) (1985), *Gijutsu to sangyō kōgai* (Technology and industrial pollution), Tokyo: United Nations University.

United Nations (1948), 'Universal Declaration of Human Rights', General Assembly Resolution 217A (III) of 10 December.

Universal Declaration of Linguistic Rights, *http://www.linguistic-declaration.org/index-gb.htm*, accessed on 1 November 2004.

Veenhoven, Ruut (1984) *Conditions of Happiness*, Dordrecht: D. Reidel Publishing Company.

Veenhoven, Ruut (1994), 'Is happiness a trait? Tests of the theory that a better society does not make people any happier', in *Social Indicators Research*, (32): 101–60.

Wallerstein, Immanuel (1974), *The Modern World-System: Capitalist Agri-culture and the Origins of the European World-Economy in the Sixteenth Century*, New York: Academic Press.

Weber, Max (1920), *Die protestantische Ethik und der »Geist« des Kapitalismus*, Tübingen: J.C.B. Mohr (Paul Siebeck). Translated by Talcott Parsons (1930), *The Protstant Ethic and the Spirit of Capitalism*, London: George Allen & Unwin.

World Conference on Linguistic Rights (1996), 'Universal Declaration of Linguistic Rights', Barcelona, Spain, 7–9 June.

World Federation of the Deaf (2003), 'Resolution of the 14th World Congress of the World Federation of the Deaf', Montreal, Quebec, Canada, 26 July.

Yama, Yoshiyuki (1996), 'Hantensuru "kishin ron" (Changing theories on "demon-gods")', *Edo no shisō* (Philosophy of the Edo period), 5: 176–91.

Yamanaka, Kōji (ed.) (2005), *Rinshō bunka no shakaigaku—Shokugyō, gijutsu, hyōjunka* (Sociology of clinical culture: Vocations, skills and standardization), Kyoto: Showado.

Yamazaki, Masakazu (1975), *Geijutsu, henshin and yūgi* (Art, metamorphosis and play), Tokyo: Chuokoron-Shinsha.

Yanagita, Kunio (1934), 'Minkan denshō ron (On popular oral history)', in (1998), *Yanagita Kunio zenshū* (Complete works of Kunio Yanagita) 8, Tokyo: Chikuma Shobo Publishing.

Yanagita, Kunio (1935), 'Kyōdo seikatsu no kenkyūhō (Folk life research methods)', in (1998), *Yanagita Kunio zenshū* (Complete works of Kunio Yanagita) 8, Tokyo: Chikuma Shobo Publishing.

Yanagita, Kunio (1946), 'Senzo no hanashi (Stories of ancestors)', in (1969), *Teihon Yanagita Kunio shū* (Kunio Yanagita collection, standard edition) 10, Tokyo: Chikuma Shobo Publishing.

Yanagita, Kunio, Tokuzō Omachi, Shunchō Higa and Hajime Shuzui (eds) ([1934]/1984), *Sanson kaison minzoku no kenkyū* (Research on folk customs of mountain and coastal villages), Tokyo: Meicho Shuppan.

Yitzhaki, Shlomo (1979), 'Relative Deprivation and the Gini Coefficient', *The Quarterly Journal of Economics*, vol. 93(2): 321–4.

Yokozeki, Yumiko (2004), 'Ghana shotō-kyōiku ni okeru kyōju-gengo: 2002 nen no shin-kyōiku-gengo-hōshin to sono imi (Medium of instruction for basic education in Ghana: The 2002 new educational language policy and its significance)', *Kokusai kyōiku kyōryoku ronshū* (Journal of international cooperation in education), 7–2(2004.10): 15–24.

Yoneda, Nobuko (2004), 'Ta-gengo-shakai ni okeru eigo no Ichizuke: Tanzania, Namibia, Zimbabwe no baai (Status of English in multilingual societies: Cases of Tanzania, Namibia and Zimbabwe)', in Ritsuko Miyamoto (ed.), *Africa-josei no kaihatsu-program sanka to gengo sentaku ni kansuru gakusai-teki kenkyū* (Interdisciplinary research on the participation in development programs and language choice by African women), Akita: Akita University, pp. 19–32.

Yonekawa, Akihiko (2002), *Shuwa to iu kotoba: Mou hitotsu no Nihon no gengo* (Sign language: Another Japanese language), Tokyo: PHP Institute.

Yoshida, Tamito (1999), '"Hikaku kōfukugaku no hitotsu no kenkyū no puroguramu furon": Kōfuku to kōfukukan: chichi ni gan o kokuchi shite ("A research program of comparative studies of happiness" appendix, Happiness and the perception of happiness: Having informed my father of his cancer)', in Hisasada Nakagawa (ed.), *Hikaku kōfukugaku* (Comparative study of happiness), Kyoto: International Institute for Advanced Studies, pp. 35–69.

Yoshikawa, Kōjirō (ed.) (1969), *Motoori Norinaga shū* (Norinaga Motoori collection), Tokyo: Chikuma Shobo Publishing.

Zenkoku Rōji o Motsu Oya no Kai (Japan Deaf Children and Parents Association) (ed.) (2004), *Rō-kyōiku to gengo-ken: Rōji no jinken kyūsai mōshitate no zenyō* (Deaf education and linguistic rights: The total picture of the claims for the rights and aids of deaf children), Tokyo: Akashi Shoten.

Žižek, Slavoj (2002), *Welcome to the Desert of the Real!*, London: Verso.

Name Index

Subject Index